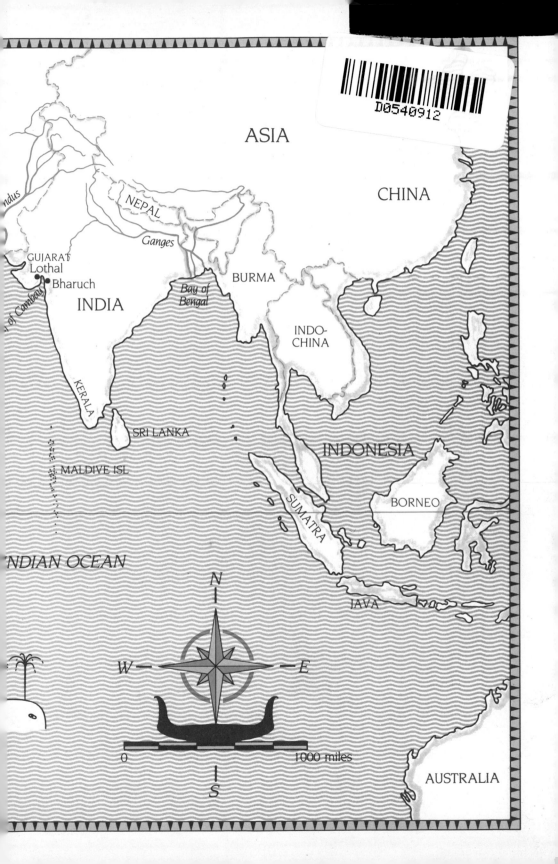

The Maldive Mystery

The Maldive Mystery

Thor Heyerdahl

London
GEORGE ALLEN & UNWIN
Boston   Sydney

George Allen & Unwin (Publishers) Ltd,
40 Museum Street, London WC1A 1LU, UK

George Allen & Unwin (Publishers) Ltd,
Park Lane, Hemel Hempstead, Herts HP2 4TE, UK

George Allen & Unwin Australia Pty Ltd,
8 Napier Street, North Sydney, NSW 2060, Australia

George Allen & Unwin with the
Port Nicholson Press
PO Box 11–838 Wellington, New Zealand

First published in Great Britain in 1986

British Library Cataloguing in Publication Data

Heyerdahl, Thor
    The Maldive mystery.
1. Maldives – Antiques
I. Title
934.9'5   DS486.5.M3
ISBN 0–04–910104–8

Set in 11 on 13 point Palatino by Bedford Typesetters Ltd, Bedford
and printed in Great Britain by Butler and Tanner Ltd, Frome and London

Contents

Plates

CHAPTER I
A Thousand Island Mystery
Buried Images and the Sacrifice of Virgins

BITS OF BLACK soil and green moss spilled over the red carpet in the President's Palace as our old potato sacks were cut open and the heavy stones rolled out. They were fresh from the jungle, and still covered by lichen and moss.

His Excellency Maumoon Abdul Gayoom, President of the young Republic of Maldives, made no attempt to conceal his joy, nor did the high officials in dark suits who stood respectfully at his side. But the servants and soldiers who had brought in the sacks withdrew puzzled, with a mixture of awe and bewilderment. Nothing like this had ever been brought in amongst the elegant furniture of the Palace. Nor, for that matter, would they ever have dumped it on the floor of their own huts.

On the carpet before us lay a row of weatherworn limestone blocks, once neatly carved out of the white island rock, but now dark grey with age, with reliefs still clearly to be seen on one side under the covering of lichen. Their opposite sides were shaped with a neck and shoulders designed to fit into a wall.

The carved symbols had been cut to stand out, by about a finger's thickness, from the rest of the stone. The most striking of these were the big sun-symbols. Big as dinner plates. A round central disc representing the sun was surrounded by a series of raised rings one enclosing the other. This has always been the classical image of the solar deity among sun-worshippers since the oldest civilisations of Mesopotamia and Egypt. Some of the stones had a more elegant decoration. They had wings added on each side of the sun, resulting in a design that resembled a modern airline emblem. The winged sun was also typical of the ancient art of Egypt and Mesopotamia.

Two of the stones were quite different and much more ornate. A row of free-standing sunflowers alternated with a raised symbol composed of vertical bars flanked by three dots set above each other, almost like numerals in Mayan hieroglyphics; and above this row was a wider band of lotus motifs running along the edge of the stone. The sunflower, too, was an emblem of the early sun-worshippers, and the lotus flower was the symbol of the sunrise not only in Pharaonic Egypt but in Mesopotamia and ancient India as well.

Clearly we had discovered something which nobody expected to see on islands that lay far out in the Indian Ocean. Even the islanders themselves admitted that they had never seen anything like these before. They were Moslems. Everybody in the Maldive archipelago was Moslem, as their ancestors had been for over 800 years, that is, since the Islamic faith had been embraced and enforced as law by the ruling Sultan in the year 583 of the Holy Prophet, or AD 1153 according to our Christian calendar. Since that time nobody would have either cared or dared to carve motifs like these in the Maldive archipelago, indeed no one can settle there without accepting Islam as their faith.

Yet, although we had barely arrived in the Maldive Islands, we had already found these non-Moslem stones. They were not easy to detect, since they were covered by moss and hidden under ferns and foliage in dense jungle. Moreover, we had found them on an uninhabited island, as far south and as far from the capital island Male (pronounced Mālĕ) and the tourist routes as it was possible to go in the 960-kilometre (600-mile) long archipelago. What we had brought to the Palace, however, was a mere sample of what we knew was still left in the jungle. At first we had brought them to the little Moslem museum in the capital, but the President then insisted on inspecting the carvings himself. He gave us a friendly reception, but when he saw the contents of the potato sacks his face lit up like a boy enraptured by Father Christmas's gifts.

He finally rose to his feet and said with pride:

'We are a young republic, yes. But now we have proof that we too have an old history, just like our neighbours on the continent!'

The stones still lay on the red carpet as we left the Palace. The guards were to carry them back to the nation's only museum where they had temporarily to be tucked away in a corner, for they did not fit in at all among the Islamic art and history to which the building was devoted.

I myself left the Palace with a beautiful whalebone model of a Maldive sailing *dhoni*, and with a personal invitation from the President to organise the first archaeological excavations ever to be attempted on the 1,200 or so islands in the archipelago that made up his nation.

I lay down on the bed in my room at the little public guest-house a short walk away from the Palace. Indeed, on this tiny capital island of Male, everything lay within walking distance.

I turned on the ceiling fan, then turned it off again because I needed to think. But thoughts seemed almost an intrusion in this pleasant tropical temperature. The sun, the sea, the white sand and the coconut palms outside all induced a sense of contentment and relaxation; even so the situation, as I thought about it, seemed clear enough. A month ago I had hardly heard of the Maldive Islands. Last week I had come here for the first time, and stopped over for one day in this same hotel before Björn Bye and I went to visit the southern atolls. Now we were back again in Male and I was lying on the same bed pondering an unexpected invitation from the President to try to unravel the lost past of his nation. At the same time, five heavy stones in dirty potato sacks were being carried from the Palace to the National Museum, and eleven more were on their way by water.

Embarrassing.

Embarrassing because I knew next to nothing about this country. For lack of time I had come utterly unprepared. Indeed, the average tourist equipped with his brochures probably came better prepared than I. Until last week these islands were nothing to me but dots on an ocean map, with names so strange that I stumbled as I tried to read them. I could not speak the local language, which they call *Divehi*, nor could I even understand the strange signs in their writing system. To me their peculiar script looked like chopped-up spaghetti tossed into lines. They

11

call it *gabuli tana*, or *thana akuru*, and it is written from right to left.

How could I, therefore, start a meaningful search for something that lay beyond what these intelligent and literate people already knew about their ancestral past?

And where among the 1,200 or so islands?

This surely was a task for someone who knew more about local problems than I did. Yet it offered a tremendous challenge. Here was a country in the middle of the ocean, a member of the United Nations, and yet with origins that were lost in mystery. No archaeologist had ever come to investigate these islands, because they were thought to be too remote from any mainland.

But I did have one advantage. I knew something about navigation and prehistoric watercraft. That was why we had found these stones in the first place. I had deliberately searched in places where it was likely primitive craft could have landed. For too long it had generally been accepted that the mariners of pre-European civilisations only hugged continental shore-lines for fear of being lost in the open sea, and for the lack of oceanworthy ships. But in recent years my friends and I had tested prehistoric types of raft ship, and sailed them across the three main oceans. During our last experiment, after sailing the reed ship *Tigris* from former Mesopotamia to the Indus Valley, we could easily have continued down the coast of India and out to the Maldive Islands. But we chose instead to sail straight across the Indian Ocean to Africa. Thanks to this experiment the Maldivians had now lured me to their country. They did not believe that pre-European navigators had only hugged the coasts. They knew that their own ancestors had crossed the ocean in pre-European times; but they did not know where they came from. They also knew that these ancestors had later been visited by maritime Arabs – Arabs who sailed the ocean centuries before Columbus. Their written history went back as far as the twelfth century AD, with their own types of letters engraved on copper plates bound together to form regular books. This is how they knew that the Islamic faith had been introduced by seafaring Arabs in AD 1153.

Now, in their forests, we had hit upon carved stones, the remains of the people who had sailed to these islands *before* the Arabs, and who worshipped the sun instead of Allah.

The President was right. The Maldive archipelago may have been young as a republic, for the last autocratic Sultan was replaced by a democratic government in 1968. Nevertheless these islanders could teach the world their own peaceful history with more than eight centuries of written records. What had happened here before then, nobody knew. It was virgin territory for anybody to explore.

If I were to investigate the mystery, therefore, I would have to start from scratch. First, I would have to find out what others already knew. But from then on I had a clear advantage. I had as a guide-post a tenable theory which had helped me go straight to those stones which the Maldivians themselves were now bringing into their museum. Certainly other scientists had visited the Maldives: some as tourists for modern sun-worship; a few to study and report on the life and language of today's people. No professional archaeologist had apparently been among them; and although a couple of enthusiasts had tried their luck with pick and shovel several decades ago, their initiative had not been followed up.

The drone of a jet engine overhead brought me to the window. A twentieth-century giant landed on the narrow airstrip recently built by Arab brothers in faith by extending a shallow islet just off Male island. German, Italian and Swedish tourists swarmed down the gangway and into the little airport building. No other nations seemed yet to have discovered this sun-baked paradise. Hardly any of these tourists would come to Male, however, or to any of the other Maldive islands where the local people lived. The government had reserved for tourists a selected number of hitherto uninhabited islands on the atolls next to Male and the airstrip.

For one reason or another it seemed as if the sun had a very long tradition of attracting people to the Maldives, even in prehistoric times. What we had found was the ruins of a sun-temple, and it was nothing but the sun itself that had led us there. As simple as that. The road had been fast and direct.

It was the sun that had brought me to the sun-temple, but it was an airmail envelope that had brought me to these islands in the first place. Slightly more than a month ago I had found in my mail box a stiff envelope with exotic stamps from Sri Lanka.

The envelope contained a large photograph. I was expecting

from Sri Lanka to see colourful pictures of palms and beaches, but this was a black and white picture showing nothing but the head and shoulders of a big stone image emerging from the ground. The head was masterfully carved and well preserved – a faintly smiling, friendly-looking figure with one strange feature that immediately caught my eye: the ears. The ear lobes had been carved to hang right down to the folds of the cloak which the figure had over his shoulders. Although it was the sculpture of a man the curly hair appeared to be tied into a small knot on top of the head.

A stone statue of a man with long ears and topknot.

I felt a sudden thrill of excitement. This was a repetition of the Easter Island mystery that had puzzled me for so long. If the picture had been taken somewhere not too far away from Easter Island perhaps there could be a distant connection between the ancient stone sculptors? On Easter Island there were hundreds of giant stone busts emerging like this from the ground, representing men with long ears hanging down to their shoulders and a topknot superimposed on the head. Certainly the style there was stiff and conventionalised. In contrast, the image in this picture was most realistic.

Impatiently I unfolded the accompanying letter to learn where this photograph had been taken. The letter was indeed from Sri Lanka, but the photograph came from an atoll in the Maldive group.

So there could be no connection. The Maldive Islands were on the opposite side of the planet, half the world away from Easter Island. When we sailed our reed ship *Tigris* from the Indus Valley into the open Indian Ocean, we had discussed whether to steer for the Maldive group.

I pulled down my globe from the shelf to check the position of the Maldives.

As I had thought. Easter Island and the Maldive group were on exactly opposite sides of the earth. Precisely 180° apart, half the earth's circumference. Indeed, the Maldives were closer to the Indus Valley than Easter Island was to Peru, and the ancient artists of the Maldive Islands could have brought the custom of ear extension from continental Asia, where it had been practised on the coast since the time of the ancient Indus Valley civilisation. The Easter Islanders had brought it from

14

Peru where it represented a characteristic custom of the Incas.

No connection. I had better pack my suitcase. I was due to fly the next day to Japan by way of America anyway.

Yet I could not dismiss the long-eared statue from my mind. I pulled out the picture once again and read the letter more carefully. It was sent by a man I did not know, Björn Roar Bye, Director of Worldview International Foundation, with headquarters in Colombo, the capital of Sri Lanka. We had called it Ceylon when I went to school. The Worldview International Foundation I knew. I had once signed on as a member because WIF's aim was to work for better understanding between developed and developing nations. WIF trained third-world students to produce their own video films for the education and edification of the industrialised world. Both worlds had something to give to the other. Communications, once by means of early ships, had helped build the first civilisations. We still had much to learn from the simple communities before we caused them to disappear.

This letter told me that Björn Bye had just been to the Maldives to establish a local branch of the Worldview International Foundation. The photo had been shown to him by a Maldive official who had noticed my name on the membership list. The voyage of *Tigris* had been eagerly followed in the Maldives in the hope that the reed ship would land there. Recently a local islander had found this stone figure on a small atoll, and the Maldive official had the idea of sending it to me. It might tempt me to come and probe the puzzle behind this evidence of ancient navigation.

I continued to study the picture. It could be an old Buddha image. Buddha had such extended ear lobes. Indeed it was Buddha who spread this custom of ear extension with his own followers throughout Asia.

Buddha was born in the sixth century BC. Ear extension did not start with him, however. In certain parts of India this strange custom was practised by nobilities long before Buddha was born. Buddha was a title adopted by an historical person, Siddhartha Gautama, who was born a Hindu prince. It was as a Hindu prince that he had had his ear lobes perforated and extended with large plugs, because it was a very old Hindu custom in noble families. But ear extension did not begin with Hindu nobles either. Big ear plugs, just like those used by the Inca nobles and the 'Long-ears' on Easter Island, had recently been excavated in large numbers at Lothal, the prehistoric port of the ancient Indus Valley civilisation.

Was it pure coincidence that remote oceanic islands like the Maldives and Easter Island had been found and settled by navigators whose gods and nobles were supposed to wear big discs in their ear lobes? Perhaps yes. Perhaps no, because we were dealing with people, and migrating families, whose remote island discoveries had proved them to be skilled, long-range ocean explorers.

Whether the statue in the picture depicted Buddha or one of his long-eared predecessors, I knew at least that I was looking at an image sculpted in the Maldives before the introduction of Islam had outlawed any art depicting the human form. What was more, the picture showed a statue buried almost to the shoulders in the ground, so how much more was there to discover through excavation?

It was now only a week since I first came to the Maldives. And only five weeks since I received that photograph. My suitcase was ready even as the photograph arrived, and a flight ticket for Japan was in my hands. There was no time to organise a visit to the Maldives, so I left it to a friend to answer the Director of WIF on my behalf. He was to say that I would come to the Maldives on a detour from the airport at Bangkok if somebody could be there to meet me with travel instructions on the day my congress ended in Japan.

It was with some feeling of uncertainty, however, that I left the airplane in Bangkok a fortnight later and went through customs and immigration. I had heard no more from the Maldives. But in the crowd outside I recognised a cameraman I had recently met in Oslo, Neil Hollander, a small man with a bushy beard and large glasses. He grabbed my hand and assured me that a side trip to the Maldives was all organised. He was coming along himself to film the unique sailing vessels of the Maldives, called dhonis. They had a curious bow, swung up high and ending in a fan shape, like the papyrus stem of ancient Egyptian ships. Neil said that he was in Asia to shoot a film about the last working sailing people in the world, so now he volunteered to join me in the Maldives. The next day we flew on together to Sri Lanka.

Another bearded man was waiting for us as we landed in Colombo. I had not met him. Tall and broad shouldered, he moved us through all the airport formalities with the audacity of a blue-eyed Viking but with a smile as peaceful as a missionary's. Björn Roar Bye was clearly at home in these tropical latitudes and in a wildly chaotic airport. He had actually come out from Norway to work for the Protestant Asia Mission, but with his knowledge of local languages and customs he had gradually ended up in the Worldview International Foundation, where he was now the head office director and in charge of all film work.

When I thanked him for forwarding the photograph he laughed. He found it highly amusing that this picture had lured me to this part of the world, since I had never been willing to come before. He drove me straight to his own bungalow home in the suburbs of Colombo, while Neil Hollander went off to a small hotel where he was to meet two other cameramen who were joining him for the filming in the Maldives.

In the home of Björn and Gretha Bye I got my first lessons about the Maldives. But first we took a trip downtown, to look for a map. In an obscure shop in a literal wreck of a building we found the last navigation map of the Maldives available in Colombo. Triumphantly we returned with this treasure to Björn's home, which was already full of other guests. Björn Bye seemed to know an infinity of local people. Roland Silva was one of them, and he had some important information, Björn explained. This tall and distinguished looking man was the Director-General of the Archaeological Survey in Sri Lanka and he had also been out to the Maldives. Silva, who proved to be a former architect turned archaeologist, was now in charge of UNESCO's ambitious programme of excavating and restoring the colossal Buddhist temples within the three historically most important sites of Sri Lanka – Sri Lanka's so-called cultural triangle.

I told him about my plan to excavate a stone statue on the Maldives, and got my first shock.

'I believe the statue has already been dug up and smashed,' he said. 'The people in the Maldives are fanatically Moslem and won't tolerate anything that is forbidden by the Koran. They even deny their own history before the day Islam was introduced.'

17

Archaeologists from Sri Lanka would have liked to dig in the Maldives but, being Buddhists, they were unlikely to get permission. They would be suspected of looking for Buddhist remains. Roland Silva could not praise the Maldivians enough as a people; but when it came to religion they were obstinate and uncompromising.

I brought forward the navigation map we had found of the Maldives. Silva agreed that this archipelago lay in the most strategic position for any navigator who wanted to round the southern point of Asia. The 64-kilometre (40-mile) strait between India and Sri Lanka was full of reefs and too shallow to permit safe sailing. To get around the Indian subcontinent sailing vessels had to go so far south that they also rounded Sri Lanka, and then they would inevitably have to force a passage through the long chain of the Maldive Islands. This chain looked like a few innocent pepper grains on an ordinary map, but the navigation map revealed the true story. Never had I seen it clearer. The Maldives lay there as a treacherous barrier. No admiral could have planned a better strategic line if he had wanted to chain off with mines a sailing route obligatory for any mariner who wanted to sail east or west past the southern point of Asia.

From the depths of the Indian Ocean a sharp ridge rises abruptly, 960 kilometres (600 miles) long from north to south. It is crowned at surface level by live coral reefs, sand bars, and small atolls set in a double row, making passage twice as dangerous. The islands are so low above the waves that, were it not for the tall coconut palms, they would be invisible until the ship was caught in the surf. Only near the southern end of this long coral barricade are there two open channels which permit safe passage through from one side of India to the other.

The more I looked at the map, the more my urge to visit these strategically located islands increased. Statue or not, I wanted to see with my own eyes what these islands might conceal. Roland Silva therefore lent me an old and very precious publication on the Maldives. I was permitted to photocopy the pages, as he knew of no other copy in Sri Lanka. I would probably not find anyone in the Maldives who had it, he stressed.

The author was a former British Commissioner of the Ceylon Civil Service, H. C. P. Bell. He had first come to the Maldives through a shipwreck in 1879. It said in the Preface that he later returned on two occasions, deputed by the Ceylon government, 'For the purpose of investigating the pre-existence of Buddhism in the Group'.[1] With this objective he had indeed been obliged to move with the utmost care not to offend the Moslem sentiments of the islanders. Mr Bell had dug some rubble mounds which he claimed to be the devastated remains of former *dagobas* or *stupas*, resembling the Buddhist temples in Ceylon.

There could be no doubt, then, that there was something to look for in the Maldives. Naturally, in his early days, Bell's digging method left much to be desired; his writings were scarcely known outside the islands; and no professional archaeologist had ever followed up what he started. Yet his notes on what the islanders had told him and what he had seen for himself would be an immense help for anyone, like us, who hoped to explore the islands.

There was one other interesting book on the Maldives, almost fresh from the press: *People of the Maldive Islands* by Clarence Maloney. It dealt with the present-day islanders, however, and not with the past; but Dr Maloney was a professional anthropologist from the University of Pennsylvania, and a specialist on South Asiatic peoples. This enabled him to launch some stimulating thoughts on the origins of Divehi, the Maldive language. Some Divehi words showed a relationship to Sanskrit and to other ancient tongues in northern India, others to peoples in southern India and Sri Lanka.

But Maloney had not known about the discovery of the long-eared statue. The great variety of physical types living side by side on these islands, and the composition of their language, had nevertheless put him on the alert. He concluded, by merely observing the present population, that 'we must be prepared to accept that the cultural history of the Maldives is more complicated than has been thought'. He suspected, in fact, that different groups of peoples had reached these remote islands independently in prehistoric times.

These were plain words. If this much could be deduced without even scraping in the ground, there should be good prospects for an archaeological search below the present surface. But here Maloney was less encouraging than Bell: 'No archaeology has been conducted to investigate the pre-history of the islands, which would be difficult in any case because of the coral sand soil and the high water table.'

Although he was full of praise for the present Maldive people, he had his reservations: 'Anthropological field work in the Maldives involves tedious travel, difficulties in gaining acceptance in numerous small islets traditionally inhospitable to outsiders, and coping with a highly conservative society that holds rigid Islamic ideals.'[2]

This was even less encouraging than what Roland Silva had said. But nothing could stop me now. Besides, if the Maldivians did not want me to come and dig, why had they asked Björn Bye to send me the picture of the long-eared statue?

Three days later the dots on the map became alive as we had our first glimpse of the Maldives from the air. From the windows of the plane it was like looking at an exhibition of green jade necklaces and scattered emerald jewellery placed on blue velvet. The Indian Ocean under us was as boundlessly blue as only the sea can be when it reflects a cloudless tropical sky. The sun, straight overhead, made the islands seem lustrous green with no shadow on the palm crowns that formed a compact roof over them. Each little islet was a separate gem set in a ring of golden beach sand and with another wider ring of glass green water outside where the coral reef approached the surface, rising like giant mushrooms from the bottomless blue.

The airliner was filled to the last seat with pale Europeans in organised tours who crawled over each other to get a glimpse of this incomparable display of nature's splendour. As for me, I was no longer travelling alone. In addition to Neil Hollander and the two cameramen accompanying him, Björn Bye had also come along and brought with him two of his Sri Lankan film students, in the hope of finding something they could photograph as a training project.

The first island slid past under us, the next grew bigger, nearer. Then the narrow airstrip came into view, all by itself in the water, with the city-covered islet of Male, green with gardens, next to it at the edge of the same calm lagoon. A slight jolt, and we had landed in the Republic of Maldives, the ancient home of a people of unknown origins.

We had come as guests to the home of a very old civilisation, literate with its own special script. Today a developing nation of some 160,000 souls, all Moslem, the Maldive Republic is adjusting itself to the jet age through a non-aligned democratic government headed by a President. It is probably the only nation composed of so many scattered pieces of land that even now no one can agree on the exact number of islands. The English navigation map indicates about 1,100 islands, a recent government count was 1,196, and a tourist guide gives the total number as 1,983. In fact nobody knows, for some islets grow out of submerged reefs and others are eaten away piecemeal by the ocean and disappear. None of them rises more than about 2 metres (6 feet) above sea level and, if not protected by natural breakwater reefs, would be washed over by the waves. Only 202 of the islands are inhabited, although others have the ruins of former habitation.

Never before had I travelled surrounded by so many cameramen: Neil was accompanied by Harald from Germany and John from Canada; Björn, by Palitha and Saliya from Sri Lanka; and now one more of his former movie students, Abdul from the Maldives, had come to the airport to help us through the customs. Abdul was working for Maldive Television. It could be seen only in Male, but about a third of the nation's population live there. Indeed land is now getting so scarce that space is being reclaimed from the ocean by the dumping of solid refuse.

A short trip in a motorboat now took the eight of us to Male, where Neil's party was lost in the chaos of dhonis that were struggling to get dock space or to manoeuvre out. Dhonis lay side by side all along the waterfront, most still with mast and sails, and all with the famous bow rising towards the sky as if they were wooden replicas of the elegant pharaonic papyrus ships.

The tourists had been taken directly to the tourist islands where they were to stay. In the daytime they could come to Male island for shopping, but they were not allowed in the capital after 10 pm. On the plane we had all been given a printed notice warning us that it was forbidden to bring into the Republic of Maldives: dogs, alcohol, and pictures of nudes. But on the tourist islands foreigners were free of all Moslem rules.

Abdul told us that rooms were reserved at Sosunge, the government's guest-house in Male. We had most of the hotel to ourselves, for there were very few rooms. Our luggage was sent ahead by taxi while Abdul guided Björn and me along the bustling waterfront to visit Abdul's boss, the man who had asked Björn to send me the photograph of the long-eared statue. His name was Hassan Maniku, and he was the Director of Maldive Television and of the Ministry of Information.

When we entered the large antechamber of the Director's office upstairs in the Ministry, the atmosphere was distinctly unpromising. A large number of young Maldive girls were sitting, noses down, typing or reading detective stories. Nobody welcomed us. We could see the boss behind a glass wall, but between phone calls and making notes he was so busy that he had no time for visitors, even though we sent in messages and signalled through the glass partition. Something was obviously wrong. I gave up and returned to the hotel. Then the telephone rang, with a message that the Director wanted to receive us immediately.

Hassan Maniku was very short by European standards, but average for the Maldives, yet broadly built with a round face that unjustly made him look like a gourmand. As his mask of officialdom melted away he turned out to be an exceedingly friendly man and, what was more, surprisingly well informed. Even so, he poured cold water on our hopes when we came to the point – the statue, the stone image with the long ears.

'The statue has already been dug up,' Maniku said bluntly. 'It was a complete bust.'

'Dug up,' I said. 'By an archaeologist?'

'By the local people,' was the quiet reply. 'They smashed the body to bits.'

This was shocking. Roland Silva's suspicions were confirmed.

'Religious fanatics,' admitted Maniku, and shrugged his shoulders. 'We have saved the head. You can see it in the museum in Sultan's Park.'

'But I want to go to the island where it was found.' I was deeply disappointed. 'Perhaps there is more to be found by digging in that same place.'

'No. There is nothing more to be found there.'

'It is worth looking. I have come a long way.'

Nothing doing. Maniku put on his official mask again. Absolutely nothing to see on that island any more. Everything had been dug up and smashed. Even the remains of some sort of old temple had been razed to the ground and smashed. Nothing. Maniku was so stubbornly negative even at the mere idea of us trying to go there by boat that I realised further discussion would be useless. Either there was absolutely nothing more to be seen, or for some reason they did not want us to go there.

At least I could see the head in the museum. Maniku grabbed the phone and gave some orders to the museum staff.

The Sultan's Palace had been torn down when the Maldives had become a republic, but an old villa in the garden had been turned into the National Museum. A couple of rusty cannons and an old German torpedo lay beside the steps at the entrance where a small army of pensioners was sitting idly at a ticket table or standing in the doorway. With instructions from Maniku to let us study and photograph the stone head, four of the old men came struggling out of the building and down the steps to the park lawn with a huge, heavy, chalky white head carried upon a length of sackcloth. It looked like a ghost peeping out of a hammock. The faces of the men reflected the disgust they felt for such a heathen sculpture, but they lowered it carefully on to the lawn.

The beheaded ghost lay in the baking sun staring at us with wide open eyes and a peaceful smile. Huge, but as realistic as a death mask. This was the head of a Buddha, a beautiful Buddha, with body and limbs missing. It had been a large monument, twice the size of a normal man and masterfully carved from white limestone, the product of a great artist. The face I recognised from the photograph: expressive, with the lips closed in a faint smile. Originally the eyes had been painted to give life to the friendly expression. The hair was adorned by fine curls and drawn up into a topknot. The ears were damaged where they had been broken loose from the shoulders, but they were still unnaturally long. It also seemed as if somebody, long ago, had attempted to cover the face and the eyes with a thin coat of white plaster, as though to prevent the lifelike image from seeing any more. Perhaps this was done by the former worshippers themselves when they were obliged to turn their backs on the venerated Buddha as a new religion was imposed upon them, eight centuries ago.

The greatest surprise, however, awaited us behind a closed door inside the little building. In two small rooms downstairs were exhibited various sultans' beds, thrones and litters. Further in, and upstairs too, were all sorts of paraphernalia of the same former rulers, their weapons, musical instruments, tapestries and fine examples of old Maldive lacquerwork. Here and there were also such curiosities as elephant tusks, deer horns, flotsam found on the beach, even a stone with a flag as a souvenir of Apollo 14's flight to the moon.

We were already dizzy from strange impressions when we came down the stairs again and made our real discovery. As the guards brought in the large Buddha head, they opened the door to a small closet where a truly weird collection of hideous demons and bizarre images in stone and wood stared at us out of the semi-darkness. The Buddha head was put back in among them, and now looked like a smiling white angel among the horrifying devils at each side, grimacing like beasts with fangs exposed and tongue stretched out to strengthen the hateful expression of their angry eyes. Good and Evil depicted in stone by different sculptors and stored side by side on a sultan's stone bed.

The guardians were quick to get out of the closet, and they gave us sidelong glances as if to check whether we understood that these were not their gods, and that they would sooner see them disposed of. The rest of the closet was filled with a pile of rusty anchor chains and other metal scrap, two broken Moslem tombstones awaiting repair, an assortment of old telephones and a dozen toy-size model cannons.

In this hotchpotch of objects two observations immediately struck my mind: the demon images next to the smiling Buddha had been carved by early sculptors who were neither Moslems nor Buddhists. Yet these sculptures also represented unmistakable 'Long-ears', wearing huge discs in their extended ear lobes.

Here, in this modest closet, inside the museum walls, lay definite proof that the Maldives had housed at least three different cultures throughout the ages. The three were represented by the Sultan's bed, the Buddha, and the demon-gods. It would be four if we counted the one that came last with telephone and cannons. Also, standing on the bed with the stone figures, was a fair-sized wooden statue of some elaborately dressed Oriental dignitary. Although of considerable age, it did not come into our count because it was clearly a water-worn piece that had been found by the islanders as drift-wood on the beach. The stone heads, on the other hand, had been carved in the Maldives from local limestone, and had served the worshippers of two different religions. None of them was Moslem. Accordingly, all of them had to be more than eight centuries old.

On the bed lay also a second Buddha head, much smaller, only the size of an apple. This too was broken off at the neck. The tip of the nose had been knocked off as well, but even so it remained a beautiful piece of sculpture, the work of a very skilled artist. It had the same quiet smile, slightly thicker lips and stronger curls, and again the ears were slit with the lobes pending like empty loops down to the shoulders. Buddha personally never wore discs or any other ornaments in his long ear slots, they hung down empty and plain as they had been extended in his Hindu childhood. It was the other images, the diabolic ones with feline teeth and outstretched tongue, that wore circular discs inserted as ear plugs. The two largest sculptures of this type were not mere stone heads, but proper *stele*, as in Mayan art, with grotesque faces on all sides, some even above each other or on the apex of the stone. In fact, with the feline corner teeth exposed, the tongue stretched out, and big discs in the ears, these images looked more like Mayan stele from Mexico and Guatemala, or pre-Inca statues from South America, than anything found on other islands in the Indian Ocean. Remains of red paint were clearly visible on one of the stele. A strange curvilinear script was carved on the surface of some of the demon figures. To Björn and me it resembled the scrolls of the Maldivian characters, but neither Abdul nor the museum guards could read these signs.

Beside the little Buddha head lay also a small stone turtle, very realistically carved, but with a square chamber on the ventral side, closed by a perfectly fitted stone lid. It was probably a sacred container for trifles of a votive nature.

Seated with full bodies, like Lilliputs among the colossal stone faces, were two tiny bronze figurines. They were within reach of a hand and small enough to disappear into a pocket should any visiting pilferer have entered the closet and realised the mighty antiquity of these objects. *'Buddu'*, the guards called them. But 'buddu' was the collective Maldive word for any image in human form, whether it represented Buddha, the Virgin Mary, Popeye, or Churchill.

One of these bronze figurines actually was a Buddha, a typical Buddha, seated cross-legged in the pose of meditation which Buddhists call *Samadhi Mudra*, supposed to depict compassion, love and kindness. The other figurine was pitted by erosion, and obviously much older. It was not a Buddha, as could be seen from the elaborate dress and hairstyle, with wide necklace and multiple rings around the wrists and ankles as well as flower ornaments on the upper arms, chest and abdomen. This elegant personality, seated on a pillow or pedestal with the left leg bent in and the right hanging down, was a Hindu deity, probably the benevolent creator and paramount lord, Shiva. Two religious competitors, Shiva and Buddha, were seated peacefully side by side on top of a Moslem bed.

There were no labels, and the guards only referred us back to Hassan Maniku. He seemed to be the only person to know, or even to care.

Maniku confirmed that all the stone and bronze images had been found in the Maldives; but none of them were found together with the large Buddha. The bronze figurines had been dug up long ago on one of the southern atolls. All the demonic stone heads had been found here in Male recently. Had I noticed the three flattish stone masks, two of them with moustaches and long ears?

Yes, I had indeed. They lay with the others on the stone bed.

One of these, said Maniku slightly amused, had been found when some workmen were digging the sewers in the street outside his own house. He had seen it just in time to save it from destruction.

'And the two big stele?' I asked.

They had been found when somebody else was building a construction wall at the eastern extremity of the island, precisely where legend claimed that a demon used to come ashore craving young virgins.

That story was also recorded by Bell. In former times a terrible *jinni*, or demon, used to come ashore from the sea every month. He came to the east cape of Male where there was a *budkhána*, an idol temple. Each month, when landing there, he demanded the toll of a virgin. When the islanders came to the temple next day, they always found the virgin dead. This frightening state of affairs continued until a pious Berber of Moslem faith arrived on a voyage from North Africa. He visited the Maldives and decided to stop the atrocity. He took the place of the virgin. As he hid in the image temple he recited the Koran throughout the night and succeeded in exorcising the jinni so thoroughly that it never came back. According to some old Maldive writings this was why the Maldivians agreed to accept the Islamic faith.

I wanted to see the place where the pagan temple was said to have been and where the two largest stele with diabolic stone faces had been found. But again Maniku was totally uninterested. There was nothing to see there now. Only new stone walls and the warehouses of a modern engine service centre. But if we cared to, we could see a human skull brought from that same place, together with the images. When they dug the foundations for the new service centre they had found the earth below full of decayed human bones. They had saved only one complete cranium because it lay on top of the largest of the many-headed stele, one with five long-eared faces.

As we returned to the museum the guards brought out a shoe box, from which they lifted a human cranium. It was a smallish head of the *brachio-cephalic*, or round-headed, form. It gave us a creepy feeling at the thought of the old legend, for it was the skull of a young woman.

Back in the hotel on this first day of my visit to the Maldives I sat down to reflect on all our new and unexpected observations. The long-eared statue I had come to excavate had been reduced to a beheaded Buddha, but instead we had found a closet full of other long-eared stone heads that belonged to a still older civilisation which had also voyaged to the Maldives independently, of course, of the Buddhists and the Moslems.

With the navigation map spread out over my knees I was tempted to take a seafarer's look at this increasingly complex Maldive riddle. Who could say that nothing more was to be detected on these islands when already so much had come to light on the first day of our visit? At the least, I did not want to leave without searching personally for other traces that might have been overlooked.

But where to start? The last government count had listed 1,196 separate islands, but there was no regular intercommunication between them. The big Buddha head had been found on Toddu island, just west of Male; the small Buddha head at Kurandu, far to the north; the two bronze figurines, however, had come from somewhere in the southern atolls; while all the stone demons had been dug up on Male itself. Yet, according to Maniku, there was nothing more to see in any of these places.

But when Maniku learnt that I would like to look at some of the other islands, he generously gave me some photostat pages. This was a copy of the manuscript of a booklet he was planning to publish,[3] a list of all the Maldive islands arranged alphabetically by name, each name followed by a brief note about any mosque on the island, as well as any ship wrecked on the local reef. In a few cases he had added the geographical name of a mound located on the island. Any mound, as Maniku would be the first to realise, must have been built by man. The coral colonies that had built up these limestone atolls had left them all as flat as tennis courts. Into some of these mounds a pit had been dug, either by Bell or some treasure hunter. Most of them still lay there as a pile of coral rubble. Probably there was nothing inside them.

But who could tell?

The number of islands seemed overwhelming for anyone who had to decide where to start looking. The navigation map was just a confusion of islets, reefs and names. Maniku's list at least had the islands sorted into alphabetical order. I looked at the first page: Aahuraa, Aahuraa, Aahuraa, and Aahuraa. Four islands with the same name. Three of them had been formed after a storm in 1955, the fourth had disappeared through erosion. I looked at the last page. Six islands were called Viligili, and six more were called Viligili with an additional suffix. Better to return to the map, after all.

The maps did not simplify the problem. Each atoll had two or more names, differing totally from map to map. To sort out this confusion all the atolls had been given yet another name by present-day officials. These new and shorter names were taken from the appellations for various signs in the local script. Yet at

28

least the position of the islands could immediately be seen from a map.

'This is where we must go to search,' I said to Björn, with a finger sweeping along the equator where it passed the Maldive archipelago. The long barrier of reefs and islands barely reached to below the equator. And precisely at the equator was that broad open passage marked on the map as the 'Equatorial Channel'. This broad channel, as I had noted before, ran straight through from east to west, without reefs, an extremely inviting passage for any sailing vessel that wanted to circumnavigate the southern tip of Asia. There was only one other channel that could permit a safe passage between the western and eastern parts of the Indian Ocean, the so-called 'One-and-Half-Degree Channel'. But I wanted to go to the Equatorial Channel.

Why all the way down there?, Björn wondered.

A double reason. For early mariners who navigated by watching the sun and the stars, nothing was easier than to locate and follow the equator. Besides, the earliest navigators were sun-worshippers. The first religion of all the oldest civilisations navigating the Indian Ocean was sun-worship. The founders of the first dynasties in Mesopotamia, in Egypt, and in the Indus Valley all claimed descent from the sun. Traces of this belief in the sun as divine ancestor survive also in the Hindu royal genealogies – even Buddha's family name linked his ancestry with the sun. From my own research in the Pacific I knew also that the Polynesian master mariners linked their ancestor god Kane with the sun and, being experts in celestial navigation, they referred to the equator as 'the golden highway of Kane, the sun-god'. For that matter, the sun-worshipping Incas had erected a monument at the equator in Ecuador to mark the road of their divine ancestor, the sun.

To all these early people the home of the sun-god and the sacred hero-kings of the past could be reached through a tunnel where the sun passed when it returned through the underworld on its daily run from east to west. It was natural to suspect that, if any navigator had reached the Maldives in the early days of solar worship, the Equatorial Channel would be of double importance to them, both as a convenient thoroughfare and as a place of special religious importance. If a solid speck of land lay in mid-ocean right on the equator, that would be a place to tempt the earliest of all navigators to build a temple to the sun.

Björn listened patiently to my reflections, then commented thoughtfully that there happened to be an airport down by the Equatorial Channel, the only one apart from the one in Male. The British navy had built an airstrip at Gan island which had served as a major military base during the Second World War. The base had been abandoned in 1976, but the Maldivians still used it for a small airplane which sometimes took tourists on the round trip from Male.

A coincidence?

Not at all. History repeats itself. With a choice of more than a thousand islands in this archipelago, the British military strategists had picked an atoll right on the Equatorial Channel because this was where all ships had to navigate if they wanted a short-cut around southern Asia. From here northwards the Maldive reefs were interlaced in a labyrinth as risky to pass as a minefield.

Neil and his two partners came in to learn about our plans. They had been filming dhonis in the harbour ever since we landed in Male that morning.

'We are leaving tomorrow,' I told them. 'For the Equatorial Channel.'

The faces of the three cameramen lit up. They wanted to join us if we had no objection. There were supposed to be dhonis with square sails looking like ancient Egyptian ships in the southern area. Up here all had changed to modern triangular sails.

To my surprise there was a flight to Gan next day. A sixteen-seat airplane was prepared for lift-off even though it looked more like a winged wagon. Asking for seats for eight was to ask for half the plane, and we would never have made that flight if Maniku had not helped us, and by leaving our provisions and half the camera equipment behind. Our number was even increased when a representative of the Island Administration, Mohamed Waheed, was sent with us to ensure our safe conduct.

As I walked alone to the airplane with seven cameramen filming my steps in anticipation of dramatic discoveries, I felt like Charles Lindbergh setting out on his historic flight across the Atlantic. Who could tell, perhaps the sequel might be the revelation of some lost civilisation on those islands down in the Equatorial Channel? It all seemed unintentionally funny.

But the adventure was about to begin.

CHAPTER II

The Great Mound of Fua Mulaku

Who Were the Redin?

AS OUR PLANE droned southwards over the archipelago from Male, sunbeams seemed to glitter everywhere around us, above and below the wings. This seemed natural now that we were approaching the golden highway of Kane, the sun-god. But, to our surprise, a long trail of low cloud lay under us like the vapour from a giant jet-plane just when we estimated we were crossing the equator. With a blue sky mirrored in a blue ocean everywhere else it looked as if the tropic sun had travelled low and scorched the ocean surface on its way from east to west. The narrow belt of low cloud could only have been caused by damp air rising due to the different temperature of the sea. The fast Equatorial Current should run just about here, changing course from east to west in company with the seasonal monsoon winds in the Indian Ocean. Perhaps this great marine river caused ocean upwellings on striking islands, or perhaps a stream of colder water was pressed through an opening in the Maldive barriers by the Equatorial Current.

At this point the pilot confirmed that we were passing over the Equatorial Channel. The next moment the little plane circled down over Addu atoll, the southernmost extremity of the Maldive archipelago. This was land's end. The atoll below us was a large ring of coral reefs and shallows on which were set at intervals low sandy islands thickly covered by coconut palms, all as if in a happy ring-dance around the calm lagoon. One of these islands was Gan, where we landed smoothly on the former British airstrip. The black asphalt gave us a hot welcome and made us hurry for the little airport shelter. Even the airport employees stood lumped together under a canopy that gave protection from the burning vengeance of the one-time solar deity. Man had left nothing of nature's shelter here. The forest was gone, and with it the canopy of foliage fostered by the sun itself to shelter and nourish all tropical life.

This was the island where Bell, in 1922, had seen a man-made mound about 9 metres (30 feet) in height, 'buried in heavy scrub jungle, interspersed freely with closely growing trees'.[4] But there was neither jungle nor mound in the flat landscape surrounding the airstrip, so we asked the oldest people under the canopy for advice. Where could we see the *ustubu*, the big mound which Bell had suspected to be the ruins of a Buddhist stupa? They gestured along the asphalt runway. Some of them had learnt a little English when the British Forces were stationed on Addu atoll during the Second World War.

'The *ustubu* was down there, near the end of the runway,' one of them said with a grin.

When Addu atoll was chosen for a military base, and Gan picked for the airport, the old mound was an obstacle which had to be removed. Not a bump was visible in the perfect landing strip.

This was tragi-comic. The islanders had managed by themselves to smash that beautiful Buddha statue, a monument to their own past. And here British bulldozers had helped them erase every trace of a colossal structure which a former British Commissioner had considered a possible prehistoric temple.

The cameramen began to laugh. Had it not been for the blistering heat of the asphalt they would have asked me to go out on the runway with them so that they could film while I pointed down between my shoes at the prehistoric site. Tragi-comic indeed; but it was also slightly embarrassing, both for me who had come to look for prehistoric remains, and for those who had deprived posterity from seeing, and perhaps reconstructing, a remarkable island monument.

Apart from our disappointed group of eight foreigners, the passengers on the flight were all Maldivians who disappeared with family and friends. There was little we could do but accept the offer of tourist facilities in one of the former air force barracks. It was now run by the Maldivians as a sort of guest-house, but today we were the only guests. A lunch of fresh, strongly curried fish in the former officers' mess helped us to regain our spirits; cans of beer were served legally as the place was reserved for foreigners; and in the shade of the verandah roof we sat down with our cool glasses to think.

I brought out my photocopy of Bell's report again to see what we had missed. It appeared that during his visit a thick jungle had literally impeded his full exploration of the colossal mound he saw. He just gave its circumference at base as about 80 metres (87 yards). The solid structure had once stood in a casing of cut coral blocks, but it had gradually been denuded. This, he said, had happened over the many centuries when it had furnished the Moslem islanders of Addu atoll with a vast supply of coral slabs, which they could use ready dressed for building their mosques and chief houses. Nothing but a big rough mound seemed to have been left in Bell's time as he wrote: 'Literally, in the case of this bare relic of a religion long extinct at the Maldives not one stone is standing on another to mark its pristine form.' And: 'The total antiquarian yield . . . from the hillock's two days "labouring", was two ancient beads, probably tossed aside by forebears of the present Muslim Islanders when they took toll of this "accursed" shrine.'

Bell had not found ancient ruins on any other island in the Addu atoll except on the northern extremity of Hitadu, an island pointing like a finger into the strategic Equatorial Channel. There he had found dilapidated coral walls from an old-time fort of non-European origin. In spite of this, some older islanders recommended us to visit Hitadu, for there was more up there than the old fort Bell had seen.

We took off again, this time crowded into the airport lorry, in high spirits in the hope of finding something preserved that far from the airport island. Hitadu was on the opposite extremity of this extensive atoll. The British had filled in the shallow reefs linking one island to the next along the west rim of Addu atoll, and a road took us through little islets with villages and coconut groves all the way up to Hitadu. Where the road ended we found a few islanders watching glittering tuna fish being unloaded from a dhoni. One of them said he knew of some important prehistoric remains.

Encouraged by his assurance, we set off into the thick under-

33

growth with our barefooted pathfinder ahead, and myself, seen by the others as some sort of Sherlock Holmes, close at his heels. After all, I had come to the Maldives to investigate a riddle, and the others of their own accord, hoping to film whatever I might find. Neil's professional group was heavily loaded for normal film and sound, Björn's training team with video equipment and, while some filmed us from behind, others ran up in front or hid in the bush to film us coming, passing, and going, towards certain hoped-for discoveries until we stopped abruptly at a clearing and my guide pointed.

I could see nothing.

'The Queen's bath!' he said with great pride, and two microphones came forth as Abdul translated.

I still could see nothing. The man took two more steps and pointed straight down in front of his toes. There was a slight depression in the ground where some brackish water had formed a shallow pool. Barely enough for a queen to dip her toe in.

'It used to be bigger,' explained our guide when he saw my modest enthusiasm. 'But it caved in when people took stones away from the walls to build houses.'

We had come too late again.

We wondered what else he had to show us. There was more to see. In another place there was a very ancient stone tower built by the first ancestors who came here.

The cameras were again aimed at two pairs of legs as they disappeared into the undergrowth. We would soon be there, the guide assured us as we began to hear the surf tumbling and rattling with loose coral fragments on a steep beach. Again he pointed. Straight down.

Covered by sparse, sun-scorched vegetation lay a short row of cut coral slabs. The cameras zoomed in at my hand as I bent down to touch them.

'But this is not very old,' I said, bewildered.

'Not very,' he agreed. 'An English officer built his house here.'

'But you said you would show us a very old tower built by your ancestors!'

'This is it,' he said, surprised at my impatience, 'this was once a very old tower. Look here!' He pointed at an eroded slab barely visible under the foundation of the former British house. It was a block quarried ages ago, sure. It could have been part of an ancient structure, maybe even the base of an old tower, heaven knows how tall. But the tower was not there. This fact was unimportant to our guide. How could I dispute his claim when he had it directly from his own grandpa that right here was the tower, built by their ancestors?

On our way back we were all silent and the cameras were turned off. Once I bent down to pick up something terracotta coloured trodden down into the trail, but I threw it away as if I had burnt my fingers when I saw it was a strip of plastic and a camera was ready to shoot.

Asphalt, plastic, a muddy puddle and a British officer's home, that was a meagre outcome for our first day's exploring outside the closet in Male Museum. I wondered if my companions were as disappointed at the day's results as I was. If so, they hid it well. Back at the dirt road we bid a hearty farewell to our friendly guide and laughed as we all crawled back on to the lorry.

We had found nothing, but one observation could be drawn from what other people had seen while the remains were still standing. Two tall stone structures had reportedly existed in ancient times on Addu atoll. Whether they were pre-Moslem temples or defence positions, they were placed at points where they could be seen from far out in the open sea, long before these low islets could be sighted. One, recalled by the islanders and probably seen by Bell in ruins, had been on a point stretching like a finger straight out into the Equatorial Channel. The other, seen by Bell reduced to a heap of coral rubble still 9 metres (30 feet) tall, had been on the opposite side of the atoll, facing the open Indian Ocean south of the last extremity of the Maldives. From these very positions seafaring enemies could be detected and friends helped to set safe course. The positions chosen were such as would have been picked for modern lighthouses intended to serve navigators rounding the southern tip of Asia. The Hitadu tower would serve those passing through the Equatorial Channel and the Gan mound those taking the longer route south of Addu atoll.

That night a young Maldivian serving us dinner in the

officers' mess told us about ruins still standing on another island in this same atoll, which could not be reached either by foot or by car. He promised to help us with a boat next morning.

In the early dawn we woke with new hope and crossed the entire lagoon in fifty minutes by fast motor dhoni to Midu island. Midu was as far from Gan to the north-east as was Hitadu to the north-west, but these two islands were separated by a long, submerged section of the ring-reef at the open entrance to the lagoon.

Midu was inhabited. The local people knew about the ruins and took us straight there. What they showed us were solidly cemented bunkers and overgrown trenches dug during the Second World War to face the Equatorial Channel. The cameramen had not even bothered to unload their equipment. Nor did they quite catch on even when I got a little excited a moment later. Nothing spectacular, and yet a new lead. A mole of crude coral blocks 730 metres (800 yards) long had been built from the sandy beach of Midu out into the shallow lagoon, far enough for small dhonis to discharge passengers and cargo at the further end. I could not help inspecting the shapeless lumps of coral and crude limestone blocks that had been tossed together to form this long white pier. In a couple of places I noted a few stones that were quite unlike the rest: beautifully squared, with classical flutings carved along one side as if formerly part of some elaborate structure. This was puzzling. At the shore end of the mole there were more of these sculpted limestones, recently set at random to serve as edges for the coral fill, but placed with no sense of the ups and downs of the fluted decor.

'Re-used building stones from some temple,' I explained to the cameramen who found the blocks to be too elegant to be part of something made by the islanders. Yet, when I began to scrutinise the crude white blocks in the high stone walls of the village gardens, the brimmed Himalaya felt hat donated to me by Björn that day must have made them think of Sherlock Holmes again. Each time my fingers stopped by one of these same elegant stones, set upside down or on edge amongst the shapeless mixture of rubble and lime, they followed with the cameras. Were these strange stones some kind of fingerprint?

Abdul asked the village people where they had found these carved stones. They went to fetch the oldest man in their community, believed to be more than 90 years old. He staggered with us to a place between some huge trees where he said there had once been two 'ancient mosques'. The stones had come from the ruins of these former buildings.

I wanted to see their present mosque. It proved to be a modest little building of crude stone fragments and mortar. No Moslem would have torn down two superior mosques built from large decorated slabs with cornices and friezes, to replace them with such an inferior structure. Nor would wartime British forces have found time or funds to build bunkers or barracks with fluted stone decoration as elegant as a Greek temple. Here was something that made no sense if we tried to explain it simply as remains from disused Moslem mosques or British bunkers; for why would religious Moslem islanders have torn down an elegant temple and treated it with such disrespect? Here, surely, we were seeing the first disturbed traces of a truly advanced civilisation which had been established on this equatorial atoll *before* the Moslems became the masters of the Maldive Islands.

The chief of Midu willingly agreed to have one of the fluted stones removed from the mole and brought to Gan for shipment to the museum in Male.

There was evidently nothing more we could do in Addu atoll, but there was every reason to take a closer look at some of the other islands in the Equatorial Channel that had not experienced the impact of modern civilisation. Most tempting of all was the lonely island of Fua Mulaku which lay all by itself, with no ring-reef, in the midst of the wide open Channel.

After many attempts at finding a dhoni to take us there, Björn and Abdul succeeded in negotiating a daily charter fee with the captain-owner of a locally built vessel of quite impressive size. To conclude the deal we had to agree that he could take along any other passengers he could round up for the crossing. The vessel, named *Midu* after the island we had just visited, was skilfully built by local people from hand-split timber of coconut palms cut on the same atoll. It was big and broad, like a giant bath tub, painted green and covered with a high deck.

When the *Midu* came across the lagoon to fetch us from Gan early next morning it was already crammed full of islanders of all ages, and looked like my childhood memory of Noah's Ark. No dogs, however, nor other animals except live chickens, and at least four generations of Noah's own distant descendants. Living quarters for crew and passengers were shoulder to shoulder on deck, where a small boy was busy baking flat Arab bread on a fireplace behind the steering wheel. The eight of us who had chartered the vessel pressed ourselves on board and dug a way for our camera equipment and other sparse possessions down on to deck level between various bundles, bags and piles of green coconuts.

We, and everything else, were separated from the ocean and secured from rolling overboard by a fragile sort of garden fencing. A canvas roof covered the entire Ark almost from bow to stern, which was comforting since last night a deafening thunder-storm with torrential rain had swept the former air force camp, and black clouds on all quarters of the horizon still showed that squalls were about.

Above the crawling multitude on deck were suspended three wooden hammocks, each like a door hanging from ropes at the corners. They were reserved by the captain for himself, Björn, and me. Our companions merrily stretched out on deck, squeezed in between giggling Maldive beauties with or without babies or husbands.

Björn, swinging back and forth as a first-class passenger above the crowd, dug out the worn photocopy of Bell to read aloud about the island we were heading for: Fua Mulaku. Bell showed that it was an atoll consisting of a single island. It was right in the sweep of the Equatorial Current, in the middle of the Equatorial Channel, and almost precisely on the equatorial line. Lying alone in its 'bliss of solitude', wrote Bell, it was justly considered by the Maldivians themselves to be the most beautiful, and most favoured by nature, of all the islands in the archipelago.

How real is the isolation of Fua Mulaku is borne out by the strange fact that even in this Twentieth Century, it remains, to all intents, absolutely unknown to Europeans . . . It is a well-nigh incredible fact, but, so far as known, remains unchallenged, that the only notices of the Island are but two: the first a bare reference by the Maghrabin traveller, Ibn Batuta, in the middle of the Fourteenth Century; the other a fuller account by the two Frenchmen, brothers, Jean and Raoul Parmentier, who likewise chanced to pay merely a passing visit to Fua Mulaku, in the first half of the Sixteenth Century.[5]

We had just passed Midu island and left the lagoon to enter the open Equatorial Channel. Out here was an incredibly fast current, listed as up to 5.5 knots. The tub started rolling, the passengers got sleepy and some women and babies could no longer keep down what they long since had swallowed. Björn, unaccustomed to the sea, lost interest in Bell and I had to read on by myself.

The island we were heading for had no harbour, no lagoon, no safe anchorage. It was the only island in the Maldives that had no exposed reef to shelter its coast. A steep beach of coral shingle, into which the feet sink at every step, falls straight down to a submarine reef. 'Within a few hundred yards of the surrounding reef there are virtually no soundings, so sheer is the drop. To such a shore, approach is necessarily fraught with danger at all times; at seasons it becomes well nigh impossible, except under gravest risk.'

We looked at the dark squalls that surrounded us on all sides, but the captain of the rolling tub was completely undisturbed, sending the cook-boy tumbling around with hot tea and with green leaves containing chopped-up betel nuts to be chewed with lime.

Halfway to our destination we lost sight of the Midu coconut palms which were the last of Addu atoll we saw behind us, but just then I sighted a black spot on the horizon ahead. I first took it for a ship until it proved to be a cluster of trees on some hillock higher than the crowns of the palms, which gradually also rose to the horizon. This started to look exciting. We were clearly heading for a completely different world, rarely visited, and here perhaps would be a prehistoric mound not yet levelled. Bell had only come in the morning and left by noon. He wrote regretfully that fate had not allowed him to unravel the secrets of what he termed 'this lovely gem of the Maldive seas, still practically unknown. Such good fortune may perchance some day fall to a luckier wanderer: for us "Isle of Beauty, fare thee well"'.

I had to close the pages and put the copy away in a waterproof bag. The palms were standing as a green wall very near us now.

We were so close to the island that we could hear the thundering surf and see it rise and tumble white all along the coast. No landing place. We all felt some excitement. At one point on the steep coral beach a crowd of people was busy launching a tiny dhoni into the foaming breakers. It was still bobbing wildly up and down as it came out to take a rope end from the *Midu*. With the dhoni tied to our side brown men from both vessels dived overboard and disappeared. They came back to the surface but kept on swimming and diving until one of them located a long rope somehow fixed to the bottom and permitting a vessel of modest size like ours to moor until the wind changed direction. There was supposed to be such a mooring rope in the open sea on each side of the oblong island, where the wind alternated from opposite directions according to the monsoon seasons.

In groups of three and four we climbed with our belongings into the dancing rowing boat and rode on the crest of the surf into the waiting crowd, who grabbed our hands and pulled us quickly up on to the steep shore before the boat with its two oarsmen hurried out in antelope jumps across the tumbling breakers to fetch the next load.

Adventures began on Fua Mulaku the same day as we landed. We had barely time to make a first survey of the most promising site when we had to come back and identify our own possessions from among the confusion of luggage sent ashore. Someone showed up with a hand-cart and, escorted by a multitude of friendly islanders while others peered from behind their stone walls, we walked through an admirably tidy village almost to the opposite coast. Here we were lodged all by ourselves in a clean, newly finished bungalow, snow white with walls of crushed coral and lime. The house had not yet been lived in except by short-tailed geckos running around on the walls and ceiling catching moths and mosquitos. Nor was there any furniture except for a lot of camp-beds brought in for the occasion.

Fua Mulaku is one of the largest islands in the Maldive archipelago with a population of about 5,600 people living in a village scattered between coconut palms and bread-fruit trees. Large leaves of banana plants and trees full of oranges, lemons, papaya, mango and other tropical fruits also peeped over the stone walls surrounding the little houses. Smoke rose from outdoor kitchen shelters. Most of the huts were white-washed, built from coral fragments and lime, but many were still made from plaited coconut leaves, tanned brown by the sun. The land, as on all the Maldive islands, was sandy and flat as a floor, although here, as we walked across the island, we saw to our surprise some glittering water and taro swamps.

Nobody had known in advance about our arrival, so we were amazed at something which later proved to be an everyday sight in the Maldives: the streets were strewn with fresh white coral sand from the beach. There were always some women bent double in the middle of the road, sweeping with short home-made brushes. They even picked up the droppings from chickens, to leave a spotless passage for all barefoot pedestrians.

There were no foreigners living on Fua Mulaku, although we were to learn of at least two others who had lived among them for some time after Bell's visit. Bell's description still held good, Fua Mulaku was blessed by nature with more fertility and more variety of fruits and root crops than all the other islands put together. The people were also exceptionally beautiful and displayed far more variety in physical type than we had seen in Male. Quite a few were remarkably tall.

It was a hot afternoon when we were installed in our new limestone home. Harald and John rid themselves of their cameras and told us to arrange their sleeping quarters as we pleased. They were more keen on an ocean bath before the sun went down. All efforts to persuade them to refrain were of no avail. They said they knew there was no lagoon. They knew there was surf and coastal currents. But they were used to that kind of peril from all the months they had filmed *jangada* rafts tackling the wild Atlantic waves, or the *shampans* in the surf of Bangladesh. They had dived from and even capsized with all sorts of primitive craft. They were not, of course, under my command. They had come with Neil to film sailing dhonis but had been side-tracked by the possibility of finding traces of a lost civilisation. So, happy at the thought of a dip, they grabbed their towels and left for the nearest sea shore, assuring us they would do nothing foolhardy.

A few minutes later I left the house too, to see where they had gone. The west coast beach was only a couple of hundred metres away, but storms had tossed up a high bank of sand and coral

41

shingle which obstructed any view of the sea from the house. Once up on the sand bar I had full view of the naked coast. Where I stood was a tiny boat turned keel up, with two islanders busy caulking some cracks. Our two friends were already far out in deep water, waving merrily with their arms. They were in the dancing waves outside the submerged edge of the shallow reef, and I found it hard for a moment to separate a feeling of annoyance at their carelessness from admiration for their courage and skill. But, strangely, they went on waving after I had waved back twice with both my arms.

Suddenly I realised they were not waving for fun at all. They were in danger.

I knew only too well that I could not manage to swim past the reef and bring anybody ashore through that surf. I would be chopped to pieces against the sharp coral wall, and so would they if they tried to get closer to the edge of the reef than they already were. They were safe only as long as they kept on treading water outside the breakers at the edge of the reef.

I ran to the two islanders who calmly went on working on their boat. The continuous thunder of the surf all along the coast made it impossible for anyone ashore to hear anyone out at sea, no matter how much they yelled. I grabbed the nearest man by the arm and turned his face, pointing at the two who were now clearly waving in despair and battling with the ocean swell. The man looked, then brusquely shook himself loose from my grip and bent down to continue his work. He and I had no language in common, so I pulled him around again and made it very clear with signs that the two out there were drowning, and that we had to launch the little boat together and row out to save them.

Now he got visibly angry and, with flashing eyes, he snarled something at me and nervously started to fumble again with his own work. So did the other man. Before I could interrupt once more, our Maldivian interpreter, Abdul, was at my side and immediately saw the danger. He yelled something to the two boatmen, who answered back without looking up from their work.

'They say they have no oars,' Abdul translated.

'Never mind,' I shouted furiously, 'tell them we can paddle this little boat with our hands!'

By this time a small crowd of curious islanders had gathered around us. I expected them all naturally to be master swimmers. None, however, showed any interest in the two men struggling to keep afloat outside the reef. Abdul hurriedly translated for me the dry statement that three of their own women had drowned last month because they had been stupid enough to take a bath at this place on the reef. But now we saw, to our great relief, a small rowing boat with two men fishing in the open sea beyond our friends. They were rowing very slowly but, it seemed, on the right course for the two who were now waving in panic as they apparently had seen the boat. The whole crowd of us ashore ran back and forth and waved with shirts and palm leaves, yelling as loudly as we could although we realised that no one outside the surf could hear us.

Now the men in the boat had obviously seen the two in the water. They headed straight for them. We all felt a vast relief. But too soon. A few oar-strokes away from the sprawling swimmers the rowing boat stopped. Next we could hardly believe our eyes. The oars slowly began to row in the opposite direction. The distance from the two men in the water increased as the boat pulled away. Soon it was so far out at sea again that we paid no more attention to it.

Abdul had by now been told that someone had run for oars at a nearby house. I suddenly noticed in the crowd a bushy-bearded face with glasses. It was Neil. He came over to me with a curious expression and asked calmly what all the commotion was about. I had hardly pointed and uttered the names of his two colleagues before he ran desperately down to the water and dived in before anybody could stop him. He disappeared in one wave and when he came up in the next he had lost his glasses and could see nothing. The following wave knocked him over and sucked him out to the edge of the reef.

When the villagers came running with the oars. Neil and the other two cameramen were all struggling for their lives, one in the tumultuous surf on the reef and two outside. The equatorial sun was fast on its vertical descent into the sea, which would leave no space for twilight, just as when the theatre lights are dimmed before a performance.

Things now happened so fast and confusedly that it was difficult to follow. Before the men with the oars reached the water, some others had pulled a hidden rowboat out from under the trees. First wading, and then paddling with their hands, they reached the two men out in the deep water and pulled one into their boat. Neil came tumbling in by himself with a huge wave, either because he was a master swimmer or because he had Allah on his side. Groping to find his way to land without glasses, he was grabbed by strong arms and pulled up on the beach, joined in the big wave by the boatmen with John. John staggered up the steep shingle slope without help, white as a moon and with all the signs of shock. A moment later somebody else came carrying Harald, lifeless as a corpse. He began to move as Björn started resuscitation and pumped water out of him in rhythmical jets.

As the sun set, Fua Mulaku was lost in tropical darkness, Harald and John got their voices back and sat up with the rest of us around a kerosene lamp to tell their story. Abdul came with the island chief and told us that the village population was furious with the two men in the boat who had come right up to the drowning foreigners and then had left them to their fate. John and Harald had seen the boat all the time from the moment a sudden undertow had pulled them off the reef. They said they had shouted 'help, help!' until the boat came and was almost within reach. Then the two rowers had abruptly turned their boat and one of them had scornfully repeated 'help, help' as they leaned to the oars and rowed away.

'Why?' we asked.

None of the islanders gave any answer. If they knew why, they kept it to themselves. They certainly did not approve of such hostile conduct, even to non-Moslem strangers.

A thunder-storm rumbled over the island all night and at 5 am our three friends had suddenly decided to break their Maldive adventure. They asked if the chartered vessel could take them back to Gan where they would wait for the first flight to Male. Björn and I agreed so long as they sent the boat back for us. Left with Björn and me was Abdul, our interpreter, and Björn's two Sri Lankan pupils with their video equipment.

As the sun rose I went back to the place of near disaster to see if it was possible to take a morning bath in the shallows without risking getting out near the abrupt edge of the reef. I was not going to take any chances, but I felt like a coward when I waded out to my knees and lay down in lukewarm water. Little more than ripples flowed in from the ocean now because the tide was low. Even so I placed myself by a big ball-shaped coral to hang on to if an unexpected sea should tumble in.

Life felt wonderful. The eastern sky was purple-red around the newborn morning sun that barely twinkled behind the coconut palms. Suddenly the water level rose. As an unexpected wave came from the beach, I felt a drag on my body and grabbed the stony coral with both hands, hanging on with all my strength. The suction increased and tore my feet off the bottom. If I had let go I would have been swept into the ocean like our friends the day before.

This was absurd, the terrific flow had not come in from the sea. Then the rushing current died down, and before anything worse happened I waded quickly back onto dry land. Now I understood why even the utmost care was not enough here. A big wave had obviously tumbled in against the steep beach somewhere further up the coast and been forced sideways along the shore until it found an open channel out across the coral ledge, just where we had found it deep enough to take a bath.

The owner of the house we had rented, a big husky islander who usually had a friendly dwarf toddling at his heels, served us breakfast of fresh, unleavened Arab bread, bananas, tea and coconut milk brought from another village house, and then we set off on our search.

The mystery of this island seemed to be concentrated around one huge man-made hill. Bell had seen it briefly and so far it had never been visited by any archaeologist. Possibly it was of the same type that had existed on Gan until the airport was constructed.

Bell had first heard of a mound on Fua Mulaku when he met a native from this island in Male after his shipwreck in 1879. His records show that, according to the islanders, there were, on Fua Mulaku, jungle-covered ruins 'resembling the bell-shaped Dágobas rising from platforms found in Ceylon, and amid them a Stone Image of the Buddha in the *sthana-mudra* (erect attitude)'.

Such rumours had made Bell conclude:

Whilst the evidence so far available is both quite insufficient, and of a nature too vague, to warrant definite conclusion, it is far from improbable that . . . Buddhist Missionaries, in the spirit of the Asöka Edicts, departing to intermingle among all unbelievers, teaching better things, carried their doctrine across the sea even to the despised and little known Maldives.[6]

When Bell finally came back to the Maldives in 1922, his brief morning visit to Fua Mulaku permitted him merely to measure the remains of the ancient structure. It was still a good 7 metres (25 feet) high, covered by trees and coconut palms. Part of the walls had been trenched and robbed but enough of the original casing masonry of hard, dressed coral blocks still remained to convince him that it was definitely the remains of a former Buddhist dagoba, or stupa. The Moslem islanders had carried away the best part of the squared facing slabs, but the big hillock formed by the inner filling of the structure nobody had managed to remove. Of the standing Buddha, however, nothing was remembered and nothing seen. Bell concluded that what he heard in 1879 'may have then been true; but nothing was known – at any rate not divulged – about any Buddhist images forty years or so later'.[7]

It was with great anticipation that we ourselves, another sixty years later still, set out to see the remains of the *hawitta*, as the islanders called it. Now there was wheeled traffic on Fua Mulaku: a few hand-carts and quite a number of bicycles. The flat island is about 4 miles long from north to south and roughly 2 miles wide. On borrowed bicycles we rode through the wide village streets and along a narrow footpath into the dense evergreen forest. Near the north-east end of the land the trail passed right by the foot of a steep, stony hillock that rose above us, thickly covered by shrubbery and palm-like pandanus trees. We jumped off and hid the bicycles in the undergrowth. Crawling up the hill on all fours we followed a ravine running up one side and ending in a crater on the summit.

The big mound had been plundered.

Certainly not by Bell during his lightning morning visit. The wound in the structure was fairly free from vegetation and filled with crude lumps of coral of all sizes mixed with a few nicely squared limestone blocks, clearly fallen in from a former outer wall.

From the top we could see only a green wilderness, and no

houses; the whole area around the hawitta had been left empty and uncultivated. There was a stony plain with some coconut palms on the seaward side, and thick jungle on the village side. Beyond the coastline the blue waters of the Equatorial Channel stretched to the horizon. An old man confirmed my suspicion that this hawitta had served him and the other island mariners as a landmark for navigation, especially when the stone walls of the hawitta had still been covered by a coat of white lime plaster.

As we crawled through the dense underbrush around the mound, we were closely followed by islanders who never for a moment let us out of sight. We discovered occasional carved blocks elegantly shaped to serve as pedestals, plinths, foundations for walls, pillars and other architectural structures, to our minds better suited to ancient Greece than on this small island. This reminded us, nevertheless, of what we had seen scattered about in the mole and garden walls on Midu.

A little further along the trail we could not miss stumbling on another irregularity in the ground, a low but wide mound that again proved to be littered with plinths, lintel segments and other profiled stones. This was the meagre remains of *Kudu Hawitta*, 'Little Hawitta', as someone in our steadily growing escort admitted. This hawitta had been much bigger, but people had carried away all the stones, another man added. We asked for permission to clear away the big-leafed plants and creeping shrubbery that covered the mound, and a number of adults and children joyfully gave us a hand.

Optimistically we asked if there were still other hawittas on the island. No, they all agreed. There were only these two.

At that moment we heard a shout from Mohamed Waheed, the usually silent officer of the Island Administration. He was standing on some elevation, hidden inside a thick wall of foliage, and called out that there was another hawitta there. Everybody seemed greatly surprised, and slightly embarrassed, insisting that this was a new discovery. To make this clear in the face of our obvious doubt, they decided to name this third ruin *Waheed Hawitta*, in honour of its proud discoverer.

Most of the area was made impenetrable by the tight growth of leathery, long-leafed pandanus palms of all heights, their edges densely set with thorns, sharp as needles. Other ruins, no doubt razed to the ground, were probably hidden in this wilderness. In the thickest part we stumbled into a deep depression. Only later did we discover that it was the remains of a ceremonial bath, possibly of the type that the queen had used on Hitadu. We noted several signs of former occupation, including very old potsherds.

In the almost barren shingle on the seaward side of the big hawitta, Björn yelled that he had stumbled upon an alignment of beautifully cut and fitted stones set in a perfect circle. The diameter was big enough for a man to stretch out inside, and each stone had been cut slightly wedge-shaped, as if intended to be the first tier for a vault built like an igloo.

With Abdul as interpreter I had made friends with a gentle elderly man named Ibrahim Said, who watched me intently as I admired the remains of the exquisite stonework. The big hawitta had been beautiful before, he suddenly volunteered. He had seen it before it was destroyed. He recalled steps that had led up the seaward wall. Also high up on that wall there had been a long line of 'letters' in signs no one understood. The line of writing had been about 2.5 metres (8 feet) long, the signs less than 30 centimetres (1 foot) in height. And then he loosened up further. I had just found a well-preserved segment of a round stone pillar about 45 centimetres (18 inches) in diameter, and asked what this could have been. It had been part of a column, I learnt, reaching to the height of a man's chest.

'For what purpose?' I asked.

'To hold betel nut and betel leaves mixed with lime.'

'But did people have to come to the hawitta to chew betel, could they not do it at home?'

'Not people. This was for the stone buddu.'

Buddu was, of course, the Maldive term for any kind of statue, and I wanted to know what this buddu was like.

He had never seen it. His mother had told him that the buddu was about 1.6 metres (5½ feet) tall. It stood on the ground close to another statue which was about 1 metre (3 feet) tall. The buddu had one hand held in front. His mother had seen it standing, before some young boys destroyed it; but she had never seen the offerings of betel, he hastened to add. He himself had never seen anything of this sort, only a small stone elephant somebody had found near the small hawitta. It was about 20–25 centimetres (8–10 inches) long and was carved from hard lime-stone, with a long nose and tusks. It was brought to the village but lost. I asked him to make a drawing from memory. He drew something that looked more like a match with four legs and hanging head and tail. But when others came to listen he had no more to say.

The midday sun was scorching, we all had empty stomachs, and a long line of bicycles and pedestrians soon headed back to the village.

It had been made amply clear to us that these people did not like to talk about things they considered to be heathen when others were present. However, with the aid of our two friends from Male, Abdul and Waheed, and the island chief, we located an elderly man who had accompanied Bell to the hawitta, and we invited him along to our house that evening. Magi Eduruge Ibrahim Diddi gave his age as 74. He did not remember much about Bell's visit except that Bell took many measurements, collected old objects and was unable to read the foreign script above the steps in the hawitta. This was surprising he said, for Bell could read both European and Singalese letters as his father was British and his mother Singalese from Sri Lanka.

Bell had not seen the image, he added.

'Which image?'

'The stone image of *Mahafoti Kalege*.'

'Who was he?'

'That was the image of the man with the fish. *Mahafoti Kalege* means "Owner of the Fish". That was the name the old islanders had given to this image. But they invented this name themselves, because the stone figure held a piece of fish hanging on a rope.'

We had never heard of Buddha holding a piece of fish on a rope. Nor did our visitor believe that the 'Owner of the Fish' depicted Buddha.

Our visitor could remember that, after Bell's visit, somebody else had come from Male and it was that person who had dug the huge trench in the hawitta. They had found four stone boxes and a stone incense burner. Each of the four stone boxes had two chambers, one full of charcoal and ashes, and the other with 'things' like gold strips. At that time many of the parts of broken stone images, such as hands, were lying about the hawitta.

Our next visitor was Ahmed Ali Diddi. He was about the same age and recalled the hawitta with a conical summit with large slabs on top. He had no comments on the writing, but had heard about the stone statue. It was called *Mahafoti Kalege* and represented a man with a piece of fish hanging on a rope. *Maha* meant 'fish', *foti* meant 'slice' and *Kalege* was not just 'man', but 'gentleman'. Allah was called *Maikalege* in their language which meant 'Big Gentleman'.

This was beginning to get complicated. As these people were Moslem, they would never carve a statue of any man. The hawitta was identified by Bell as a Buddhist structure, but Buddhists would never offer betel nuts to a man with a fish on a rope.

Instead of inviting the old people to visit us, which would involve long walks for a generation who did not know how to use a bicycle, we went in the evening to the widely scattered huts of the elders, and sat with them in their wooden hammocks to hear their stories. We realised perfectly well that whatever they told us would not be as dependable as archaeological remains which we could see with our own eyes. There would be many reasons to be sceptical about details in their stories, whether intentional or not. On these islands, to touch upon other religions than Islam was a most delicate affair. Besides, human memories were not always reliable. Our objective was to extract from their statements any fragment of information which might imply that other people, besides their own ancestors, had been present on this island in former times.

Ali Mussa Diddi was 75. He had been present when the big hawitta was plundered. He had seen the human bones they found. Just under the present ground level they had dug up a slab and under it was no box but a skeleton with a skull. They had taken the bones and buried them near the mosque. He had also seen the double-chambered stone boxes which he said were thrown back with the rubble into the hawitta while the contents were taken to Male. He had seen *Mahafoti Kalege* standing near the small hawitta. It was still there in Bell's time, but he did not touch it. It was the statue of a naked man without beard or hair, with the penis broken, and with a piece of fish on a cord. He had also seen the elephant. It was definitely an elephant, about one foot tall.

The stories of *Mahafoti Kalege* were reconfirmed as we went from house to house. Abdulla Mufeed had heard a tale explaining how this statue came into being. His grandfather had told him that, long ago, people coming from the Arabian side lost their way at sea and arrived on this island. Later one person named Ambolakeu went to fish and his wife was standing onshore. Just as he was to give fish to his wife, a jinni passed by and threw coral sand at them, so that both were turned to stone. One man and one woman. Abdulla had seen them himself, but after they had been broken. Both had very big heads with long faces. The legs and arms were shorter than on ordinary people. They had big ears, small eyes and no hair or beard. They looked like Japanese. The woman had a smaller forehead than the man, but a very long face too. The man had one hand coming forth with outstretched fingers holding a very short rope with a round slice of fish. The woman was nude with small nipples and a groove for sex. The man was also nude but with his sexual organs broken. They had been standing on stone pillars near the small hawitta before they were destroyed. The woman had no name, but the man's name was 'Owner of the Fish'. Abdulla had seen the elephant too, big as a rabbit with four legs, teeth and trunk.

It seemed obvious that the legend of the jinni throwing sand, and turning the fisherman and his wife into stone, was invented by a people who had found the statues already standing on the spot. Not knowing their origin or function they created their own explanation.

Our interview with old Abdul Rajmal, 90 years of age, was less successful. The old man spoke a local dialect which our interpreter from Male did not understand, and he had to resort to assistance from younger relatives. Soon the old man's house and garden were full of people and our host, who had previously spoken freely, suddenly could not remember anything. Nobody recalled anything. To make an effect I uttered a magic name:

'*Mahafoti Kalege!*'

They all reacted. A young boy at my side repeated the name and pointed with a broad smile towards the north-east cape as he mentioned the word: hawitta. Many in the crowd laughed shyly, but a man above middle age suddenly came rushing out of the door waving a stick. He drew a circle in the ground in front of my feet.

'This is what *Mahafoti Kalege* looked like, a round stone with a hole in it! It was nothing other than the kind of anchor stone they used here in former times.'

I ventured to ask why they had called a round stone 'Mr Piece of Fish', and the man had a quick answer that settled the discussion:

'A piece of fish can have any shape.'

We thanked our hosts for their good company and interesting information and rode off into the village darkness. The streets were wide, straight and long, and the houses set far apart, so at night we saw only the glare from occasional paraffin lamps. Otherwise there was nothing but the silhouettes of the huge banana leaves groping for the sky, with the still taller, crooked bread-fruit trees that seemed to spread their lobate foliage among the stars.

In another part of the village we had better luck. Muhammed Maniku, 70 years old, was not afraid to talk. In former times, he said, Singalese fishermen from Sri Lanka sometimes stopped here 'to give thanks'. They were very religious. His father had seen Singalese fishermen who stayed over on this island to offer fish to the statue. Raw fish. They had had 'good contact' with the statue. He himself had taken part in the digging of the big hawitta, but had little new information to add except that the man who had come from Male had seen the writing on the wall, which he said resembled Tamil signs. They resembled Singalese signs, according to what Abdulla Mufeed had told us before. He had heard this from old people who had sailed to Sri Lanka and who had also told him that the hawitta looked like a Singalese temple, and that Singalese sometimes came and lived nearby.

Back in our own house we had a late visit from our fine host, Kennari Ibrahim Diddi, a strongly built middle-aged man, a former sea captain, and one-time official representative of Fua Mulaku in Male. Kennari was a calm and authoritative person, with experience of the world. When asked if he had heard of any statue on the island he said he knew the man who had buried one.

'Wasn't it two?' Björn asked.

'Oh, you mean the woman figure?' our host blurted out. He then added that there must once have been many figures. When they dug the large hawitta they had found arms and fragments of other statues. But the digging had been a search for treasure only, so all this had been thrown back into the first trench and buried there. If we wanted to know more he could take us to an old relative who had been the foreman during the digging.

Hussain Kalefán, who was 73 and the relative to whom Kennari was referring, told us that a certain Adam Naseer Manik had come long after Bell's visit. He said he had been sent from Male to dig the hawitta. Hussain had therefore helped him to find workmen and, as they dug into the hawitta, they found some stone boxes with lids on. There was gold inside which the visitor had taken to Male. Deeper down there had been another stone box containing a small image. This image was not taken to Male, nor was it destroyed. It was not the same image as *Mahafoti Kalege* with the fish, it was only about 30 centimetres (1 foot) tall. Nor was it like Buddha, but naked, and standing with hands and long fingers straight down the sides. It had eyes, nose and mouth made to look more like a man than a devil, and it had no ears and no teeth exposed. The 'leader' from Male had not cared for it. In any case, it was forbidden to show a human figure in Male. People could be put in jail for less, even if they only drew a human figure in the sand.

This was important information. The statue was said to be still there, in the same stone box, left under the coral rubble they had thrown back into the wound in the hawitta. It could be easily recovered without damaging the old structure. All we had to do was to dig where it had been dug before, and extract the stone box.

We chose Kennari as foreman for a team to reopen the trench, but first we wanted our companion Waheed from the Atoll Administration to obtain authorisation from Male. Each atoll had an atoll chief who had daily radio contact with Male. Waheed spent hours with the little radio in the chief's office trying to get our message through. Finally we got word back. They had appointed a National Moslem Committee to decide whether the hawitta could be reopened. We must not touch the mound until we had heard from Male again.

In the meantime, we lost no time in obtaining more information from the village people. Another old islander, Ibrahim Didi Kalo Sehigé, had looked into the stone boxes as they were extracted from the hawitta. Each of them had two chambers and a vaulted lid jutting from the walls like the roof of a house. In one he had seen gold in a brass tin, in another a fire burner with charcoal and ashes. He confirmed that a small standing statue had been left buried in its own stone box.

An old woman, Kadija Ibrahim Kalifan, was pointed out as the widow of the chief at the time that the gold was taken from the hawitta. It was taken by a person she referred to as a 'leader' from Male. Everything he had found in the hawitta he had kept in her home until he left the island. He had only shown her two bowls full of amber and small gold objects, and some charms that had to do with witchcraft. But she knew they had also found a skull and other human bones. These had not been buried near the mosque, but beside the hawitta.

Björn Bye and his two Singalese students were tape-recording songs and rhymes, when a middle-aged man, Ahmed Mussa, contributed a very rhythmical poem that proved to be known even to the young people on the island. This was the first time we heard about the Redin.

Probably nobody would have thought of, or even volunteered to mention the Redin, had it not come to us in a local poem. It was a rhyme praising their own island, with one particular verse dedicated to the great hawitta:

> *Redin taneke hedi ihao*
> *Hawittai dágebó singhala maumore ko.*
> *Etá buddé hutte dò*
> *balang damá huri etó.*

Abdul translated with help from those versed in the local dialect:

> It was here the Redin once created
> the hawitta, very old, built by Singalese.
> There was a statue there you see,
> shall we go and have a look
> whether it is there . . .

The reference to a possibly hidden statue seemed clear enough, but the reference to two distinct originators of the hawitta at first seemed to make no sense. Bell had identified the Fua Mulaku hawitta as a former Buddhist stupa of the very ancient Singalese type he had seen in Sri Lanka. So it was reasonable to accept the poet's claim that it had been built by Singalese. But who was Redin? And if the Singalese had built the hawitta, how could it first have been created by Redin?

It was only a long time afterwards that the implications began to dawn upon me. During those first days and nights in a strange community of mixed secrecy and confidence, there was too much to digest to draw meaningful conclusions. We also received a visit by a young islander from the northern atolls, sent here as a school teacher, who wanted me to know that, on this island, there was more knowledge of early history and more non-Moslem beliefs than the people dared to admit to outsiders.

He was probably right, yet new fragments pertaining to the island's past continued to fill my notebooks. I was particularly keen to obtain information on the mysterious Redin. Then, in rechecking Bell's report, I found a casual reference to Redin in a note concerning a mound Bell had visited on an island in Haddummati atoll: 'No tradition exists regarding this mound, beyond the attribution of its construction to so-called "Redin", as the reputed ancient builders of all such colossal work.'

So Redin was not a person, but a people. Later Bell says about another such structure up in the northern atolls, at Miladu island: 'From superstition, the Islanders are afraid to dig into the mound, which they call *"Redinge Funi"*.'[8]

Redinge Funi means 'Redin's Hill'. The two atolls where Bell had heard about Redin were at opposite ends of the long chain of the Maldive Islands. And now we learned that Redin was also remembered as the initiator of the large mound on Fua Mulaku.

In our efforts to learn more about the days of the legendary Redin people we found, to our surprise, that it was a general conviction among the population that, when the Redin created the hawitta, Fua Mulaku had been an atoll with a lagoon inside. In very ancient times, they all said, ships could sail right into the middle of the island and anchor or dock where now there was cultivated land. They had heard from their ancestors how, very long ago, a terrific storm had tossed up coral blocks and sand that blocked the entrance to the lagoon and gradually transformed it into fertile fields with a freshwater lake in the centre. They were so firm in this belief that they took us to the place on the south coast, now an uninterrupted steep boulder beach, where the entrance was said to have been.

They also took us inland to a beautiful freshwater lake, some 274 metres (300 yards) across, from which ditches ran through boggy marshland in all directions to flood the taro fields. Bandara Kuli was the name of the lake, the first and only I had ever seen, or even heard of, on a coral island. The surface, smooth as a mirror, reflected an unbroken picture of green tropical foliage, banana leaves, and coconut palms. In here the Redin were supposed to have sailed before sharks and lobsters were locked out and the coral rock garden at the bottom was replaced by dark and fertile humus. This explained why it was well known throughout the archipelago that no other island in the group was blessed with such a variety of tropical fruits, flowers and vegetables as Fua Mulaku.

Somewhere in the midst of this verdant paradise were supposed to be the remains of an ancient buried wharf which we never managed to see.

It was hard to rid oneself of the vision of this inland lake when Muhammad Ali Diddi spoke about the former Fua Mulaku lagoon. His grandfather had told him that very, very long ago Fua Mulaku had lost its lagoon and changed to become only land.

'This change took place before we became Moslems,' he said. 'When we embraced Islam there were already people living in the centre of the island.'

At that time there was a fisherman called Ambola Keu, or Ambola Keola. He came sailing into the inside of the island and there he passed from one side of the lagoon to the hawitta side where he met two old men with very long beards, down to their chests. They were not Moslem. They were clad in white garments made from leaves. Abdul first translated these as banana leaves, but corrected it. The material was pandanus leaves. The custom of this earlier population was to soak the narrow strips of pandanus leaves in water, then peel them and hammer the strips together with a wooden club to make a kind of cloth, smooth as silk. The clothing of these two men covered only their sexual parts. They both used walking sticks and had the appearance of religious people. Ambola Keu had been fishing, and the two old men commanded: 'Give fish!' They did not beg or ask gently. Ambola gave them pieces of fish strung on a rope. They hung the fish on their walking sticks over their shoulders and walked away.

When the grandfather of our informant had heard this story, he asked:

'Who were these people that Ambola Keu met?'

'They were the people of the hawitta.'

The place where Ambola had anchored was at Iduga Koletere, now dry land inside the island.

The connection between the episode describing Ambola's meeting with the people of the hawitta and the lost statue of the 'Owner of the Fish' was unclear. But the ancient fisherman, Ambola Keu, had the same name as the fisherman in the legend who was bewitched by a devil into the stone statue *Mahafoti Kalege*.

The same informant was vague in his memory of that statue. 'It is destroyed,' was all he recollected. 'All the statues were destroyed.'

'Who made the statues?'

'The Redin. The Redin made both the hawitta and the statues.'

'Who were the Redin?'

The old man shrugged his shoulders. They might have been Singalese, at least they spoke a language different from the Divehi of the Maldivians. The Redin were on these islands first and the Maldivians came later. The Redin were white people. The colour of their hair was brown. Our informant touched Björn's chestnut-coloured hair to emphasise what he meant. They had big hooked noses and blue eyes. A tall people, with long faces. They made statues and worshipped them.

He confirmed that a different statue had been found inside the big hawitta, but he thought that one had been destroyed. 'The Owner of the Fish' and the female statue had stood next to the small hawitta. He knew nothing more about the Redin.

We returned to Hussain Kalefán, the foreman of the old dig, and asked him if he had heard about the Redin. We were seated with his family inside his house, and everybody around the table looked at each other in silence as if they did not understand the question. But as the adults hesitated, a bright little boy stepped forward from behind me and exclaimed:

'Redin, sure, he lived here.'

The parents seemed embarrassed. The father ignored this strange remark. He tried to side-track the discussion by suggesting that Redin was just the name of a mythical people. I wanted to know what the Redin looked like, but nobody knew. Perhaps they had only been some Hindu, our host suggested. As the boy kept on insisting that he had seen Redin in this house I asked his parents if they had had a Hindu visitor. They both laughed shyly and said no, but a foreigner like us had come to the island and had stayed in their house. His real name was Michael. They had only nicknamed him 'Redin' because he had brown hair and looked like a Redin.

We were grateful to the little boy for this unintended piece of information from his father. So, the image these people had of the Redin was that they had brown hair and looked like us!

Legendary references to seafaring people with fair skin and brown hair are well known from pre-Columbian Mexico and Peru, and even on Easter Island. Certainly these early seafaring stone-masons in the legends had not come from Europe. But people fitting this description had also existed outside Europe. There were brown-haired people with fair skin in the Middle East and western Asia. The only thing we could deduce with certainty from what these people told us, was that the present population on Fua Mulaku did not believe that the big mounds had been left by their own ancestors, but by an earlier people who looked to them like foreigners. So a strange old legend, common in other parts of the world, was also present on these lonely islands in the Indian Ocean.

We were soon to learn that probably every adult on Fua Mulaku, and most people throughout the Maldives, had heard about the Redin; but few admitted openly that they believed in these ancient stories. To the modern Maldive youth the word Redin meant no more than did jinni and other terms for spirits and fairies. Soon it will be too late to save even the last remnants of pre-Moslem legends in the Maldives.

While we waited for permission from Male to reopen the trench where the islanders said the small buddu had been reburied in its box, the village people began to disagree on whether or not it was wise to search for that pagan figure again. Some of them were suddenly eager to assure us that it would be a waste of time. One old man came to testify that it was not true that a buddu had been found in any of the stone boxes. On checking his reliability we learned from the foreman of the dig at that time that this 'eyewitness' had not been anywhere near the hawitta when it was dug. The foreman himself confirmed that he had seen the buddu. We therefore returned to the old man. He now admitted he had only told us what he had heard from a trustworthy person who had actually been at the site and assured him that he had seen no buddu. When Björn and Abdul went to locate that eyewitness, they found to their surprise that he was a blind man.

There was no reason to upset the superstitious among the local people, nor had any permission come from Male to reopen the trench. We decided therefore to forget the hawitta for the time being. The *Midu* had returned from delivering the three cameramen to Gan, and we wanted to proceed now to the islands along the northern edge of the Equatorial Channel. Departure proved impossible, however. The *Midu* had rested safely at anchor in the lee of the island since its return, but when we wanted to leave Fua Mulaku we found that someone had fiddled with the engine and the propeller would no longer turn. The captain reported laconically that the *Midu* would remain here forever unless someone lent him a compressor. There was no such thing on Fua Mulaku, and unless we wanted to settle there indefinitely, we would have to get one from Gan. Sixteen men in an open dhoni rowed all the way across the Equatorial Channel to Gan and came back two days later with a compressor.

In the meantime, we explored the island in search of other traces of the Redin. Whoever they were, they must have left something behind other than the colossal hawitta.

CHAPTER III
The First Fingerprint
Voyages through Space and Time

A FEW HUNDRED yards from the big hawitta, a tiny old mosque lay abandoned all by itself at the side of the forest trail. By any scale it was small and modest, but even more so in comparison with what was still left of its titanic neighbour. The Redin who had built the pyramidal colossus would surely have frowned at the modest house of worship that took its place when Mohamed's faith reached Fua Mulaku.

The contrast in dimensions between these two old religious shrines seemed to testify to the victory of faith over purely physical might. Whoever the Redin were, they had put an enormous amount of wealth, skill and physical labour into their mountainous structure. The mosque, in contrast, had been built with minimal effort by some mason who had quite simply fetched the ready-shaped stones from the fine walls of the giant Redin structure.

This was confirmed to us by the village elders. The little mosque was the oldest Moslem structure on the island. The fine polished limestone slabs in its walls had been shaped by the Redin to form the fitted walls that had once covered the loose fill which was now all there was left of the former temple. When Islam was embraced by the local people, they had stripped the blocks from the hawitta and carried them to this place to build the first mosque to Allah. In front of this mosque was the tombstone of Yusuf Naib Kalegefan, who had converted the people of this island to Islam. Yusuf was the son of Yahya Naib Kalegefan who had come sailing from some distant land soon after Male had been converted.

The walls of Yusuf's mosque had attracted my attention from the very first day. Never had I seen more beautifully carved and polished limestone slabs, fitted together as if cut from cheese rather than from the solid island bedrock. Yet some of the slabs, jutting out at the corners, revealed that they had not been designed for use here, and one wall was simply patched together by small bits of limestone cemented with burnt lime, as was customary in the village houses.

A closer examination revealed that Yusuf had raised his mosque on the foundation platform of an older, classical structure. The stones in the base were elegantly fluted, and were still assembled as when first set in the ground.

Eager not to miss any track of the old Redin, we followed the paved path that normally runs from the door of a mosque to a sacred well in front of it. At Yusuf's mosque, this path was so elaborately fitted from carved blocks that it seemed to be part of the pre-Moslem works. It actually by-passed the little well and disappeared among some shrubbery. We followed it and found a big rectangular basin among the bushes, glittering full of water.

The basin proved to be an elegant structure, almost buried under soil and turf. It was built like a small swimming pool, with polished slabs closely fitted together. The base of the mosque, the path and the pool clearly belonged together and were from the same period. The local people confirmed that worshippers in former times had submerged here for ritual baths. Today, it was never used except occasionally for profane washings.

One conclusion could already be drawn from the superior masonry that we ascribed to the pre-Moslem period. Evidently the masons of the hawitta period were not a mere handful of savages who had landed here by chance at some remote time in antiquity. The remains along this forest trail were the work of skilled architects and professional masons who had settled this island on a voyage from some area where their ancestors had already developed a degree of culture. Here, in the Equatorial Channel, we were beginning to find the first tracks of civilised prehistoric navigators.

Yusuf's mosque was not the only one on the island. In the village area there were bigger mosques, but they were more recent and therefore built like the village houses from crude bits of broken coral and lime. We remained profoundly impressed by the fitted masonry in the walls of Yusuf's mosque until we stumbled upon a large semi-buried structure in front of the village mosque of Kedeere.

The Kedeere mosque itself was just a small shack surrounded by a modest Moslem graveyard. We again noted magnificently fluted temple stones reused at random as border stones between tombs and pathways. By following a slab-paved path from the doorsteps we were surprised to come to a large sunken enclosure. A broad and majestic flight of stairs built from huge carved blocks brought us down to a roofless room part-filled with gravel. In the centre of this gravel floor was a small stone-lined Moslem well, filled with water. The original floor of the room could not be seen, as the walls disappeared down into the gravel. The high walls around us were fitted together so tightly from large polished blocks of masonry as if to make a watertight enclosure.

The Moslem well in the centre was obviously a secondary feature dug down into what must be a half-buried ceremonial bath. The bath itself was square with all walls 5.3 metres (17 feet 4 inches) wide and oriented exactly north–south, east–west. Standing in the partly buried basin, we could not see over the walls.

The megalithic stairway descended the east wall, and was broad enough for a man to stretch out across. The stones used were truly large, even though they were cut as straight and smooth as a panel of glass. We measured one that was 2.45 metres (just over 8 feet) long, 63 cm (just over 2 feet) wide, and polished to an even thickness of 10 centimetres (4 inches). For hard limestone from the island bedrock to be cut with such precision made us marvel. Although fitted so closely that a knife-blade could not enter between them, these blocks were all of different sizes and not always rectangular. Many had one or more corners stepped in as shoulders and yet matching their neighbours as closely as the pieces in a jigsaw puzzle.

This sunken structure was indeed an important piece of that jigsaw puzzle which had brought me to these islands. It was more than a piece in a puzzle, it was a fingerprint. The slabs in Yusuf's mosque had been looted from the old hawitta but had not been reset with the original precision. These walls had never been taken apart, however. They were original. The people who had designed them had used an exceedingly difficult technique by following an important aesthetic or magico-religious tradition known only to a few restricted pre-European civilisations. It was unknown anywhere in Europe. Unknown indeed to the best masons in most of the world. In a very conspicuous manner, this peculiar masonry tradition followed the distribution of the people who had once built reed boats.

These walls carried my thoughts back to distant places I had visited in my efforts to trace early human migration routes by sea. They had been typical for people with notedly maritime cultures, in fact for ocean navigators. The first time I saw such walls was on the world's loneliest speck of land, Easter Island. Next time, it was in the former Inca territory of South America. Then on the Atlantic coast of North Africa, in Asia Minor, and lastly on the island of Bahrain in the Persian Gulf. Each time I saw them, these walls were associated with reed ships, and each time they came closer to the Indian Ocean. Here I had finally seen them on an island far out in the Indian Ocean. Thus they were spread around half the world's circumference, with Easter Island and the Maldives representing antipodes. Contact would seem impossible. But no. When I came to think of it I had covered all these same ocean gaps myself in prehistoric types of vessels.

In the whole Pacific Ocean they existed nowhere else except on Easter Island. The lost civilisation that had left the long-eared statues there had erected them on megalithic walls fitted together with this very special technique.[9]

Nothing like it was found anywhere in the Pacific hemisphere except on the nearest mainland of South America. The long-eared statue sculptors who had preceded the Incas in Peru had built megalithic walls in this very manner, and they were navigating their open coasts in reed boats and balsa rafts. Their reed boats, too, were the same both in shape and material as those on Easter Island. The similarities were so striking that numerous scholars tried to explain them either as a strange coincidence or as due to prehistoric contact between Peru and Easter Island. That such contact could have taken place, I proved in 1947 when we sailed on an Inca type balsa raft, the *Kon-Tiki*, from Peru to the Tuamotu archipelago, twice as far as to Easter Island.

My next encounter with this peculiar masonry technique was quite unexpected. I had come to Lixus in Morocco to meet builders of the local reed boats before I built a reed ship of my own for tests in the Atlantic. Nowhere else on the Atlantic coast of Africa did reed boat building survive except in this former Phoenician port of Lixus. I had come to study reed boats, not to look for stone walls, but on top of a high promontory where the navigable Lixus river enters the Atlantic, colossal stone walls of megalithic masonry rose against the sky. I was amazed to find here the same peculiar stone-fitting as in Peru and on Easter Island. A year later, in 1970, we sailed from this same African coast to Barbados in the Mexican Gulf with a ship of papyrus reeds, the *Ra II*.

Who had left behind the prehistoric ruins of Lixus?

Nobody knows. But archaeologists agree that they were either built by the early Phoenicians or by some unknown Phoenician predecessors. Whoever they were, there is general agreement that the founders of Lixus had come sailing from the distant Middle East to build their astronomically oriented megalithic temple to their sun-god. Ages later the Romans reached this port and built a temple on top of the old ruins to their own ocean god, Neptune.

Since nobody disputed that it had been possible to sail from the inner Mediterranean to the Atlantic coast of Morocco, as the Lixus people had done, it would have been superfluous for me to repeat this voyage. The mariners of Lixus must have sailed in fleets of prehistoric craft from Lebanon through the Straits of Gibraltar to settle just where the powerful Atlantic current starts its flow straight to tropical America.

Since the architects and masons who built the Lixus sun-temple had their roots among the great civilisations of the Middle East, it was not surprising that they were masters in handling colossal stones. Megalithic temple walls of giant blocks brought from distant quarries were common in the Middle East. They were typical for most of the civilisations that suddenly began to sail the inner Mediterranean in the millennia just before European history began.

But what about the type of stone-fitting, the 'fingerprint masonry', I had followed backwards from Easter Island to Lixus?

Once again reed boats put me on the trail backwards through history. While searching for reed boat illustrations in the tombs and temples of the Pharaohs, such stone-fitting came to my notice exactly at the spot where we built the *Ra I*. There, just behind the great pyramids, some of the megalithic walls in the *mastabas* and sun-temples were built in this way. But in Egypt this kind of masonry was not common.

Having tested the Egyptian type reed ships *Ra I* and *Ra II* in the Atlantic, I next went to Asia Minor, this time to study local reed ship designs before I tested a Sumerian type in the Indian Ocean. In Asia Minor, among the Hittite ruins, I felt I had come to the source of the masonry I had been tracing backwards. It would not be surprising if this specialised stone-fitting art had started with the Hittites in view of their great age and cultural importance.

But who were the Hittites, and where did they live?

Until archaeologists discovered their ruins in modern times, nobody knew. And yet the Hittites were a people who merit recognition by all civilised nations, since the arts and crafts that have made cultural progress possible from early antiquity have reached the modern world through them. The Hittites were the predecessors of the Phoenicians and lived where Lebanon and Syria are today. Their home centred around the narrow stretch of land in Asia Minor that separates the Mesopotamian rivers from the Mediterranean Sea. They were the middlemen who brought the art of writing from its inventors in Sumer to the Phoenicians on the Mediterranean shore.

The Hittites were not the inventors of the basic traits in their own civilisation. They had adopted ideas that came up the navigable twin rivers, the Euphrates and the Tigris, directly from Sumerian ports on the Persian Gulf. The Sumerians had taught them to build temples to the sun, to carve large stone statues with inlaid eyes, to write with both hieroglyphic and cuneiform script, and to build large ships that could sail the sea. A cylinder seal incised with reed ship designs, precisely like the reed ships on Sumerian cylinder seals, has been found by archaeologists in Hittite territory on the upper reaches of the river Euphrates.

The Hittites prospered by commanding the trade between the eastern and western worlds of navigation in early antiquity.

Only 200 kilometres (125 miles) separated the navigable upper reaches of the Euphrates from the Mediterranean. The Sumerians themselves had prospered from maritime trade by reed ships sailing in the Persian Gulf and up the twin rivers straight into Hittite territory. The Hittites carried the merchandise on the short distance overland to their own Mediterranean ports, and from there to Egypt, Cyprus, and elsewhere; but the Hittites were extinct and forgotten long before the ancient Greeks began recording history.

From the Greek historians we learn that the Phoenicians were the first to build sailing vessels and navigate the open sea. Today, we know, thanks to archaeology, that this was only what the Greeks believed. Ships had sailed the seas off the shores of Lebanon and Egypt long before Phoenician times. Prepharaonic petroglyphs and pottery decoration from Egypt illustrate large reed ships with double cabins, sail and rigging. And when the first splendid Hittite sun-temples were recovered from under the sand in Asia Minor, tall ships with sails were found carved in relief on the stone walls. They had been carved centuries before Phoenician times and yet they had sails and rigging as complex as those used millennia later on the caravels of Christopher Columbus.

There, in Hittite territory, ended the visible traces of the fingerprint masonry. There was no such type of masonry in the Sumerian territory down by the mouth of the Tigris and Euphrates, even though most of the Hittite skills had been inherited from the Sumerians.

I had been so sure that Hittite territory was the source for this fingerprint masonry that I assumed the Hittites to have been the original inventors. It seemed reasonable that this art should have evolved in the rocky hill country of the Hittites in upper Mesopotamia. In lower Mesopotamia, where the Sumerians dwelt near the Persian Gulf, there was a total absence of rock. The Sumerian territory was an enormous plain of sand and mud. Therefore the Sumerians had to build their colossal stepped pyramids from sun-baked mud bricks and their statues were carved from imported stone.

In 1977, I had the reed ship *Tigris* built on the river of that same name, in the midst of former Sumerian territory in order to sail to Dilmun, the legendary Sumerian fatherland. Nearly 5,000 years ago the Sumerians had written on their clay tablets that their forefathers had landed in Dilmun after the Great Deluge. From Dilmun they had come by sea in *ma-gur*, their largest kind of reed ship, to form the first Sumerian dynasty at Ur in lower Mesopotamia. According to the writings on numerous tablets, Sumerian merchant mariners constantly returned to the sacred fatherland of Dilmun for the purpose of trade.

Dilmun remained but a legendary name until it was recently identified by archaeologists as the island of Bahrain in the Persian Gulf. About 100,000 large and small burial mounds from the Sumerian period inspired the Danish archaeologists, P. V. Glob and G. Bibby, to bring a major team of excavators to Bahrain. They discovered, completely buried in sand, a prehistoric harbour city and a temple of beautifully cut stones, built as a smaller version of the ziggurats or stepped pyramids in Mesopotamia.[10]

As we landed in Bahrain with *Tigris*, Geoffrey Bibby flew down to see the kind of reed ship that had frequented Bahrain from Mesopotamia in the Dilmun period. He took us down into the streets of his buried city.

The city was laid out in orderly blocks with streets running north–south and east–west, in the manner that is characteristic of sun-worshippers. The main gateway opened from the city square straight on to the port, which is also characteristic of a maritime population.

Bibby pointed out the shallow coral bottom of the harbour, where no keeled ship could have entered. He therefore noted with interest that the double bundle body of our reed ship, with its very shallow draught, could easily have come in here at high tide and rested firmly on the bottom, ready to load or unload as the tide went out.

The Dilmun people, too, had clearly been reed ship builders. Bibby showed me that the last old-timers on this island still went sea-fishing from reed boats like those of Easter Island, Peru, Lixus, Egypt and Mesopotamia. I was therefore not altogether surprised when the fingerprint masonry also turned up in Bibby's excavations.

It was on this island of Bahrain that I was to pick up the tracks I had lost by moving down river from Hittite territory into the mud flats of Sumer. Some of the oldest stone walls in the port city Bibby showed us, deep below the present ground level, were fitted together in precisely this way. If the Sumerians had come from this island, they would have known this distinctive stone-shaping art while they still had access to quarriable rock. The mere fact that the Sumerians frequented Bahrain for trade, which they carried up river to Hittite territory, shows that there was no geographical barrier between the Dilmun people and the Hittites.

Since the Sumerians had ancestral links with Bahrain, and since the Hittite culture was younger than the Sumerian, I felt sure that Bibby was showing us something closer to the source than anything I had seen before; but I was not a little puzzled that we seemed to go further back in time with each step we took towards the east. Bahrain was halfway between Sumer and the Hormuz Strait, the gateway to the Indian Ocean. And yet Bahrain was certainly not the place of origin of this eccentric masonry form. There was not even any stone on Bahrain of the type that had been used for fitting these peculiar walls together. Bibby told us that this fine limestone could be found nowhere on the island. Hundreds of thousands of tons of quarried blocks must therefore have been brought by sea from some locality not yet identified.

With permission from the government of Bahrain to visit the prison island of Jidda, a few miles offshore, however, we found the missing quarries. Large areas of the limestone hills on Jidda had been carried away by experts in both stone work and navigation. The seafarers who had built the port city and the mini-ziggurat on Bahrain were no primitive drift voyagers. They must have come from some part of the world where the people were already expert in selecting the best kind of rock, in the art of carving it to shape, and in transporting it by sea to the building site. Some of the blocks brought from Jidda to build the structures on Bahrain were truly colossal and perfectly shaped. But none of the masonry impressed us more than what we saw when Bibby took us down the steps to a large ceremonial bath he had excavated at the foot of the mini-ziggurat. I wrote at that time:

> Bibby looked rather surprised when I kneeled down to examine the perfectly plane and smooth surfaces of his

Dilmun blocks and the way they were fitted together ... all were made to fit adjacent blocks with such precision that no crack or hole was left between them. My friends from *Tigris* looked at me like some kind of Sherlock Holmes trying to find fingerprints or tool-marks that might lead us on the track of those who did it. The beautifully dressed stones were shaped and joined together in a special manner I began to know all too well by now. I had to tell my puzzled companions why these stone walls had any bearing upon our voyage and upon the voyage to this same island by the people who had once made them.[11]

From Bahrain with its pre-Sumerian port, mini-ziggurat and bath, we had then sailed on with the *Tigris* out through the Hormuz Strait and into the Indian Ocean. First we visited Oman, where we were shown a recently discovered mini-ziggurat in the midst of the Sumerian mining area, and reed boats of Sumerian type still used by the fishermen on the nearest coast.[12] But we saw no fingerprint masonry there.

From Oman we sailed for Pakistan and the Indus Valley, where we went to visit the partly excavated ruins of Mohenjo-Daro. The long forgotten Indus Valley civilisation, with Mohenjo-Daro as its capital, began to bloom just after the first pharaonic dynasty in Egypt and the first Sumerian kingdom in Sumer had been founded, approximately 5,000 years ago. My interest in Mohenjo-Daro lay in the fact that, in the period from about 2500 BC to about 1500 BC when the Indus Valley civilisation suddenly disappeared, a close maritime contact had been maintained with Bahrain and Mesopotamia. A large number of seals with the still undeciphered Indus Valley script had been found on the islands in the Persian Gulf and in Mesopotamia, all the way from Ur down near the sea and up into Hittite territory in modern Syria. A Mohenjo-Daro seal depicted a reed ship with cabin, bipod mast and twin rudder oars, just like those in ancient Sumer and Egypt, and just like our *Tigris*. Sailing their reed ships between Mesopotamia, Bahrain and the Indus Valley, the merchant mariners of old could have carried tons of cargo and provisions while avoiding the hardships and risks of overland transport through deserts, mountain ranges and territories with hostile tribes.

The reed ship had thus been present in Mohenjo-Daro, and the ceremonial bath too, but without the fingerprint masonry. As in Sumer, the river plains of Mohenjo-Daro were without quarriable rock. Like the sun-worshipping city builders of Mesopotamia and Bahrain, the founders of Mohenjo-Daro had also laid out their blocks, squares and streets according to the north–south, east–west plan. Among its main structures was a centrally placed terraced temple mound with a big ceremonial bath at its foot. The bath was deep, approached by broad stairways down one wall, and with benches all around the base of the walls it immediately recalled the bath we had recently seen on Bahrain. But the Indus Valley bath was built from burnt brick made watertight by asphalt and in this respect differed from the bath on Bahrain.

When I saw the old ceremonial bath on Fua Mulaku, I was reminded not of the Mohenjo-Daro bath but of the more distant one on Bahrain. The voyages through space and time that had brought me step by step backwards to this corner of the world flashed through my mind as I patted the smooth fingerprint walls and followed the patterns of the tight fissures with my finger nails. It was impossible not to remain fascinated by the close resemblance between this Fua Mulaku structure and the one in Bahrain.

Was there any relationship? Could the early navigators, who used Bahrain as a midway station for trade between Meso-potamia and the Indus Valley, also have found their way down to the Maldives?

The distance from Lothal, the main Indus Valley port, to the Maldive archipelago was no longer than from that same port to Mesopotamia. Nor was it any longer than the last leg of our own voyage with the reed ship *Tigris*, when we sailed non-stop from the Indus Valley to Djibouti in Africa. It is well known that the Indus Valley civilisation spread its influence down the west coast of India. One would think that, intrepid sailors as they were, they would have explored their own coast eastwards just as successfully as they navigated westwards to distant Sumer.

If so, they would inevitably have hit upon the Maldive barriers, and found there this passage through the Equatorial Channel. As passionate sun-worshippers and keen astronomers studying the path of the sun, they had a double reason for finding this Equatorial Channel interesting.

A fantastic possibility then dawned upon me down in this old bath. I had almost forgotten that I had also seen a prehistoric swimming pool in Peru, the largest of them all, and also with a broad flight of stairs down one wall. It had been built from sun-baked bricks by the pre-Inca sun-worshippers of Chan Chan on the Pacific plains of Peru. The architects of that bath had also built large and small step pyramids of the ziggurat type. Furthermore, they lived in the main centre of pre-Inca reed boat navigation. A common motif in their pottery decoration was ancestral heroes who travelled by sea on large reed ships. And their moulded ceramic jars always represented their own royal ancestors as men with huge discs in greatly extended ear lobes.

Could there be a connection?

The idea seemed at first too fantastic to consider seriously. I had long suspected that Middle East culture had reached tropical America by sea centuries before Columbus, but direct from Africa, not from distant Asia. There were also those scholars who had speculated on prehistoric voyages from India, by way of the Pacific, to America. I myself, like almost everybody else, had rejected such conjectures as geographically without sense. By the time the prehistoric voyagers from India had reached the Asiatic shores of the Pacific, they would still have half the circumference of this planet left to cross before reaching America. The Pacific coast of south-east Asia and the Pacific coast of South America are antipodes. Furthermore, upon entering the Pacific any prehistoric type of sailing craft would be pushed back by the prevailing winds and currents. In this part of the world they head full force from tropical America to tropical Asia, set in permanent flow by the rotation of the earth itself.

Nobody seemed to realise that America lay much closer to India westwards by way of the Atlantic Ocean; nor that this course would, furthermore, be favoured by the elements.

Now, as we had discovered that prehistoric seafarers had established a foothold on the Maldive Islands, we could see that they had been in a good position to sail on even to America. The winter monsoon from the north-east would give Maldive sailors a fair wind for the southern Cape of Africa and there the Atlantic Ocean begins. At any time of the year the South Atlantic

Current and the south-east trade winds would carry them straight on to the Gulf of Mexico. The Gulf of Mexico actually lies there like a magnet, attracting flotsam from all parts of the African coast. With the reed ship *Ra II* we had come from North Africa with the North Equatorial Current and the north-east trade winds. We could have come as easily from South Africa by the South Equatorial Current and the south-east trade winds. These two mighty Atlantic Ocean rivers converge off the coast of Brazil and flow together into the Gulf of Mexico.

With the Maldive archipelago as point of departure and a course that followed the elements, the geographical picture became drastically changed. Navigation became possible. I could no longer maintain my former view that voyagers from southern Asia could not have had access to tropical America.

But what really made me scratch my head and wonder what might have happened were the long-eared images that had lured me to the Maldives in the first place. We had now linked them with the builders of the fingerprint masonry. Together with the fingerprint masonry and reed boats we had traced the custom of ear extension back from Easter Island to Peru and Mexico, but so far no further. The custom of elongating the ear lobes until they hung to the shoulders was still in use on Easter Island when Captain Cook arrived, although not practised by any other island people in the Pacific. The Inca nobility also extended their ear lobes with the same kind of discs until the Spaniards arrived, and claimed that they had been told to do so by their legendary sun-king, Con-Tici-Viracocha. According to Inca history he ruled a long-eared people who lived in Peru until he sailed away into the open Pacific.

Although ear extension was not used in Mexico when the Spaniards came, the Mayan stele and the Olmec and Aztec statues and reliefs abound in images of men with long beards and huge discs in their ear lobes. The mural paintings in a Maya temple at Chichen-Itza depict a people with white skin and yellow hair landing by boat among hostile people of dark skin, and all of them have long, pendant ear lobes. Obviously, as shown in images on pottery and stone from Mexico and Peru, ear extension had a long tradition and wide distribution within aboriginal America. Yet it only occurred within the limited area where aboriginal civilisations had suddenly begun to worship the sun and to build pyramids of ziggurat type, living in organised communities with city streets laid out in squares with houses built of baked brick, precisely as in the early Middle East.

I had been looking in vain for the custom of ear extension among the pyramid builders in Mesopotamia and Egypt, among the early mariners who had settled Cyprus, Crete and Malta, among the remains of the Phoenician seafarers, and the founders of Lixus. None of them seemed to have practised it. I had a list of well over one hundred culture traits peculiar to pre-Columbian Mexico and Peru, and so special that they were unknown elsewhere in America. Yet all of them reappeared within the restricted territories of the earliest Middle East civilisations. The only item missing from that list was ear extension. Although it was shared by the earliest civilisations in Mexico and Peru, I could not locate it among seafaring civilisations on the other side of the Atlantic.

Then, a year after the *Tigris* expedition I returned to the Indus Valley, this time to see the recently discovered brick-walled harbour of Lothal, the main port of Mohenjo-Daro and the Indus Valley civilisation. Lothal, on the Indian side of the Pakistan border, is the oldest known man-made port in the world, flourishing from about 2500 BC to about 1500 BC. Scientists at the University of Baroda were sorting out the material they had excavated from its docks and warehouses. There was a drawer full of round discs with grooved rims, like colossal vertebrae made from ceramic. They looked precisely like the ceramic ear plugs of prehistoric Mexico and Peru. In Inca times they were made from pure gold. We had excavated them ourselves on Easter Island, carved from thick shell. I was in not a moment's doubt as to what these archaeologists had dug up at the Lothal port, but asked them just the same.

'Ear plugs,' was the answer. 'You see, these ancient mariners pierced their ears and expanded their ear lobes to insert these large plugs.'

So the Indus Valley mariners were 'Long-ears'!

The Hindu nobility had later copied the custom from them, and afterwards Buddha and his followers had spread it far and wide in Asia. From the time the Indus Valley people began sailing the Indian Ocean this peculiar custom had thus been practised on the coast, and even by sailors roaming the ocean. No wonder then that long-eared images had been left by ancient sculptors in the Maldives.

Not until later did I learn that ear extension had survived on the Maldive Islands until recent times. Maloney, who studied the local customs, quotes in his book an early visitor who stated that Maldive women had their ears pierced, and he adds: 'Some people remember even now that their grandmothers' ear lobes extended nearly to their shoulders.'[13] With 'Long-ears' inhabiting the Maldives the road was open too for another strange custom which followed the stone masons who had voyaged in reed ships on the open seas in prehistoric times.

As I walked, therefore, up the ceremonial stairways of the Fua Mulaku bath and faced the glittering blue sea of the Equatorial Channel, I felt as if the air was loaded with excitement and possibilities. Since we, as novices in reed boat navigation could have crossed these oceans, why could not the experienced 'Long-ears' from Lothal have done the same? Who could ever tell what traffic had passed through this Channel in the course of the millennia; what kind of watercraft had first been beached on this lonely shore, and what kind of people had built the great hawitta and bathed together in this splendid pool?

We mounted our bicycles and pedalled along a footpath into an uninhabited wasteland south of the village area. Here we left the bicycles in an open field full of evidence of former habitation. The stony terrain was arid and treeless but low dryland shrubs covered the traces of walls and tombs.

In the midst of the area lay a large circular basin sunk deep into the solid ground and lined with carved slabs plastered with lime. We measured the diameter to be 20.6 metres (67½ feet) and the circle was so even and smooth that the islanders believed some prehistoric masons had carved it all from one giant piece of rock.

Well over a metre down from the rim a ledge ran all around the wall like a bench, and below this the wall continued down another full metre to the bottom. There was fresh clean water below the bench, although the bottom itself was covered by a thick coat of mud. The east wall was intersected by a stairway running down into the pool.

What could this old structure have been?

The islanders seemed to be as ignorant of the former function as we were. They just knew it as *Vasha veo*, which Abdul translated as 'the round bath'. They suggested that some former people had used it for sacred rituals, and pointed out what seemed to be the remains of a totally shattered temple just a few steps east of the stairway.

Even this type of large and circular bath I could recall having seen before. It was another feature characteristic of the seafaring people who had lived on Bahrain in prehistoric times, the same people who had built the square ceremonial bath with the fingerprint masonry. Why the early Dilmun people built themselves two such completely different forms of ceremonial bath was a puzzle in itself, but here, on Fua Mulaku, the same two types reappeared together once again.

It was too early to draw conclusions, but high time to be alert and search for other traces on these islands which had so far been overlooked by historians. It was certainly too early to conclude that the Dilmun seafarers, or 'Long-ears' from Lothal, had come to Fua Mulaku. But I had seen enough to be convinced that the Maldives was another of the many maritime way-stations for some of the great seafaring civilisations that had roamed the high seas centuries before European maritime history began.

When our captain reported that the propeller of the *Midu* was working once again, we embarked and temporarily left Fua Mulaku. We headed for the islands lining the northern edge of the Equatorial Channel, full of anticipation at what we might run into there. We left at night, so that we could reach the islands on the other side at sunrise.

Against a tropic sky where the Southern Cross twinkled amid a host of constellations, the low atoll of Fua Mulaku showed up merely as a rugged silhouette of feathery palm crowns that barely rose from the sea. The individual crowns slowly joined to form a long black wall that diminished in size and sank behind our stern.

Five hours later, just before the sunrise, we sailed slowly into the calm lagoon of Gaaf atoll, formerly known as Huvadu.

CHAPTER IV

Pyramid in the Jungle

A Sun-temple on Gaaf-Gan

AS THE *Midu* entered the narrow passage between two islands in the Gaaf atoll, the sun rose from a calm lagoon and we sailed close inshore along the sandy beach of a long and low island, densely covered by jungle interspersed with palm trees. Not a house to be seen. For no obvious reason this fertile island was uninhabited.

The name was Gan, the same as the airport island we had first visited in Addu atoll, on the opposite side of this channel. We decided to call it Gaaf-Gan since it was on the ring-reef of the extensive Gaaf atoll. There was a third major island in the Maldives, also called Gan. That third Gan was in the nearest atoll to the north. All three islands, according to Hassan Maniku, had important prehistoric mounds. The largest, he believed, was on the island we were now passing. It had not been seen by him, nor by Bell, but, he wrote, it was known to the natives of the neighbouring island as '*Gamu hawiththa*', or 'Gan's mound', and was said to be just under 60 feet high.[14]

I had asked Maniku in Male how three important islands in the Maldives came to have the same name, and what did Gan mean? I was given the surprising answer that, in the local language, Gan and Gamu were but different grammatical inflections of the same name. The proper name of these three islands would be Gamu, and *gamu* was an old Sanskrit word for 'settlement'. Divehi, the Maldive language, contains many Sanskrit roots, and Sanskrit was the old Indo-Aryan language that had spread from the Indus Valley region about 1500 BC, at just about the time when that civilisation collapsed. But as the island was completely uninhabited, it seemed strange to name it Gan if that meant 'village' or 'settlement'.

76

A narrow channel, where surf entered the lagoon from the open Equatorial Channel, separated Gan from the much smaller island of Gadu, which was thickly populated. There 1,600 islanders were lumped together in a village that covered all the land, whereas they rowed over to the uninhabited Gan only to fetch food.

We anchored in the lagoon off Gadu and were set ashore in a local dhoni. Friendly people housed us in their community house, where camp-beds with home-made reed mats were set up on the earthen floor which was shewn with a thick coat of clean white coral shingle.

My first question was why the large island of Gan had no population. The amazing answer was that Gan had been populated very long ago, but one day an invasion of huge cats had come ashore from the ocean. These huge cats had been ferocious and the people of the island had either been killed or had escaped in their boats. Nobody had come back to live on the island since. Even today people from Gadu island only go there in daytime.

Cats were the only domestic mammal in the Maldives, in fact, the only terrestrial mammal known to these people in former times. But the cats that had come from the sea were hardly normal household cats, but some sort of man-size demons in feline form.

The people of Gadu told us also that the forest of Gan was full of ruins. Nobody had ever dug them. It was true that there was a big mound, but it was not called *Gamu Hawitta*, or 'Gan's mound' for there were several mounds on Gan. They distinguished the biggest one as *Bodu Hawitta*, which simply meant 'large mound'. The real name was *Vadamaga Hawitta*, and it had been built long ago by a people called Redin. All sorts of things were supposed to be hidden inside it.

The chief of Gadu came to us together with an unusually tall man, clearly of some status in the community. His name was Hassan Maniku, the same as our learned friend in Male, so to distinguish between them Abdul referred to him as the 'owner' of Gan. Nobody actually owned an island, he explained, but this Hassan held Gan on lease from the Maldive government in order to harvest the coconuts. The people of Gadu picked the coconuts for him and gave one-eighth of the harvest to him as the 'owner'.

We lost no time in expressing our desire to visit the island, and the 'owner' seemed more than pleased to take us there. In a small dhoni we rowed across with him and two of his men. Dancing over the smooth swells rolling in from the Equatorial Channel through the open entrance to the outer sea, we struck bottom in the shelter of a sandy bar jutting into the lagoon, and waded ashore in lukewarm water. Peaceful ripples from the large lagoon washed against a white beach of fine coral sand. Like all the other Maldive islands, Gaaf-Gan was a low and flat platform of coral bedrock that rose no more than 2 metres (6 feet) above the level of the Indian Ocean. It would have been constantly awash from the big waves of the Equatorial Channel had it not been sheltered by a wide and barely submerged coastal reef. Arrested by this shallow limestone shelf, the ocean waves would rise as surf and tumble in defeat, reduced to feeble rows of ripples before they reached the dry land.

About an hour of pleasant walking brought us, first, through an open grassy plain scattered with tall coconut palms, then along a good footpath walled in by thick jungle on either side. The wilderness off the trail was so impenetrable that it could conceal any man-made structure an arm's length away. Between the branches, foliage and thorns there was no opening for any beasts bigger than slim lizards. But high above the dense jungle roof, brown bats as large as rabbits hung upside down in the trees and palm crowns. Scared by our voices, some of them fluttered away over the forest like witches unfolding their cloaks. Clearly these flying foxes were the only warm-blooded creatures to live on this island since the big cats had driven the humans away.

The fable of the big cats from the sea puzzled me. No seals or other marine creatures could have scared away a people who fought even the largest sharks without fear, yet it was too easy for an outsider to laugh off the story of the large cats as a tale invented to explain why Gan had been depopulated in the distant past. For by talking to the 'owner' of the island, and the others who believed in this tradition, we quickly understood that we were not dealing with infantile or primitive people, but with the heirs to a civilisation which was as old – possibly older – than our own.

The people of the nearest large land, Sri Lanka, called themselves *Singalese*, the 'Lion people'. There never had been lions on Sri Lanka, but the local Singalese claimed descent from ancient sea voyagers who came to Sri Lanka from India and celebrated a legendary lion as their royal ancestor. For this reason the Singalese carved lion statues and used lion symbols such as ferocious masks with feline teeth to distinguish themselves in war and peace.

Lions would indeed be 'very big cats' to Maldive islanders who had never seen any of the larger feline species. And there was every reason to believe that the Lion people had come to the Maldives. Bell recognised the big hawitta on Fua Mulaku as a ruined Singalese stupa. The broken Buddha heads and the Buddha bronze figurine we had seen in Male were proof enough that Buddhists had come here before the Moslem period. And yet these Buddhists had found people of a still older religion. The Lion people of Sri Lanka were devout Buddhists. No other Buddhists lived closer to the Maldives. Singalese raiders masked as lions might have been the large cats from the sea who were sufficiently ferocious to scare an entire population into flight.

I was close on the heels of the 'owner' when he stopped and pointed into the jungle. Abdul translated what he said. Down there, near the other coast, were the ruins of a 'Buddhist castle'. Very little was left to be seen.

I asked if the Redin had been Buddhists. But no, the Redin were those who had built the hawittas. Somebody else had built the 'Buddhist castle'. When we got back to Gadu in the evening he would get some of the really old men together who might tell us what they knew.

We reached a small opening in the forest where again we got a glimpse of the sea. Turtles had dug big craters in the sand. In the short grass at the centre of this glade was a deep stone-lined well where our companions were drawing clear drinking water with the half of a coconut tied to a long rod. An overgrown trail turned off towards the inland. Here the 'owner' asked his two companions to go ahead in front of him. From here on they had to cut a fresh passage with their long machete knives.

This slowed us down markedly. Proceeding step by step we had time to admire the huge trunks of jungle trees that surpassed in dimensions all we had seen so far. Lianas hung like ropes from the jungle roof, and the thick branches that stretched

79

out from the trunks were embellished, like moss-covered shelves in a flower shop, with orchids and parasitic ferns. It was hot. Hot and damp. Not a breath of air found its way in here. Nothing moved the foliage.

Glistening with perspiration we were fighting mosquitos when the men ahead stopped and made room for me as they pointed with their long knives. At first I could see nothing but the green jungle in front of my nose. Then I noticed something unusual, almost black, hidden among the foliage. It looked like chunks of black coke heaped up into a pile and abandoned for ages, shrouded in greenery and cloaked in moss.

The pile was much wider than it had seemed at first. One more step ahead and I could see black stones covered with green moss wherever I could catch a glimpse through the foliage, right and left. We could not see how tall it was, as it completely disappeared upwards in a cover of green.

This had to be Gan's large hawitta. Björn and I made no effort to restrain our enthusiasm when we saw how the pile continued upwards so high that we had to bend our heads back to try to detect its full height. We were standing at the base and yet could gain no more than glimpses of dark stones above us as we began to crawl up the slope on all fours, wriggling between the branches and ferns.

When I got my feet up as high as the heads of the people on the ground I began to crawl over thick roots that twisted between the stones. A huge jungle tree grew here, right out of the side of the mound even though it seemed to be a solid pile of stone. Crude lumps of limestone and broken branches of coral had been piled up to form the hill. Once as white as snow, the coral and limestone had all turned greyish-black from age wherever it was bare of moss.

The stones were loose, so we crawled up on our hands and knees, grabbing hold of big ferns, stems and roots, careful that no boulders should roll down on those following us. Our vision was hindered by all the stalks, with huge leaves resembling rhubarb, that grew in profusion up the slope, and made it as hard to see what was below us as what was above. My impression, however, was that I had reached the height of a three-storey building when I began to see over the jungle roof.

As I rose to my feet at the summit I was most surprised to find myself standing between the sprawling roots of a colossal jungle tree as large as any giant we had seen down on the ground. It took four of us to join hands around the trunk, which rose into the blue sky above us like a majestic spire. It seemed to have been added by nature to heighten the impressiveness of this ruined temple mound.

If the summit tree had been an oak I would have guessed its age to be 500 years or more. Jungle trees often grow very fast, but this tree was growing on top of a compact rock pile high above the jungle soil. A few extra centuries would seem to be necessary for a jungle tree even to take root and establish itself on the top of such a lofty man-made structure.

Not a single carved stone, nothing of interest but the huge tree, was found on the summit, so we carefully scrambled down the steep talus slope the way we had come up. The slope seemed to be at the maximum angle that permitted sliding boulders to come to rest. This could very well have been what it always looked like, a crude pile of stones thrown together with an enormous amount of labour, a monument like the royal burial mounds of the Vikings. But it could also represent the shapeless remains of a pyramid after the retaining terrace walls had crumbled or been removed.

Down again at the foot of the mound, the 'owner' and his two friends sat down well satisfied with the day's excursion. They had fulfilled their promise to take us to the *Vadamaga Hawitta*, and there was nothing more now to show us. But they had heard that there were many valuable things buried inside this hawitta. We, on the other hand, were itching to see more of this place.

One of the men had brought some green coconuts which he now scalped with his long knife as if they were ostrich eggs. Björn and I drank ours to the last drop, then we eagerly crawled in opposite directions into the thickets surrounding the foot of the mound. Here the ground was so packed with fallen stones that trees were sparse and there was room for us to wriggle in between branches and big ferns.

Our first discovery was a 4-metre (13-foot) wide ramp that ran part of the way up the south side of the mound. Clearly this had been some sort of ceremonial approach to the upper part of the structure which soared high above the landscape. The question

81

posed itself again: had it always been a rough mound, or was this some sort of walled pyramid?

On the northern slope I detected sparse remains of a retaining wall. A dozen moss-grown blocks, all cut square, still lay undisturbed on top of each other in a straight row, blocking the rubble behind from sliding down. I was surprised to find that this remaining wall section formed a straight line. The hawitta on Fua Mulaku had a circular base, as one would expect from a Buddhist stupa, but this straight section suggested that this pyramidal structure could have been square. For me it began to resemble the stepped pyramids with ceremonial ramp approach of Mesopotamia, Bahrain, Oman and pre-Columbian America.

I excitedly called Björn who struggled around from the opposite side.

'Yes,' he said, as I pointed. 'Yes.'

He sounded rather distracted. He was not looking at my wall at all, instead he began to point at something else:

'But what is *this*?'

I looked to the left, higher up, where he was pointing. There was a huge open eye staring back at us from under a root. My first thought was that this was part of an old stone image, for image eyes were often carved like this among ancient sun-worshippers, with circles of increasing sizes enclosing each other as in a shooting target. This wide open eye under the tree seemed as bizarre and alive out here among the ferns and leaves as if we had found a one-eyed goblin peeping out of the mound. The circles showed up in relief right through a thin coating of green moss which clung to the surface of the stone like its skin fits the flesh of a beast.

'But what *is* it?' Björn repeated impatiently when he realised his discovery had left me speechless.

'A sun-symbol,' I exclaimed. 'We came down here to look for traces of sun-worshippers at the equator, and here they are. Concentric circles around a central disc. That's the symbol of the sacred sun throughout ancient Asia, Africa and America.'

'So, what more could you ask for?' Björn laughed and slapped me on the shoulder in triumph.

Our island friends came to share our joy, cutting right and left with their machetes. They stared for a moment in silence at the strange stone, every bit as surprised as we were. Then they began to pull ferns and cut branches all around the base so that we could check all the stones that had fallen from the hawitta. We soon restricted our search to the blocks that had been dressed to shape, for the others were only part of the fill and were too crudely cut ever to have been decorated. Every stone we turned over was rolled back into its original position.

Soon we heard a yell from one of the men with a machete. Under a fallen fern lay another square block with the very same sun symbol. Near it lay yet another. The next one I found was of a different type. On each side of the solar rings three 'fingers' were pointing outwards, as if the sun was meant to have wings. The winged sun-disc was a common symbol for the supreme god, the sun-god, among the stone sculptors of ancient Meso-potamia and Egypt.

More sun-ornamented stones appeared, of both types. There was even one cornerstone with solar symbols on each of the two adjoining sides, which clearly showed that the structure, so far from being round, had straight walls and square corners. All the other sun-stones had a neck at the rear of the squared block that could be set into the wall in such a way that the carving projected with the sun-symbol on the slightly convex front side. This was a technique well known among the temple builders in both the Old World and ancient America.

We had still not exhausted these discoveries at the foot of the mound when, exploring the ground a little further away, I stumbled upon a faint rise in the flat terrain. Worked stones were lying partly buried and partly exposed. Another slight elevation was found on the opposite side of the big hawitta. The one due east, the other due west of the main temple mound. The worked slabs indicated the former presence of some related buildings, perhaps subsidiary temples.

In the pile to the west of the big mound were several long and flat stones beautifully decorated by master stone sculptors. There was not a single sun-disc here, but flowers. Sunflowers! Elegant little sunflowers raised in high relief, set in a row along the edge of stones which were fluted like lintel or ridge pieces. Between each flower and the next was a peculiar symbol, varying slightly but always consisting of vertical bars flanked by dots, mostly resembling the numerals in Mayan hiero-

83

glyphics. They could indeed have been Mayan numerals if not for the fact that there were bars on each side of the dots. The flower relief, too, symbolic as well as ornamental, I had seen on ancient Mayan temples and, more often still, in Hindu religious art.

'Look at the turtle ornament,' I exclaimed, and showed Björn the broader bands of tongue-shaped reliefs that ran parallel with the rows of flower and staff-and-dot symbols. We recalled the little turtle image, dug up together with the demonic stone heads at the sacrificial place in Male. We both imagined we saw the row of crested sea-turtle shells with hind flippers set side by side along the very edge of the stone, but the head and front of the turtles were not carved. Slowly it dawned on me, however, that we were mistaken. These were not sea-turtles at all, but the continental lotus flower decoration typical of the great ancient civilisations of the Old World. Here we had another exciting fingerprint in front of us in the jungle. There were plenty of sea-turtles in the Maldives, even on this island, but lotus did not grow here. The lotus flower was a decorative symbol shared by the ancient Egyptian, Phoenician, Mesopotamian and Hindu civilisations. Long before it spread to Europe to decorate the capitals of Greek columns, it had been widespread in the Middle East and south-west Asia as one of the most persistently used ornamental symbols of religious architecture. To these ancient people the lotus stood for the rising sun.

Sun-discs, sunflowers and now lotus flowers! What more could we ask for?

It was becoming ever clearer that neither motifs nor architectonic technique had been born on this little island, or elsewhere on these atolls, but had been imported in developed form by navigators from distant lands.

The island 'owner' was disturbed at the thought of what would happen to these sculpted stones now that they had been found. Anything considered to be heathen remains was always destroyed, he said. We recalled the beautiful Buddha which had been quickly beheaded, and the images of Fua Mulaku that had disappeared without trace, and knew he was right. It seemed best to place these carvings therefore in the security of the Male Museum. None of them had been found in their original place in the wall anyway. Between all of us we managed to carry thirteen stones back to the boat, leaving one to be fetched the next day.

The fading light told us that the sun was sinking towards the western horizon, although not a single ray penetrated the thick jungle roof. On our way back to the landing place we took a side trail to visit an old and abandoned Moslem cemetery. Some of the slabs marking the tomb edges had clearly been taken from some earlier non-Moslem temple. The cemetery had not been maintained, for the beautifully carved Moslem tombstones and their old Arab inscriptions were either half buried or broken. When the 'owner' casually pointed out a highly ornamented stone that commemorated the person who had introduced Islam to this atoll, I was struck by the complete lack of either fear or veneration the islanders showed towards these relics, even though they pertained to their own creed.

Immediately afterwards we stepped over the almost buried remains of a stone border. The whole area showed signs of former habitation, but everything was thickly overgrown by turf and forest.

'The Buddhist castle,' said the island 'owner' and nodded to left and right.

Whatever this might have been, it had been carefully demolished, for nothing more than bumps could be seen in the ground.

We reached the little boat and rowed over to the village on Gaaf-Gadu. The only warm-blooded creatures left on Gaaf-Gan were the huge bats. As the sun went down, they lifted their heads and began to fly around over the tree tops.

The kerosene lamps were lit in our room in the community house by the time our friend the 'owner' fulfilled his promise and brought two old men to see us. They were indeed old. One of them had difficulty in both walking and talking, but once they were comfortably seated in two wooden armchairs their brains seemed to work well, albeit slowly.

Ibrahim Futa said he was about 104 years old, whereas Don Futa gave his own age as 102. When asked what they knew about Gan they had both heard that the people there had died or fled when the big cats came from the sea. The big cats were *feretas*, a monster, part cat and part human, that sometimes used to come ashore from the sea in former times. Nobody living today had seen *feretas*.

The Redin had built the big hawitta. But the Redin were people and not *feretas* and it was not the Redin who had been chased away by the *feretas* either. Some other people had lived there after the Redin and before the *feretas* came. These people had a ruler, a queen called *Khanzi*. She built smaller hawittas but also used the big one built by the Redin. She was a very dark lady, tall and large. She had a son called *Khanzi Bodu Takuru*, and he had a great voice when he spoke to people on Gadu.

Björn, who had lived for some years among the people of South India, whispered to me that *Takur* is an old benevolent god among the Santal tribes, and that it is also an Indian word for 'priest'. We already knew that *bodu* meant 'big'. *Khanzi* then remained as the common name for the queen and her son, which suggests it might have been a royal title or a family name.

The two old men made it clear that Khanzi had ruled her own people. They were big in stature, like she was. They had lived on Gan before the Singalese came. The Singalese had come to Gan later and driven the Khanzi people away, who then fled to Wadu island in the same atoll. For some time now the Singalese had occupied Gan. These Singalese from Gan even went to Wadu and killed the Khanzi people there.

Although nobody identified the Singalese with the big cats in plain words, it was specifically said that the 'kingdom of the cats' had started when the Singalese drove the earlier Khanzi people away from Gan. The 'kingdom of the cats' would then be the kingdom of the Singalese, the 'Lion people'.

This was beginning to assume the character of a detective puzzle, and it was tempting to suspect that the dark and tall Khanzi people were Hindu from India since they had named their own prince Takur after an Indian god. It made sense that Hindu settlers had been driven away by Buddhist Singalese from Sri Lanka, since we had already seen archaeological proof of both having left their images in the Maldives.

But if the Khanzi people had come from India and the *feretas* were 'Lion people' from Sri Lanka, who then were the Redin who had come to these islands first of all and built the big mounds?

The legends of the Khanzi and the cat people referred to

people who had fought each other in the Maldives before the Moslem faith was embraced in AD 1153. As this took place so long ago, it was tempting to dismiss the stories as fairy tales, except for the fact that the Buddhist and the Hindu images had actually been found. I checked my notebook and found that the two small bronze images stored with the big stone heads in the Male Museum closet had both come from Gaaf-Gadu, from this very island. One of them was Hindu, the other was Buddhist. The Hindu one was the older and more eroded. That supported the hypothesis that the Hindu, in agreement with the Khanzi tradition, had come here first, and the Buddhists, alias the cat people, later.

The introduction of Islam over eight centuries ago marked the beginning of the present era also to these people. They still recalled the name of the first person who converted their ancestors from Buddhism to Islam. His name was Al Fagir Hafis Hassan Fali Takur, and it was his tombstone they had pointed out for us next to the 'Buddhist castle' on Gan. The location of his burial adjacent to the Buddhist sanctuary could indicate that he was not himself an immigrant Arab, but a local islander converted from Buddhism to Islam. The 'Takur' added to his Moslem name might even suggest some royal Khanzi relatives among his ancestry.

From the days of the Moslem missionary, Al Fagir, images of any sort were forbidden, the old men reminded us. They knew that their own ancestors 'in the Singalese time' had images of Buddha sitting with crossed legs. The Khanzi people, they said, worshipped other kinds of images. Even today the people from Gadu, when digging in the yam fields on Gan, still found such old images.

I was surprised to find these people speaking about a Singalese, or pre-Moslem, period in their atoll as if it was common knowledge. Although the sultans in Male had, through the centuries, done their best to erase any memories of periods ante-dating their own genealogy, their success had clearly decreased with the distance from the capital island.

Both the Redin and the Khanzi people had worshipped fire as well as images, said one of the old men.

No, only the Redin worshipped fire, corrected the other. According to him the Khanzi worshipped only images.

For a moment the two old men could not agree. There was even a vague suggestion from one of them that the Khanzi were here before the Redin. But in the end they agreed that the Redin had been the first. And the Redin had worshipped both fire and images.

The last point our two old informants repeated before they staggered away was that there were supposed to be many valuable objects hidden inside the *Vadamaga Hawitta*. They agreed that this big building had been much higher before, with stairways running way up on one side. Don Futa had heard from old people that this hawitta had in former times been square, and flat on top where there had been a 'room'. This room had caved in because it had been 'hollow'. In all likelihood it had been a small shrine or temple on the summit, but they remembered nothing further.

When the old men left we were fetched by the village chief for a late but sturdy meal of turtle eggs and curried fish served by the women of the house. Then we returned to our beds on the white shingle floor. The last things I saw, before I blew out my lamp, were the two glassless windows crammed full of curious faces of both sexes and all ages. They had probably never seen a foreigner go to bed before. Their human faces gradually faded into those of the cat people and the Redin, as I drifted smoothly into a dream world from which not even a cloudburst of mosquitos could wake me.

Shortly before the sun rose I was called back to life by a delightful smell of tea and freshly baked Arab bread. I sat up and found our spectators already back at the windows. Or had they been there all night? I managed to wriggle on my trousers and made it clear that I needed to visit a certain place. They showed me through a narrow door into a tiny garden plot with exceptionally big tomatoes, and with walls so tall that nobody could peep over. There I was handed a heavy iron crowbar that stood waiting for visitors. I caught on, and ran a hole into the ground: one deep and narrow toilet per person per visit. No wonder the size of those tomatoes!

It was still early morning when we climbed into a nutshell of a rowing boat to return from overcrowded Gadu to uninhabited Gan. Our friends of yesterday came with us again. Today they by-passed the first sand-bar where we had landed the day before as they found the tide high enough for us to pole and row on along the very shallow lagoon side of Gan. This would save us a good deal of walking.

The shallow water by the shore in the lagoon was so calm and clear that the corals which almost scraped the bottom of our boat seemed to be out of the water. Broken bits of coral tossed up on the beach lay there like dead bones and as white as the sand they had helped to form. But in the water they revealed wonderful colours as we slid along a spectacular rock garden which we could touch with our hands. There were no limits to the forms and the colours. Corals, corals and more corals; a petrified nature with no sign of waving seaweeds or soft sea anenomes. Some lay there, as round as eggs or mushrooms of all sizes; others were as flat as trays, curved like fans or shaped like jars, while most of them branched out like fantastic, crooked shrubbery or even elegant candelabra. Seen as a whole, the bottom shone at us in all the colours of a giant painter's pallet. Yet, while warm and spicy perfumes were wafted to us from the jungle ashore, the beautiful corals had a nasty fishy smell if we lifted them out of the water. These fancy-shaped apartment houses, with their myriad minute coral polyps waving from the windows, were designed for the marine world where tiny multicoloured fish fluttered about sniffing at them like peaceful butterflies. Larger, predatory fish shot away from our keel as if caught with guilty consciences, while the little fish seemed perfectly at ease, or at the worst hid within the branches of the sharp corals. I was surprised at the complete absence of seaurchins and starfish, which are otherwise so common in such marine gardens.

We hung nose down over the gunwales until the boat hit solid limestone and we had to jump out and wade ashore. We were early, and yet the 'owner' showed us traces in the sand of boys who had already walked around the shoreline collecting turtle eggs. Today was the great weekly day of harvest. Soon all the people from Gadu would be coming over to cut yam and give our friend his one-eighth share. He would also get one-eighth of the turtle eggs. He expected they would gather today about 400 turtle eggs from three turtles. Every month about thirty-four turtles came ashore at Gan to lay eggs. They came back and laid eggs every thirteen days, and some 30,000 eggs were collected on Gan every year. But turtles were rapidly disappearing from the Maldives now. The thirty-four left on Gan were marked and the 'owner' considered them almost like his own chickens. Indeed, all the Maldive islanders were seriously concerned now by the fact that, what had been one of the most important sources of food for their ancestors, would soon be gone.

'Why?' we asked. And I later posed the question to the Minister of Fisheries in Male.

Previously the people of the Maldives never caught the turtles, they only ate the eggs. Then, a decade ago when tourism spread to the Male area, turtle shells became popular items as souvenirs. Besides, the Maldivians had also broken the old rules, and begun to eat turtle meat. Sales of complete turtle shells were now prohibited by law, but objects made from turtle shell could still be sold legally in Male. But who could control turtle hunting on a thousand uninhabited islands?

We crawled over some deep turtle nests dug just above the beach where the jungle started, and for a while a hardly discernible forest trail helped us to proceed inland. Then two men had to chop a trail through, step by step.

Finally we stood next to *Koli Yavali*, the second largest hawitta of Gan. Another huge rubble heap, where there was hardly a worked stone left to see. The mound still stood 5 metres (16 feet) high although it had totally lost its original shape when the dressed facing stones had been removed. But on the south side the elevated remains of a former ramp could be seen, and the base seemed to have been square. Low down on the east side was a depression as from a caved-in niche full of beach sand.

The mosquitos soon drove us back to the shore where the blue lagoon invited us for a refreshing bath. No sand here. The rugged coral bottom cut our feet like broken porcelain. Yet we had to wade far out in sun-warmed water hotter than we were to get wet halfway up our legs. As we lay down among the corals, at least the mosquitos left us. While we lay in the water the 'owner' sent his two trail-breakers further along the coast and inland to fetch the one carved stone we had left behind yesterday.

We lay there with our heads roasting and bodies boiling for an hour, until the two islanders came trotting back along the shore with the stone. But it was the wrong stone. It was not the

90

one with the concentric solar rings we had left behind yesterday, but one on which the sun also had wings.

They had simply found another sculpture.

No sooner did they realise their mistake than they were off again to look for the right stone. Almost an hour later they came back again, this time with one sun-stone each. There was evidently no shortage of these stones around the remains of the sun-temple.

That second evening on Gadu we were to hear about cannibals. We had already heard cannibal stories in Fua Mulaku. Somebody on that island had found masses of human bones while digging the foundations for a house, and the people of Fua Mulaku believed it was the remains of what they termed a 'bone-house'. This was a place where the bones were left from people who had been eaten.

It is strictly against both Moslem and Buddhist beliefs to eat human flesh, but the story constantly recurred. Old Abdulla Mufeed insisted that there had been cannibals even in Moslem times. He told us an incredible story about a woman whose husband had served her bits of flesh cut from his own body, saying it was chicken meat. When she saw the wound and understood that he had fooled her, she killed him, and ate him. Later she lured children to her door with some goodies, then caught them and ate them as well. She ate people for about three years, then committed suicide.

Whatever the origin of this tale, it seemed to reflect some memory of horrible events that might have been witnessed by the forefathers of these islanders, prior to their conversion to Islam. We heard, word for word, the same strange story from old Mohamed Diddi, but according to him that woman was not alone in her tastes. Together with a midwife and other women friends, the whole group had started eating human flesh. To catch their prey they used their beds as traps, and placed sharp sticks in holes in the ground underneath.

This was expressly said to have happened after the introduction of Islam, whereas the 'bone-houses' were associated with recollections from pre-Moslem times.

The cannibal stories we now heard on Gadu did not refer to local events. Old Don Futa recalled a long story about ten men from Addu atoll, on the south side of the Equatorial Channel, who got lost at sea. After a very long time they came to the land of *Azékara*, where there were cannibals. Some people brought them to a big house where they were given plenty of food to get fat. Then over a period of time, they were taken away from that house, one by one, until only two were left. These two followed secretly behind their last friend when he was taken away; they saw that he was brought to the chief's house, and found out he was eaten.

Later that night they went to the window of the chief's house and found the chief sleeping. A fire was burning in the middle of the floor with two hot iron bars. They discussed what to do and then killed the chief with the hot iron rods. Through the window they escaped from the guard and ran to the ocean beach. There they lost each other but one of them, Kiruduni Alibeia, hid in a refuse heap by the shore, where he slept for some days until he was able to continue his flight, and then came to some very good people. From them he sailed with a ship to Karachi. At that time people from Karachi used to come to the Maldives with their boats, and Kiruduni at long last returned home by way of Sri Lanka and Male.

We were breathtaken at the ground covered by this story, but not altogether surprised, for we had heard numerous tales of Maldive sailing ships going to all corners of the Indian Ocean, right until very recent times. All the people present confirmed that Azékara was a well-known Maldivian name for a very distant land known to their ancient ancestors. One of them was convinced that Azékara was somewhere in Indonesia, or even perhaps the old name for Indonesia itself. It made no difference when we pointed out that a voyage home from Indonesia would not go by way of Karachi, which was in Pakistan and on the far side of the Maldives. Our argument made no impression. They knew very well the direction of both Indonesia and Pakistan, and although he came back by way of Pakistan his cannibal adventures had been in Azékara.

In former times there were merchant ships that sailed regularly back and forth between Indonesia and the Indus Valley ports. Our informants assumed that Kiruduni Alibeia might have worked as a sailor on such a vessel before he returned to his own group.

We asked many people where Azékara was. Most of them believed, as did our first informant, that Azékara was in Indonesia. At first Azékara made us think of the land of the Aztecs. The Aztecs of Mexico practised human sacrifice and religious cannibalism on their sun-pyramids until long after the Moslem population had replaced the former cultures in the Maldives, but Mexico was too far away to permit a return voyage. The distant Azékara had to border the Indian Ocean, either in Indonesia as these people believed, or somewhere in East Africa.

Azékara was in fact well known in ancestral traditions throughout the Maldives. That there had formerly been overseas voyages between the Maldives and Indonesia could not be doubted. Prehistoric voyagers from Indonesia had even traversed the entire Indian Ocean and settled on Madagascar, off the East African coast. The Malagasy people and culture were not of African, but of Indonesian origin, and the Maldive archipelago lies exactly halfway between them.

'Of late years,' Bell had written of boats built by the Maldivians, 'more than one vessel, albeit unintentionally, has sailed as far as the East Coast of Africa, when driven out of their course, in adventurous voyaging, by the treacherous winds and currents which render navigation of the "Equatorial" and "One-and-Half-Degree" Channels always hazardous for the seaworthy, but small, Maldivian barques.'[15]

In a footnote Bell adds the last example which happened during his visit. Three boats from Midu island in Addu atoll had then sailed into the Equatorial Channel bound for Male. They were trapped by foul winds and currents and driven westwards across the Indian Ocean, but they finally made the East African Coast in safety. The crews of the three vessels were reshipped to Ceylon (Sri Lanka) and came back to Male in 1922, the year of Bell's last visit.

All Maldive voyages to distant lands were certainly not the result of mere hazard. Some of the descendants of old boat builders and seafarers impressed us with their knowledge of ports around the ocean that surrounded their own microworld. Ports in India, Yemen and Somalia, hardly known to us, were known to several of these heirs of an old mid-ocean civilisation. And it was by no means due to modern influence.

In his early writings, Bell was equally impressed. He quotes
the first Europeans known to have described their encounter
with the Maldive population: the French brothers Parmentier
who rounded the south cape of Africa in 1529 in the two ships
Pensée and *Sacré*, and hit upon Fua Mulaku in the Equatorial
Channel. They were given an honourable reception by a devout
and amiable person assumed to be the chief or archpriest of the
island. In their narrative they wrote that 'The chief Priest, who
was a man of much discretion and knowledge . . . showed the
Captain in what quarters lay the countries of *Adam*, *Persia*,
Ormus, *Calicut*, *Muluque* and *Sumatra*; and proved himself to be
both learned and well travelled'.[16]

All this was known on an islet in the Equatorial Channel even
in the early days of Columbus's generation. *Calicut* was an
important port on the west coast of India and was only reached
by Vasco da Gama on his historic voyage thirty years before the
French Parmentier brothers came to Fua Mulaku; whereas the
Arabs had established an oversea trading centre in Calicut since
the seventh century. *Ormus*, or Hormuz, is the important strait
from the Arabian Sea into the Persian Gulf, the maritime gateway to Mesopotamia. The country of *Adam* is a clear reference to
Mesopotamia, where both the Christian visitors and their
Moslem informants placed the Garden of Eden at the confluence
of the rivers Tigris and Euphrates. By referring to *Sumatra* and
the *Moluccas* the old sage on Fua Mulaku showed that he was
familiar with Indonesian territories as remote from the Maldives in one direction as were Persia, the Hormuz Strait and the
land of Adam in the other.

We now began to see more and more clearly that the Europeans were the latecomers in this ocean. When they claimed to
have 'discovered' the Maldive Islands, they were only very late
visitors to an old maritime sultanate.

When we left our new friends in Gadu to embark and return
once more to Fua Mulaku, it was late in the evening. A heavily
loaded dhoni took us out to the tall and broad vessel anchored in
the lagoon, as always full of patient islanders. A squall came and
it was difficult rowing with the little boat so deeply laden with
people and stones. The sea was so rough even inside the big
lagoon that we were tossed mercilessly up and down against the
tall wooden hull of the anchored vessel, as we pushed with

poles to avoid being crushed. We had to struggle to keep our balance as we handed our heavy potato sacks up to our helpers who were lying prone on the deck.

The captain from Addu atoll had complete faith in his wooden vessel, however, and neither darkness nor the rough weather deterred him from weighing anchor, so we left the protected lagoon for the treacherous Equatorial Channel. We saw only shadows of land on either side and heard the rushing sound from the reef as we sped into open water outside the lagoon. It was 3 am when we left the ring-reef of Gaaf atoll, and 10 am when we were back at our familiar anchorage in the open sea behind Fua Mulaku.

There was no reply yet from Male. Until the Moslem Committee answered our request we could not look for the image said to have been reburied in the Redin mound. We spent the day waiting in the village, and I made use of the opportunity to ask people if Fua Mulaku had always been inhabited. This time the blind man was the first one to speak. Fua Mulaku had been abandoned twice. The first occasion was before Moslem times. Some creatures called *feretas*, which come from the sea and kill people and eat them, had driven the entire population away. Only one woman had remained and seen them at close range. She had hurt one fereta with boiling hot *aros*, a sweet she was stirring with a stick. The ferata had run away from her house and never come back. When the island population returned she told the others that the fereta walked on two legs and had the face of a man.

The next time Fua Mulaku was abandoned was in Moslem times. The village used then to be near *Vasha veo*, the big circular bath we had seen. A fever came to the island with some voyagers, and people started to die. Some left for the island of Midu in Addu atoll. A people called *Rannin* lived there then. There was still the remains of a pool made by the *Rannins* in Midu. Fua Mulaku was left with no people for eight years this time. The Sultan's government in Male learnt about it, and a religious man came and brought the people back to Fua Mulaku from Midu. The island was then resettled by families organised in four groups. The first one led by *Musculi Kalege*, which means Old Man; the second by *Matti Atti Kalege*, a man of high standard; the third by *Ali Adalfi Kalege*, who always chewed betel nuts; and the fourth by *Bul Hadakene*, who took care of people's heads, hair and headwear. The island was divided into four parts, each with its own mosque.

That evening we received a reply on the radio-telephone from Male. The Moslem Committee had decided that we should not

Page 1: With this photograph the Maldive mystery was born. It was sent to the author with a challenge from a stranger: Come to an island far out in the Indian Ocean and solve a riddle. Who made this statue found buried on an island where Islamic law, for more than eight centuries, has rigidly forbidden all art showing the human form?

Page 2, above: Together with Björn Bye *(left)* who sent the challenge, the author rushed to the remote Maldive archipelago only to find the stone statue already dug up and broken by religious fanatics. Only the head was left, and found to represent a beautiful Buddha carved in local limestone.

Below: Two bronze figurines had been dug up by the islanders. They revealed that Asiatic seafarers had navigated the open ocean while Europe was still in the mediaeval ages. The Buddha to the right, together with the broken stone head, showed that Buddhism had a foothold on these remote islands before the Arabs arrived with Islam in 1153. The eroded Hindu god to the left testifies to even earlier visits from mariners before the Buddhist period.

Page 3: A rounded *(above)* and a squared *(below)* limestone stele were carved on all sides with multiple masks of demons with feline teeth and outstretched tongues. They all had large discs inserted in their elongated earlobes. Between the masks the surface of the stone was covered with the unintelligible signs of a forgotten script.

Page 4: Evidence of prehistoric civilisation.

a: Our first discovery was sun symbols cut into limestone blocks scattered about the foot of a round temple mound in the jungle.

b: Among the fallen blocks were also many carved like stylised death masks.

c: Some stone walls showed traces of metal clamps that had formerly held the blocks together, proving that the prehistoric architects had an advanced level of civilisation.

d: This was also evidenced by the discovery of a stone plaque with rows of symbols resembling hieroglyphic script.

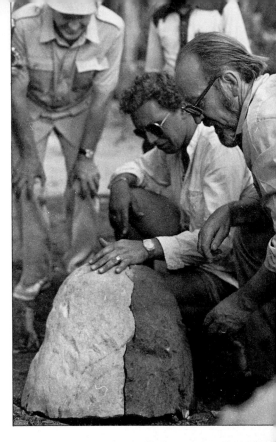

look for the buried statue. We should not touch the old pagan hill. It was better to let this sleeping dog lie.

Our eight-day charter of the good ship *Midu* from Addu atoll had expired, and the next day we crossed the other half of the Equatorial Channel on our way back to the airport island of Addu-Gan. We selected the five finest specimens among the stones from the sun-temple of Gaaf-Gan, which we brought with us in the airplane to Male. The captain of the *Midu* promised to bring all the others next time he sailed north for the capital.

We had found what we had come to look for in the Equatorial Channel. After slightly more than a week's absence we returned to Male with proof to the effect that early sun-worshippers, long

Page 5: A large abandoned bamboo raft drifted ashore on Viringili during our visit. The type of craft, together with the writing on a label we found in the cabin, revealed that the raft had drifted from the coast of Burma, 4,000 km from the Maldives. We took it as a possible pointer, because Burma had been the most important area for the early spread of Buddhism when it descended to the coast from Nepal via the Ganges valley.

Page 6, above: Two of the twenty-three complete or broken phalloid sculptures found in a test trench on Nilandu island. To the left Professor Skjölsvold studies a composite specimen – are they phallus images or phalloid models of *stupa* temples? To the right Johansen has dug up a large fragment which perfectly fits another discovered on the surface in the underbrush.

Below: Two of our Maldive assistants with samples of the many miniature stupa towers we discovered through excavations.

Page 7: Walls of quarried blocks appeared below ground as we dug around an artificial mound in the forest. They proved to be the foundations of a pyramidal structure, once with an interior full of beach sand, faced with sun-oriented walls which had been torn down when Islam reached the islands. From the left, the author, Loutfi, Johansen and Skjölsvold.

Page 8: Who were their ancestors? The Maldive Islands were a kingdom of unknown origin until AD 1153 when the Arabs came with Islam and established a sultanate which closed the nation to foreigners until the Maldives became a republic open for tourism in the 1970s. The marked variation in physical types therefore reflects the complex origins and oversea contacts with many nations around the Indian Ocean in prehistoric times.

before the Arabs arrived, had built temples to honour the sun on the equatorial line. Another old civilisation with a different religion had preceded Islam. The Maldive origins were complicated indeed. The people on these islands had been converted time and again, until they ended as Moslems.

What we least of all suspected was that more surprises awaited us behind the door of the little closet in the museum. When we pushed open the door to help the guards store our sun-ornamented temple stones on the floor in company with the non-Moslem images, we noticed that the door hit a pile of broken stones. The pile was tucked away in the corner behind the door and could not be seen when the door was open. I had noted these stones on our previous visit but taken them for broken bits from the wall which the museum custodian had swept out of sight after some repair. But this time, having seen the nature of broken limestone rubble from the ruins of slab-covered temple mounds, Björn grabbed one of the biggest fragments from behind the door and turned it over.

'How strange – Ai-ai, what is this?' I heard him mutter.

In front of our feet lay a corner fragment of a stone plaque with one side polished flat and smooth as a marble floor, and covered by engraved symbols.

'Hieroglyphics!' I exclaimed. 'This is obviously hieroglyphics. But they are different from the Egyptian. What they resemble most are the hieroglyphics from the Indus Valley.'

Above the line of strange hieroglyphic signs was an ornamental row of swastika symbols, a symbol typical of the early Indus Valley civilisation and which only later spread to Nazi Germany. Originally it was an Indus Valley symbol for the sacred sun. Below the hieroglyphic line, emerging from the broken edge, were the remains of a large wheel with numerous spokes: the well-known sun-wheel of that same early civilisation. And around the outer edge was a broad frame with the characteristic lotus decoration, again another ancient symbol for the divine sun, the rising sun. Sun-symbols in three varieties dominated the stone tablet.

Yet it was the central line of hieroglyphics that more than anything else struck the eye. First, the marine symbols: a fish-hook, a conch, and two fishes, each carved standing upright.

The fish was indeed one of the most common signs in the undeciphered Indus Valley script. There were also two barbed sticks resembling rods for hooking fish. Then there was something else also common among the Indus valley signs, which resembled a beaker but was believed by scholars to represent a sacred drum. Centrally placed in the line was a complex sign in the form of a jar with a neck, from which emerged three arrows with triangular heads. The arrow was an important sign in the Indus Valley script.

The row of hieroglyphic signs continued to the broken part of the tablet, which was missing. Some other strange nondescript symbols were incised beside the broken sun-wheel.

Important pieces were missing. They were not among the stones behind the door.

When we showed the stone to the museum custodians they merely shrugged their shoulders. This was nothing particular, just something old found somewhere in the Maldives. That was all they knew.

Where was the rest of the broken plaque? Missing?

Nobody knew. But the fractures were clearly recent, so it seemed probable to us that the rest of the plaque was still where these pieces had been found. Somewhere on one of these many atolls lay the fragments that would make this hieroglyphic plaque complete.

'We must launch an expedition,' I heard myself exclaim as we rose from squatting beside this precious fragment.

'No way out!' Björn laughed.

We were still overwhelmed with all we had seen during the week, and had not yet digested our discovery behind the museum door, when word of it all came to the ears of the President.

And this was how the stones we had brought to the museum in soiled potato sacks from Gaaf atoll came to be first opened on the red carpet in the President's palace.

This was also why the President, every bit as excited at what we had found as we were, asked me to start excavations.

'An archaeological excavation here is not an easy project,' I said to Björn when my first enthusiasm at the discovery of the broken plaque had subsided. The President's request for me to start excavations had been as much a surprise as had the Moslem Committee's refusal of our request to reopen the trench in the Fua Mulaku hawitta. To look for that reburied image would have been an easy matter. But proper archaeological excavations had to be done with stratigraphic precision, with special tools and professional supervision, to ensure that nothing was damaged and all was minutely measured, mapped and put on record.

Did these people want to know their own buried prehistory, or did they not?

It did not yet dawn upon me that we had stirred up a hornet's nest. Nor did I quite grasp that Maldive society, civilised for so long and finally moulded into a rigid Moslem fraternity by eight centuries of conservative Sultans, had begun to be overrun by jet-age foreigners little more than a decade ago. The locks had been opened, almost overnight, to the outside world, and the young Republic was in a melting pot of old and new. There were those who shared the former Sultan's philosophy that it was best to let sleeping dogs lie; but there was also the progressive group of younger leaders who wanted to find their own roots, establish their own cultural identity, and know the truth of their mysterious unwritten history. From what we had learnt, they all felt strong ties and a sense of debt to the Arab world for the faith and cultural revolution that the magic year of AD 1153 had brought them; but they knew as well that they were not all of Arab descent. Their ancestors had been converted, but not replaced, by the Arab seafarers.

The following morning we were due to leave the Maldives, and our flight reservations had been confirmed. But the President asked us to delay our departure for a day, so that I could give a public lecture in Male about our discoveries. The national television station was closed for the occasion to ensure a full auditorium in Male. The questions from the audience reflected the growing desire of the young Republic to know what had happened in their own archipelago prior to the sultanic period, about which they were well informed.

The hawittas, the image carvers, the Redin, these were all concepts which they had known about but which had never been touched upon in public. I had been invited to come and see a statue before it was smashed to pieces. Now, once again, I had been invited to come back and search for the local truth. This was a challenge I had to accept.

So I did accept.

Next day Björn and I left the Maldives. It was late November 1982. I wanted to be back there again by the end of January, and bring a team of archaeologists to begin excavations before the rains started. The rains in the Maldives start in the spring, at the time when the monsoon reverses its course from north–east to south–west.

The sun and the monsoon winds had sent the early voyagers on the first expeditions into these open parts of the Indian Ocean. The sun still suggested the best place to search, and the monsoon the best time to come, for a modern archaeological expedition.

CHAPTER V

Archaeologists Come to the Maldives

Should Sleeping Dogs Be Disturbed?

A STRING OF atolls in the Indian Ocean, a thousand islands nobody could count accurately. They were emerging again from beyond endless blue horizons, just as I saw them appear when I came on my first visit three months before. A mini-world of its own. A pond of water-lily leaves adrift in the mid-ocean.

Yet this time I saw the islands with the telescope of mind and memory. Down there I had seen unexplored hawittas, hidden images, tablets with strange signs. Flying foxes hanging upside down in the jungle trees. Mosques and ceremonial baths. Entire villages with traditions about the Redin and feretas that had never been recorded. I could hardly wait to get off the plane, and down to the Equatorial Channel.

Björn Bye had joined me in Sri Lanka once again with his two Singalese videotape assistants. Martin Mehren, an old friend from Norway, the first since Fridtjof Nansen to have crossed Greenland on skis, had also joined our party and volunteered to help keep track of the expedition accounts. I always finance my expeditions with books and films. This time Swedish state television were covering the costs in advance against TV world rights and permission to send along two cameramen. They were due to arrive the next day.

The two Norwegian archaeologists who were to take charge of the excavations were not due until three days later. I felt I might need this extra time to prepare for the expedition's departure from Male. Telephone messages and telegrams never seemed to reach the person for whom they were intended.

Other than the President's oral invitation and my own acceptance before I left, it had been an entirely one-sided flow of messages, stating who was coming, when and how.

On the stop-over in Sri Lanka before flying on to the Maldives I had already begun to sense problems in the making. Björn met me with the news that our Maldive contact, Hassan Maniku, had just arrived in Sri Lanka, and that he would be away from the Maldives for exactly the period when we would be there. It was to him that all our messages and correspondence had been directed.

'Hassan Maniku, why are you here when we are coming to look for old remains in your country?' I asked him when we located him in a private villa in Colombo.

We were offered tea and exchanged the customary Arab courtesies before he seemed sufficiently at ease to answer.

He was tired of politics. He had held his responsible position too long. Probably he would resign as Director of Maldive Ministry of Information and Television. At any rate, now he had come for a vacation in Sri Lanka with his family. He very much regretted that he could not be with us on our survey of his beloved islands, but he knew we would be taken good care of. This had been ordered by the President.

At the airport in Male we were met by a tiny girl from one of the government offices. Sweet and helpful though she was, she knew nothing except that she had been told to take us by motor dhoni to Male island; but she was afraid it might be difficult to find vacant rooms in any hotel.

On the pier in Male we happened to run straight into, apparently by chance, the President's personal adviser and right-hand man, Abbas Ibrahim. Short and broadly built, with his modest and winning smile, he was a real gentleman and one of the most likeable persons I had met. I knew him not only from the President's office but also as a fellow board member and the Maldive representative of Worldview International Foundation. As Director of WIF Björn knew him well too, and regarded him as one of the most capable and influential men in the Maldives.

Mr Abbas had been present in the Palace when we unpacked the sun-stones, and he was well aware of the President's invitation. It was just bad luck for us that the President had left for Egypt.

There was not time to look for a hotel. We left the girl in charge of our luggage while Abbas took us to meet the important man who now occupied Hassan Maniku's office.

Behind the familiar glass walls in the Ministry of Information we were now received by the Minister of State for Presidential Affairs, His Excellency Abdulla Jameel. After cordial greetings he explained that the provisional Moslem Committee, which had been unwilling to let us look for the stone image in Fua Malaku, had now been officially replaced by a group of fifteen persons who formed the new National Council for Linguistic and Historical Research. Mr Jameel regretted that this National Council was ignorant about what we wanted to do, for no real archaeologists had visited the Republic so far, and in the absence of the President, nobody had the authority to make decisions.

The glass walls around us must have vibrated at the conflicts in my own mind. The official representative of the Maldive government on the other side of the desk was an extremely pleasant and polite person, now speaking on behalf of a committee that had the right to act against a foreigner coming to dig up an image forbidden by Allah and yet found on their own soil. On the other hand, the same foreigner would never have come to start excavations if he had not been expressly requested to do so by the head of that government.

The two Maldivians were friendly and sympathetic, and understood that this problem had somehow to be solved to our mutual satisfaction. They immediately ordered rooms to be booked for us at the Hotel Alia, and it was agreed that we should all meet there for further talks in the cool of the evening.

In the hotel we were never left alone for a moment. Maldive visitors called to make certain that we did not feel abandoned and reassure us that everything would work out with time and patience. There was Abdul, our lively young interpreter from last time, and the more serious, middle-aged Mohamed Waheed who had been sent with us then by the Atoll Administration.

Most impressive was a new acquaintance, Mohamed Loutfi, a high official from the Ministry of Education and one of the fifteen members of the new National Council for Linguistic and Historical Research. Mr Loutfi was a tall, broadly built man, above middle-age, with a friendly face and with a stature and dark skin that reflected what he later told us. His ancestors had been brought as slaves from Hadaramot in South Yemen twelve generations ago, to serve as a select bodyguard for the Sultan in Male. They later revolted, became free men and married into Maldive families. Mohamed Loutfi could claim therefore, with characteristic good humour, royal sultan blood through both of his parents. He surprised us by his impressive knowledge of Maldive history and of the whereabouts of all sorts of local prehistoric remains. He surprised us even more when he confided that he had been chosen to be our guide when we began our archaeological survey of the islands. Obviously then, in spite of the President's absence, there was still some hope.

Dark clouds collected over the Hotel Alia again in the evening, however. When our helpful friend Abbas arrived with Jameel, the latter informed us that neither of them had authority to let us dig anywhere. In the absence of the head of state it was up to the board of fifteen to decide. He would call them for a meeting as soon as they could all get together in Male.

At that moment I visualised the whole expedition ending on the rocks before we had even got started. I said calmly, but in very plain words, that I was not willing to sit down for a discussion with fifteen men who would never agree on anything anyhow. Time was precious, I had to put faith in the words of the President, with Mr Abbas as witness. In three days' time the archaeologists would be landing in Male on short-term leave from universities and museums in Norway, and any day lost by delay in Male would have to be deducted from the available days of field work.

Abbas hurriedly assured me that everybody wanted to carry out the President's wishes. The last thing he had said to Abbas before he left was that everything possible should be done to ensure all the help we needed. They had even booked the government hospital ship to take us around for a full month, and Mr Loutfi would show us anything we cared to see. The problem was only that we were not allowed to dig.

I expressed appreciation for this marvellous opportunity for my party to be taken around on a cruise, which we would all certainly enjoy immensely. But I added that the archaeologists were bound to feel embarrassed if they came on a tight leave-schedule from distant Norway, without permission to dig. Such a situation, I said, would inevitably result in a scandal for all concerned. There was still time to send a telegram to stop them.

Abbas was desperate and Jameel seemed most uncomfortable. More cool soft drinks were ordered and Abbas asked me to be sympathetic, for, never having had any archaeologists working here, they did not know what it would involve. The National Council did not understand exactly what we wanted to do.

I realised this was an unusual situation. With Maniku obviously out of office, the formal paperwork sent by us had gone astray, or at least had resulted in nothing like a written dialogue, although our island hosts never denied for a moment that they had expected us and that they wanted us to come.

It was getting late. Since Abbas and Jameel said it would be against the wish of the President if I stopped the archaeologists coming, I could see only one way out. During the night I would write a contract in longhand, specifying everything the archaeologists would want to do, what we expected from the local government, and all the rights and duties that affected both parties. This proposal was accepted.

Before office hours next morning my draft was ready. It was fetched by Abbas for typing and subsequent study by the National Council.

Shortly afterwards an airplane landed with one of the two cameramen who was to join the expedition. The other was left behind at the airport in Sri Lanka because somebody had stolen his passport. On the same plane came also the first journalists who had heard rumours that an expedition was planned.

Björn and I sneaked out by the back door. Although time was more precious than ever, there was nothing we could set in motion before we got the green light from the responsible Moslem group. So for once we had time just to look around. We knew what we wanted to see. We walked right through the town of Male, which filled the coral island from coast to coast since it was only one mile long by half a mile wide. The city streets, all without pavements or road cover, to let the rain water sink through and into all the wells, formed such a labyrinth that we were forced to take bearings from the sun. We wanted to go to the extreme east cape where in pre-Moslem times the demon from the sea came ashore at full moon craving Maldive virgins.

Today's Maldive virgins were peacefully pedalling their bicycles between puddles for fear of soiling their clean school uniforms, the only risk being that of bumping into one of the occasional Male taxis which swerved from side to side to avoid the same puddles. The men seemed as peaceful and inoffensive as the women. No shouting, no quarrels, no arrogant behaviour. 'Peace be on you' was the wish brought from all the little mosques into the Moslem community, and it seemed to work.

And yet Male was no longer the quiet place it must have been only ten years earlier when this country was opened to the outside world. The long wharf on the lagoon side and the central shopping area were as busy as if they had been in existence for a hundred years, although the waterfront was still dominated by home-built dhonis, and the streets by imported bicycles. But motorised transport was rapidly coming in.

So far most of the houses in Male had a single floor, in the shopping streets many had two, and in the centre cranes were busy lifting iron bars for the first three- or four-storey government buildings. Among them was a new and truly colossal mosque donated by other Arab nations and designed with a golden dome that would shine in the tropical sun far out over the surrounding ocean.

In this busy part of the town small tourist shops selling turtle-shell carvings, black coral necklaces, shells, shark jaws and model dhonis had begun to sprout like mushrooms, and in between them were shops which, country-store fashion, tempted Maldivian visitors from other islands with everything under one roof from oil drums, corrugated iron and nylon ropes to soft drinks, chewing gum, tinned goods and plastic bottles. In a machine shop they sold fresh tomatoes from the Canary Islands and cucumbers from Holland. In another place we saw a whole shelf full of cans of air freshener!

In the daytime the very few foreigners visiting from the tourist islets could easily be spotted by their red, perspiring faces, as they hunted for souvenirs or looked in vain for a bar or sheltered place to sit down.

Most of the city area still consisted of modest village roads flanked by low huts of crushed coral and mortar. Many, however, were painted in pale colours – light blue, light green, pink and yellow. A few homes still had walls and roof made of the plaited leaves of coconut palms, but today these were more usually kitchen annexes. In the baking sunlight windows were rare or absent, but through open doors we could see people sitting on beds or in wooden hammocks, often with a couple of bicycles by their beds. Perhaps because it happened to be a Friday, the Moslem holiday, transistor radios were blaring music or voices at full blast from almost every home.

Each house was usually linked to its neighbour along the road by a high coral wall which enclosed a luxuriant tropical garden. Tall coconut palms, huge banana leaves, crooked branches of evergreen bread-fruit trees and magnolia towered everywhere high above these modest buildings, and left the impression of a large park or botanical garden. The damp sound of an empty bucket dropping into a well was followed by splashes as the bucket was lifted higher than the garden wall to pour cool fresh water over someone enjoying a shower.

These were clean people. Again we noticed the long-robed women bending double to sweep the dirt road from side to side with their short wisp brooms. When they rose and walked away they moved as if they were gliding along on roller skates, their bodies straight and motionless – characteristic of women accustomed from childhood to carry trays and water jars on their heads.

Somehow the whole atmosphere reminded me of Polynesia – Polynesia at the time of Gauguin, where barefoot women with brown skins, long black hair and Victorian dresses reaching to their ankles radiated feminine charm that bewitched the seafaring visitors. The setting of palms and banana plants undoubtedly reinforced this impression. But in spite of their choice of dress – like the Polynesian *vahines*, in the brightest and most alluring colours rather than black – the Maldivian women were renowned for their chastity, at least if approached by a non-Moslem.

In most of Male the men too were dressed in Polynesian fashion, with a loin cloth wrapped around the waist. Rather colourless compared to what the women wore, this loin cloth usually also reached to the ankles, more rarely to the knees. One young man made us jump, however, as he zoomed by on a motor bike, unconscious of the noise he was making because he was enjoying his own taped music on headphones. Young men here did not look very different from young men in the outside world; and their parents would certainly like to see them go straight out of school uniform to white-collar jobs in government offices.

Nobody greeted us as we passed, but Maldivians do not greet each other. Their language has no word for a salute, although the Arab salutation is beginning to win ground.

We were approaching the eastern extremity of the island. Beyond the crossroads we could glimpse the blue sea. Down there was the liveliest part of the Maldive capital. The bustle and clamour along the harbour started daily before sunrise with the din and clatter of boat engines and motor bikes, mixed with the rumbling of drums and chains on decks and pier, loud radio music, and shouts from all the people ashore and on board who were attempting to make themselves heard above the hullabaloo of a thousand other male and female voices.

In the blue water outside the harbour wall dhonis of all sizes came and left, fast and slow, a few still under sail, most with rumbling engines. At full tilt speed boats jumped savagely over the waves as if life were at stake, as if they were scared by the old demon of the sea. The air was trembling with noise from all these fast, faster and fastest vessels which followed the recipe of the outside world, for our generation seems to feel the need to frolic in the global supply of combustibles while there are still some to burn.

We reached the waterfront at the point where the harbour and all its turmoil ended, and the open ocean lay before us.

Here, on the eastern cape, the road followed the sea with a naked reef on one side and a very high wall on the landward side. Here too were pages of Maldive history. Partly embedded in the coral reef, and partly awash, lay one old cannon next to the other, tossed away with no concern for the value of scrap metal. There seemed to be more than a dozen. But quite apart from scrap, each of these cannons could be a collector's item of immense value, welcomed anywhere else in historical museums or by collectors of arms and antiquities. They were Portuguese cannons and marked the beginning of European history in these waters. They had been thrown down on to the reef over 400 years ago or, more exactly, in 1573, when the Portuguese intruders were driven away by the Maldivians after fifteen years of occupation. This was the only period in Maldive history when the archipelago was under foreign rule.

109

The tall wall on the other side of the road was new, yet it enclosed fragments of a much older era of local history, though passers-by would normally only notice the big sign on the gate: 'Maldives Engine Service Centre'. The wall, taller than ourselves, was built from the usual crude chunks broken from the coral reef and bound together by mortar. But a few of the stones, haphazardly set in among the rest, had an appearance very familiar to us by now. They had been worked square with traces of decorative mouldings. Reused temple stones. Displaced fragments of Maldivian prehistory.

We were not in doubt about the origins of these building blocks. This was as far east as it was possible to go on this island. This was where the virgins had been brought in pre-Moslem times. Out there in the endless expanses of ocean had appeared the many lights under the full moon which marked the monthly appearance of the evil jinni from the sea.

The big gate was left half open. Nobody there. Some boats and engine parts lay scattered around. A small boat was propped up by some stones. One of them was an old temple stone, while another one lay tossed on to a pile of rubble and refuse.

A young man came out of a shed.

No engine trouble? Why then had we come? He was surprised. If this was the place of the images and virgins?

The young Maldivian gave us a suspicious look as he wiped an oily hand on his blue jeans and with polite but fumbling gestures brought us back to the gate, which he slowly bolted behind us.

We had found the place. We had seen stones from the jinni's temple and the pagan footmarks set in the wall. But Allah's youngest generation had exchanged modern engines for former idols.

We walked back by following the ocean shore all around the island, and soon came to the fill-in area. Vast coral shallows, barely awash, extended offshore with short reeds growing on parts already reclaimed from the sea by large quantities of refuse. A hand-cart was just being rolled out and dumped. Two men were burning what would otherwise have floated away, and raked the ashes into the shallows. Most of the area seemed to consist of rubble from torn-down houses mixed with common waste.

The new beach was a world of plastic, tins, glass, rags, rubbish. It stank. Like rotten eggs. Spray bottles, Coca-Cola, broken pots, rubber tyres, sandals, plastic, plastic, plastic.

A nice-looking woman was squatting washing her arms. Others were coming from the houses to rub and clean their pots. They searched for the cleanest areas, for in some spots the lagoon water was as black as the bottoms of their cooking pots. For sure, man with all his modern means could not compete with Allah in creating an attractive coral island.

But what should these poor people do? As in the rest of the modern world, the people in this country try to move from out-of-the-way places to the capital. The capital in the Maldives happens to be a small island. In Male there is no farm land or hill country to expand into, only what can be recovered from the Indian Ocean.

Far out in the sea we could make out the contours of some other palm covered islands. They were the tourist islets, ensuring cash economy for the modern Maldives. Inland we saw a huge yellow truck-crane passing like a prehistoric dinosaur behind the houses.

Back in the hotel we noticed a strange smell from the water as we took a much needed shower. It smelt just like rotten eggs. We asked the owner. He assured us politely that with time the bad odour would disappear, but his well was still new and the hotel was built on land recently recovered from the sea.

We waited in vain all the rest of the day, expecting to receive our contract back signed by the Moslem Committee. Nothing happened.

Nothing happened the next day either, when the archaeologists would be departing from Norway. I called the friendly Mr Abbas and told him that I wanted to telephone the President, wherever he was. But nobody had his number in Egypt. And besides, it was not necessary to call since the President had told them to give us all assistance. The ship we were to use was waiting in the harbour, ready to go as soon as we had the digging permit. Unfortunately, Abbas added, more and more voices on the Council were against any digging by the archaeologists. To show me the extent of their goodwill, Abbas took me to the wharf and showed me a beautiful ship at anchor outside the harbour wall, all nicely painted white, and green below the water-line. Across the broad stern was painted '*Golden Ray*, Male'.

This was the government's hospital ship, donated to the Maldives by the British forces when they left Addu-Gan at the end of the Second World War. Abbas explained that the *Golden Ray* was almost 24 metres (78 feet) long and manned by eleven Maldive officers and crew. She was just waiting to take us on a tour anywhere we desired.

This did not make the situation any easier for me. I went to bed that evening knowing the archaeologists were due to arrive in Male the next afternoon at 1 pm.

Next day was Sunday, but the shops were open. In despair I appointed Björn quarter-master general, and with lists all ready we began shopping for an expedition of at least twenty-two men who would be cut off from further supplies for thirty days. After an hour and a half a messenger from the Ministry of Information came and told me that I was needed immediately for a meeting with his boss.

I rushed to the Ministry of Information, only to learn that the meeting had already been convened somewhere else in Male. I rushed to the address they gave me, only to learn that the meeting had been cancelled, as it was not necessary.

Back at the Ministry I now found a handwritten note that 'Dr Hydral' was to come to the Amini Building at 12.30. This was exactly when I was due to be at the airport island to meet the archaeologists.

Björn was therefore delegated to fetch the archaeologists by boat while I headed for the Amini Building. As I had refused to sit down and discuss with a fifteen-man committee what I had come to do on request from their President, Abbas had asked if I were at least willing to talk to two members of that group, and I had agreed. For balance I now went to the meeting in company with Arne Fjörtoft, the Norwegian President of Worldview International Foundation, who had come from Sri Lanka with the journalists to see us off. His personal friendship with Mr Abbas had made him an important helper in the strange wrestling match that now seemed to be going on.

In the Amini Building we were met by two exceptionally pleasant and friendly government officials, both representing the newly formed National Council for Linguistic and Historical Research, formerly referred to as the Moslem Committee. One was Mohamed Loutfi, the well-informed, swarthy giant who had said he would be coming with us; the other was Mohamed Waheed, a solid and strongly built man with kind eyes and a big black bushy beard.

I was about to sit down at the long conference table when I was stopped by the two others. A little office girl was running in and out of the room and moving chairs about. The two Maldivians were to sit on one side, and my friend and I on the other. But the two pairs of chairs facing each other across the table did not seem to satisfy her, and she kept on putting an extra chair at the top of the table as well, which she then removed, until she finally came back and put two chairs side by side at the narrow top of the table.

I now realised that the two who had received us were not those who really counted, as they suddenly straightened up at respectful attention when two other men arrived. The new arrivals entered solemnly, as in a two-man procession. Obviously they wanted to show that they held high office in the community. In fact equally high, which is why the little girl had been told in the end that they should both be seated side by side at the head of the table.

One was introduced to us as the Honourable Mr Moosa Fathhi, Chief Justice of the Maldives High Court, and thus a Moslem with supreme authority since Maldive law is entirely based on the words of the Koran.

The other was introduced as the Honourable Mr Mohamed Jameel, and although he acted as if we had never met, I knew him as the President of the National Council who was to decide what we could do when we weighed anchor with the *Golden Ray*.

These two, representing the top religious authorities in the country, held a power that perhaps equalled that of the democratically elected President.

As the meeting began the two at the head of the table remained stern and silent and left the introductory speech to Mohamed Waheed. He went out of his way to be polite and positive on behalf of his superiors who did not seem to understand English. He apologised for the island mentality, as they were very afraid, he said. Many people were of the opinion that the hawittas had been left in peace for hundreds of years, so why take risks, why not let this continue?

We were not there to plunder the hawittas, I explained. If they did not want us to, we would not even touch them. We would be just as interested in looking for other remains, for instance early habitation sites, any refuse from former times that could tell us something about their own ancestors. This was what the President had wanted us to do.

A big cloud seemed to drift away. We could dig anywhere we wanted within the Republic, as long as we let the hawittas alone. To my surprise, after some discussions between them in Divehi, unintelligible to us, the friendly speaker turned back to us and said in English that we could even excavate hawittas. But if we wanted to dig more than three of them, we had to send in a new request.

Various amendments were now made all through the contract I had proposed, but nothing of any importance. I left the meeting greatly relieved, and rushed to the hotel to meet the archaeologists who had come with Björn from the airport. At 4 pm the National Council was to send the amended contract back to me, retyped and signed by the responsible authorities.

I waited the rest of the day, but no contract came back. In fact, it never came back. I never saw it again, nor any other paper signed by the National Council or any other government office. But Mr Loutfi came with a broad smile and assured us that now we could sleep soundly, there were no more problems. They had left it to him to decide where we could dig, and I could trust him, so I needed nothing in writing.

That evening, after dark, I was permitted to inspect the *Golden Ray* which was to be ready for departure by 7 am the next morning. It was a fine ship with a large room down below ideally suited for the storage of digging equipment and provisions. Appropriately, this former hospital room was also full of field-beds. There were even three small single-berth cabins on deck in addition to a berth behind the steering wheel, reserved for the Maldive captain.

But on inspecting the single small wooden lifeboat, I found a hole in the bottom big enough to put my head through. It had clearly been in contact with a reef! I refused to go to sea without any kind of landing craft. It was already late at night, and I was told not to worry because there was a walkie-talkie radio on board so we could always talk to the atoll chief when we reached any island, and he could send out a dhoni to take us ashore.

But I refused point blank. We could not depend on some chief ashore each time we wanted to land, particularly since the majority of Maldive islands were uninhabited. Besides, there was hardly any more dangerous navigation area in the world, with its labyrinth of tidal currents, submerged reefs and sand bars. The one argument that finally resolved this issue was that, with my experience of the sea, I was able to insist that it was an offence in international law to navigate the ocean with twenty-two men on board a ship that did not even possess a life raft.

Telephones rang and messengers criss-crossed Male by bike all night. As the sun rose a big, flat-bottomed metal launch, ideally suited for our purposes, was towed out and tied by a strong rope to the stern of the *Golden Ray*.

It was hard to get out of bed for all the sacks, crates and baskets mixed with shovels, jerry-cans, cooking pots, jungle knives, coils of rope and kerosene lamps; all our new acquisitions had been delivered yesterday and were piled up high around our beds. Here were all the larger tools the archaeologists had not brought from Norway, field equipment, provisions and medicine. As the expedition members and our Maldivian friends started to carry it all on to big hand-carts waiting outside, I checked with red marks all the items already cancelled by a blue stroke on the various lists in my notebooks. Nothing was missing that we could not do without. In high spirits we helped the owners of the carts to manoeuvre the towering loads through the town and down to the docks.

It took time to row it all on board, and it was 8.30 am instead of 7 am as agreed when the anchor chains of *Golden Ray* began to rattle and Mr Loutfi looked anxiously at his watch.

'We are an hour and a half late,' he said. 'We will not get as far as I hoped before the sun sets. And the captain wants us to anchor in some lagoon before night. It is too risky to move between all these reefs in the dark.'

The captain of the *Golden Ray* was a little wiry Maldivian above middle age by the name of Mohamed Maniku, who liked to be called Pakar, since the Maldives were full of Mohameds and Manikus. Pakar was a mariner of few words, hardly any of which were English. But Mr Loutfi himself turned out to be an experienced navigator. He had his captain's certificate and, as some sort of comptroller of the Maldive schools, he knew the whole archipelago better, we were to learn, than anybody else in the Maldives. Loutfi represented the government, and Captain Pakar had to take orders on the itinerary from him.

In addition to Loutfi, Mr Kela Ali Ibrahim Maniku had climbed on board with us, an Ethiopian-looking gentleman with a well-trimmed black beard and glasses, who introduced himself as Project Officer of the Atoll Administration. His ministry had selected him as our English-speaking liaison officer in dealings with the chiefs on all the islands.

Now, and only now, as the ship began to move, did we get a chance to relax and tell ourselves that we were really off on our 'dig'. As the long row of dhoni masts behind the mole began to slide away, together with the houses along the water front in Male, I had my first real chance to welcome the two archaeologists. We lined up along the railing to watch the scattered flotilla of little palm-clad isles anchored at the Male ring-reef while we alone moved away and out of the calm lagoon.

Behind us lay a ring of purely tourist islands around the Maldive capital. They seemed like satellites occupied by visitors from outer space, for here, and only here, were the only non-Moslem beings in the archipelago.

We felt immense relief as the *Golden Ray* entered the smoothly rolling swells of the open ocean. Yet there was land and reefs on both sides behind the horizon. We were steering south-westwards, obliquely across the waters that separate the two submerged ridges of Maldive atolls and shallows which run side by side from north to south for almost 900 kilometres.

Deck-chairs were brought up, and with Pakar at the wheel and all his crew at their jobs, the rest of us settled down in the open space on the aft deck to discuss our plans. Loutfi agreed that our best choice would be to set course for the Equatorial Channel where we knew there was so much to be found. He estimated that with our speed reduced to 5.5 knots by the launch in tow, and by the captain refusing to move at night, we would need three days to get there.

Young Abdul, who again came along as interpreter, and his two fellow students from Sri Lanka, Saliya and Palitha, did not hide their joy at the chance of returning to Fua Mulaku. Their memories of the tasty fruits and the beautiful girls on that island were soon shared with the crew from the bridge to the engine room.

Most of the palefaces in our party lay stripped to the Moslem legal minimum on deck, trying to recover what they had lost during a dark Nordic winter. The one who had lost the least was clearly my old friend Martin Mehren, a passionate skier and golfer who spent more time in the open than in his office. He had joined the expedition purely for fun.

The real core of this enterprise were the two archaeologists. My long-time friend Professor Dr Arne Skjölsvold was to lead the excavations. He had joined me for the first time on the Galapagos expedition in 1952, and later for a full year on Easter Island and other parts of Polynesia. With his long beard, and glasses on the tip of his nose, it was easier to see that he was an absent-minded university professor and head of the archaeological faculty at Oslo University, than it was to guess that he was also the hardiest expedition companion and greatest merrymaker in any party. He had just returned from further excavations on Easter Island, but the university generously allowed him another clear month off for the Maldives.

He had personally picked his assistant, whom I did not know, a second-generation archaeologist named Öystein Johansen. To anyone who did not know that this smiling young man was already a noted field archaeologist and director of a provincial museum in Norway, he might have passed for a super-blond Nordic actor, the way he posed for the cameras in the bow. But it was the two cameramen who had picked him out to point as they filmed the tumbling dolphins that swam in fan-formation in front of our bow, like huskies before a sledge.

With these two cameramen fresh out from the deepest forests of central Sweden, our mixed party of travellers was complete. Bengt Jonson was a former lumberjack, and Åke Karlson a former waiter in a neighbourhood country inn. They had first met when Åke had asked Bengt to come and cut down a tree in front of his house. The tree is still there, for the two started discussing films, and ever since they had roamed the world together shooting and producing their own documentaries. Bengt was still the big jovial lumberjack, holding a microphone in his large hands as if it were an axe, and Åke still the elegant waiter who could manipulate his cameras past every obstacle as though he were carrying a tray through a crowded restaurant. Both visibly enjoyed every minute of life. It was easy to see by looking around that, with this crowd, we were not going to have a dull moment on board or ashore.

With the salt air and the soft rolling of the ship our appetites rose to a zenith with the sun. The skinny Maldive cook looked as if he hated eating, but our noses were now telling us that his taste for good food was far superior to his own appetite. The tall Maldive mess-boy was a comedian. He looked like a slim Italian, and had worked for Italians on a Male tourist island and learnt one Italian word, *mangiare*, 'eat'. With a pot and a big spoon he came marching in like a soldier with a drum, beating and announcing: *'mangiare, mangiare, mangiare'*, to which he added the only three English words he knew: 'Food is ready!' Before I knew it Martin and the two Swedes fell in behind him, and soon we were all marching towards the mess room clapping in time and repeating the magic words with great appetite. Our ages ranged from Martin's well over 70 to Abdul's 22, but clearly nobody was going to worry about the difference on this journey.

Well satisfied with the tasty Maldivian lunch of fish, rice and curry, we passed the afternoon dozing in the sun, watching the glittering flying fish and tumbling dolphins, and looking in vain for sharks or whales.

In the early afternoon a long string of low palm islands appeared ahead of us on the starboard side. This was the Ari atoll. The sun was still high as we passed close to the beautiful but uninhabited Digura island. Then we entered into the Ari lagoon through a reef with broken coral blocks rising out of the water like swimming animals. Following the ring-reef on the inside we passed other incredibly spectacular palm islands, none of which showed any sign of life, until Loutfi and Captain Pakar agreed that we had to anchor while we were still in the shelter of the lagoon. With our late start this morning we would not manage to cross the open channel and reach another safe anchorage before sunset.

The anchor rattled out and Loutfi told us there was still time to go ashore. Two islands were within easy reach. We could choose between Maamigili island, which was inhabited and where we would have to pay for fresh coconuts to drink, or Ariyaddu island which was uninhabited and where we could climb for the nuts ourselves. Martin immediately suggested the uninhabited island where we could have a swim in the clean lagoon. When Loutfi added that the uninhabited island of Ariyaddu had once been the home of the Redin there was no longer any doubt.

I was surprised at Loutfi mentioning the Redin. What did he know about the Redin on this island? Nothing, except that, according to Maldive traditions, they had once lived there. Others had lived there after the Redin, but even that was long ago. The government had records, which began more than two centuries ago, of all the inhabited islands, and Ariyaddu was depopulated before then.

As we approached land we noticed a big dhoni coming out from behind a sand-bar and packed so full of people that they were standing with no room to sit down. We next noticed a few soldiers in uniform who had remained behind on the beach. As our launch hit the sandy bottom and we all waded ashore, Loutfi asked the soldiers, in his own language, what was going on; he was told that this island belonged to the Minister of Defence. He had ordered the undergrowth to be cleared as he wanted to start test plantations and an experiment with poultry and goats.

The clearing was well under way and we were permitted to walk where we pleased. Big trunks of pandanus palms and piles of cut firewood lay everywhere, otherwise there were extensive fields of burning in the surprisingly stone-strewn ground. Only the coconut palms were left standing. This gave us an excellent opportunity to see far and wide between the trunks of the palm trees, and we had hardly left the sandy beach before we found the first remains of former habitation. The further we went inland the bigger were the shapeless piles of limestone blocks and broken coral. Clearly, former buildings of impressive size had been torn down and the building materials scattered over the ground.

In one place were the foundations of a small mosque, carefully laid out to point in the direction of Mecca, but the building stones must have been taken from some earlier and larger structure.

For the first time in the Maldives I noticed square blocks with shallow depressions from dovetailed mortices at each end – the traces of former metal clamps intended to hold the stones tightly together. Not only had the clamps been removed or had fallen out, but when the stones were reused in the mosque they were placed together in such a way that the mortices in one stone no longer matched those in another.

Nearby was a huge, flattened rubble mound which Loutfi confirmed was the scattered remains of a long since devastated hawitta. Next to it was a deep depression in the ground where the soldiers had thrown all sorts of branches and leaves they wanted to burn. Much to our excitement we discovered that this was a large, circular ceremonial bath. One fair-sized section of the wall was still exposed as soon as we removed some leaves and branches, whereas the main part of the bath was totally buried. The walls in the bath had been built from perfectly shaped rectangular blocks with the empty mortising sockets still to be seen in their original positions, like butterfly designs at all joints between the building blocks.

At only one place in the world could I remember having seen this particular kind of stone jointing, and that was the prehistoric Phoenician port of Byblos in Lebanon. The blocks from the former harbour construction, slightly submerged outside the present port, had been joined together precisely in this way, and there the 'butterfly' joints of bronze were still in their original sockets. Whoever the Redin had been, they had been sufficiently civilised to be familiar with copper or bronze. And they must have had contact with the mainland since no form of metal could ever be locally available within an archipelago formed entirely out of coral. The Phoenicians were not known to have sailed beyond the Mediterranean and the Atlantic Ocean, except when the joint Egyptian–Phoenician fleet of Pharaoh Necho circumnavigated Africa in about 600 BC. Yet this highly characteristic 'butterfly' type of prehistoric stone jointing was so specialised that the Maldive Redin must have learnt it abroad from people who, directly or indirectly, had contact with the Phoenicians.

Loutfi had heard that a stone phallus of the type which the

Hindu called a *lingam* had been found on this island. It had been measured before it was destroyed and was said to have been 'one foot and three inches long, and one foot in cross-section at the base'. He asked the soldiers if they had heard about this sculpture and one of them volunteered to show us where it had been found. We walked right across the island to a place where there still was a large and tall hawitta which had been plundered in the past, for a big crater had been left in the centre. At the side lay a finely carved, stepped pedestal block with a square depression on the top. The soldier told us that this had been the base of the stone that Loutfi had heard about. The base of the *lingam* stone.

Before we left the Redin island we witnessed a spectacular sunset behind the palms. Next morning, as the sun rose, we were on our way out of the lagoon.

CHAPTER VI

Excavations Begin

The Buried 'Phallus Temple' on Nilandu

AT BREAKFAST we were all laughing over our luck. We would never have stopped at the island of Ariyaddu if we had not been delayed in our departure from Male. And had Loutfi not happened to mention the Redin, maybe we would have chosen to visit the other, inhabited, island.

'Who do you think the Redin were?' I asked Loutfi who was beaming with satisfaction when he saw how pleased we were with the discoveries.

'I do not know,' he answered with a broad smile.

'But do you think they were real people?'

'Yes, I do. Our ancestors said they were real people.'

As we left the table the two archaeologists, Loutfi and I went up to Captain Pakar in the wheel-house. The navigation chart lay open in front of us, and so did the blue ocean. We were out on the ocean side of the western row of the Maldives.

'Where do you want to stop next?' asked Loutfi as he let his dividers straddle down the chart towards the equator.

'Will we pass any other island where the Redin are said to have been?' I enquired.

'Sure,' said Loutfi, and took a close look at the map before he pointed. 'There,' he said, 'at Nilandu.'

I looked at the archaeologists. They read my mind.

'Why not,' said Arne Skjölsvold. 'Let's stop at Nilandu.'

I went to fetch Hassan Maniku's list of all the islands. 'Nilandhoo,' I read, 'in Faaf atoll. Inhabited. East of the centre of the island is a ruin measuring 146 feet in circumference and 4 feet high.' There were other prehistoric ruins also, and a mosque built by the first Sultan of the Maldives in AD 1153–66. The note ended: 'Digging here a stone "box" with a bright red powder and a golden statue was found.'

'It was a golden cock,' Loutfi added. 'It was brought to Male but lost.'

At 10 am the *Golden Ray* anchored in the open sea off the Nilandu reef. If nothing else, we wanted to hear the story of the golden cock from the mouths of the local people. There was a village on this island, according to Loutfi, of 760 inhabitants. They had already spotted us from the beach, and through the walkie-talkie Loutfi was informing the chief of our intention to come ashore.

A dhoni came out to pilot our launch in across the reef through a long and shallow channel cleared of protruding corals. The water was crystal clear. It seemed clearer than the air, and all the fantastic shapes on the bottom showed up as if seen through a magnifying glass. We marvelled at the beauty all around as we moved through the bottle-green shallows over the reef which sheltered the golden beach of the palm island from the assaults of the sky-blue ocean.

At the head of the pier we were received with hearty hand-shakes by the chief, the second chief, and all the men of important rank in the little community: first the customary exchanges of questions of well-being and good wishes in Arab style; then we started walking along the pier, towards the village. Loutfi now began to pass on the questions we had already posed to him to some of the elder men who seemed to have the sole privilege of answering.

Sure, somebody had come from Male and they had dug up three boxes of stone, covered by stone lids. They were all a little more than 30 centimetres (1 foot) square. Two had been carried away unopened. But one was destroyed as it was opened and it contained a golden cock. There was also a metal plate with some script, but the script could not be understood. All were sent to Male.

Loutfi was visibly embarrassed when he had to confess that nothing like that existed in Male. Yet the chief insisted that nobody on the island had taken anything. The official records, he said, showed that the golden cock and the metal plate with the inscriptions went to Male. He was willing to show us the place where they had been dug up.

We walked in from the beach between the palms and immediately entered the wide and admirably clean sandy streets of the little village. All the women and children were lined up along the road as we passed, or peeping from behind the doors of the little houses. As if to excuse their curiosity, the chief told Loutfi that no foreigner had come ashore on this island for seven years.

Walking along I noticed that we ourselves were staring at the spectators along the road at least as much as they were staring at us. Some of the women and children were remarkably beautiful, and not only the youngest men in our party exchanged glowing comments to that effect. There was in particular one young woman sitting on a bench, stoically smoking her water-pipe, and another tall one with long flowing hair standing with a little baby clinging around her neck, both of whom could have competed victoriously at any beauty contest in the world. Neither of them reacted, however, to the cameras that were directed at them.

Not all the people were equally good-looking, indeed they showed a remarkable variation in physical features. In general the Maldivians must be considered handsome by any international standard, yet most of them are so exceedingly short, reaching only to the chest of the average European, that they would have appeared like dwarfs except for the fact that they are always extremely well proportioned. For this reason they often look like teenagers until they become old.

The majority, as in Male, look like Singalese or Indians. Among the taller types there are those who could pass for Arabs, Jews, Ethiopians or other people from Asia Minor and East Africa. The real beauties were commonly tall and remind one of the fair-skinned European type of Polynesian more than of any people in the neighbouring territories of southern Asia. In contrast to Polynesia however, these beauties made no move to tempt the visitors with their feminine charms. Their Moslem faith was stronger than any temptation. Abdul joked happily with Saliya and Palitha as Buddhists, and Öystein Johansen as a Christian, at the fact that here he would be the only one who would have a chance.

The local men who accompanied us barely had time to assure us that there were no sculptures of any sort, nor any other old objects left on this island, when an innocent-looking little boy who ran along with us contradicted them by telling us that he had a fragment of what Abdul translated as a 'statue'. To the embarrassment of the elders he ran off and came back with what seemed like a neck and shoulder fragment of an image. The boy drew in the sand something that resembled a bust when he told us what this figure had looked like before he broke it.

As we tipped him some Maldive coins for his courage in showing us his fragment, other kids ran off and returned with more pieces of worked stones, but they were too fragmentary for us to say more than that they had not been shaped by nature nor, very likely, by any Moslem. Since they all got their reward anyhow, it became too much for the adults and a man came with a big chunk of a smoothly vaulted limestone fragment. Öystein Johansen gasped.

'A phallus fragment!' he exclaimed. 'I wrote my thesis on prehistoric phallus distribution, so I know what this is!'

We were all amazed. Loutfi admitted that this was supposedly the shape and size of the *lingam* they had found on Ariyaddu, but which was lost. The sculpture was broken lengthwise with one half missing, and when we showed the islanders with signs where the missing part was broken off, two young men disappeared into some nearby shrubbery, digging with their hands, and soon they came back with another big fragment of a phalloid stone of the same size. The two big pieces did not fit together but there were obviously other fragments lying around in the neighbourhood.

The archaeologists were excited and wanted to dig in this area. These broken sculptures certainly represented vestiges from some pre-Moslem cult. Here was firm evidence which supported Loutfi's report that a *lingam* stone had really been found on the last island we had visited – even though it had since been lost and we had merely been shown the carved base, representing the feminine parts. If these were truly the broken parts of *lingam* sculptures, then they would have been carved by Hindu worshippers, for phallus worship, which is unknown to Moslems, never pertained to Buddhism. Since we had found Hindu images as well as Buddha figures in the museum closet, we were all convinced that our new discoveries represented phallus images of a Hindu type.

Loutfi agreed that the archaeologists should start work right here. He strongly recommended that we stopped for a day or two on this island to investigate this very area. There was no reason to object, and we decided to start operations there and then.

Just a few steps away was a low sandy mound which would hardly have been noticed, as it was thickly covered by undergrowth, had it not been for the fact that the islanders told us this was where the stone boxes with the golden cock had been found. We told the chief that we wanted help to clear the low mound. He said that he would round up as many men as we needed next day, but he could give us twenty women right now to clear the undergrowth. Next moment a crowd of barefoot women in their long colourful gowns swarmed into the thickets with jungle knives, cutting left and right and pulling the long leafy branches away from the site.

Soon the whole area lay clear but for the big trees and palms, and in the midst of it was the mound where the golden cock had been found. It seemed to be nothing but a heap of loose white beach sand. There was also a fresh pit in the ground a few steps away where the men had dug up the phalloid fragment. We stopped them from touching anything more as all digging was to be done by the archaeologists.

From the islanders we got some coils of fine rope twisted and braided from coconut husks. Then the archaeologists staked out the limits of the test pit they intended to dig and marked it off with tight ropes. No sooner did they start scraping the loose sand with their trowels than they hit sculpted stones which they brushed clean and found to be fragments of still more phalloid sculptures. As one of these was lifted out from the ground, it proved to match perfectly the first fragment the islanders had brought us. With the two pieces held together the sculpture was complete and not a single chip was missing. It appeared a perfectly shaped and smoothed phallus. Its identity could not be mistaken, with the little hole on the top and the ring around the shaft representing circumcision.

As the digging proceeded still more phalloid fragments appeared in the same trench, and in between lay also some

peculiar limestone carvings in the shape of the strangely seg-
mented towers customary on top of Buddhist stupas as well as
on Hindu temples. It looked like one umbrella, or mushroom,
set on top of the other in diminishing sizes from base to top. We
termed these sculptures 'umbrella towers' when we found that
they were almost as common in the trench as were the phalloid
stones.

Miniature towers of this kind in ancient Asia were commonly
buried as votive offerings. But these were not buried as offerings. On the contrary, as with the phalloid images, they had
been broken and thrown away as undesirable objects. From the
way all these fragments lay together in confusion it was obvious
that they had been tossed there haphazardly, later to be deliberately covered with beach sand.

By the time the day's work was ended we had recovered from
the one test trench five phalloid stones, out of which two were
complete and set on short cylindrical bases, and we knew that
there would be more to be found when work was resumed the
next morning.

Before we left the dig, however, we had learnt from the local
people that the name of the low mound where the golden cock
had been found was *Fua Mathi*, which was translated as 'Testicle
Height'.

While at first we had all unhesitatingly accepted the phalloid
stones as *lingam* sculptures and assumed the Testicle Height to
be the remains of some sort of fertility temple, Skjölsvold was
impressed by the many little 'umbrella towers' found with the
phalloid stones, and called for caution. Stones just like these had
been found by archaeologists in Sri Lanka, too, and there the
phalloid type of stone with an 'umbrella tower' on top represented a miniature stupa.

The Testicle Height had been built from beautifully cut stones,
but, when Islam was introduced by the first Sultan of Male,
these pagan buildings had been stripped. The worked stones
were used to build the nearby mosque, which was the second
oldest in the Maldives. The oldest was the one the same Sultan
had first built in Male.

While the archaeologists were cataloguing the day's finds
Loutfi and I went to visit this mosque. It was big, and in every
respect surprisingly impressive for such a small community.

127

Inside we found the mosque decorated with beautiful hard-wood carvings in arabesques which dated from the original building period, well over 800 years ago. Certainly the local people would never have built such an edifice today. Part of the walls were magnificent, fitted together from perfectly shaped and dressed blocks of large dimension. Certain sections had been reassembled entirely as in the dismantled temple, and the result was another example of the spectacular 'fingerprint masonry', the same story, in fact, as on Fua Mulaku. The first mosque had been conveniently built, probably in record time, by stripping ready-made blocks from a non-Moslem temple.

As they brushed the sweat away, the archaeologists were quite overwhelmed at the result of the first day's digging. In Norway they could dig for a whole season and be happy if they hit upon even as much as this. Here, on an atoll in the Indian Ocean, they had dug a test pit and immediately hit upon all those phalloid images or stupas and 'umbrella towers', which were now lined up along the trench.

Johansen, who as a phallus expert knew how rare similar objects were in Europe, was literally beaming. Loutfi was no less pleased and amazed. Only one such *lingam* had ever been seen in the Maldives before, but it was lost. Here we had five, already numbered and secured for the Male Museum.

Seeing that these long hidden oddities were not only toler-ated but also made all of us happy, even the Nilandu islanders began to rejoice with us. This had to be celebrated. And not just with coconut juice but also with something to please the eye and ear. In the main village street the little girls of the island had been lined up for a dance, with their long black hair falling down over spotless white school dresses with blue neck ties. A man and a girl were squatting in front of them with drums carved from coconut wood covered with ray skin. As we arrived they started a rhythmic drumming and the girls began a lively Maldive song to which they all danced. It was a regular South Sea atmosphere, enjoyed every bit as much by the village spectators as by us.

Before we went back on board Björn Bye and I ran to have a quick dip in the crystal clear water between the beach and the reef but, almost as soon as he dived in, Björn sprang out again with a yell. Something had hurt him so badly that the pain was to last for several days and a scar remained on his arm. He caught a glimpse of the creature and found another of the same sort stranded on the beach. It looked like a crystal vase floating upside down with the rim broken into sharp teeth of a brown colour, as if dipped in paint. The village medicine-man came running with a cocktail of herbs to soothe the pain. *'Tatun Fulhi'* explained the islanders, which Abdul translated as 'sharp bottle', it was the local name for this strange whitish coelenterate, which, although it had a hard jagged edge which cut, seemed to be a distant relative of the jellyfish.

Next morning we were ashore early to start fencing in the archaeological site. While one of the archaeologists continued the trench where more phalloid fragments and 'umbrella towers' appeared, the other staked out a 2-metre (about 6-foot) wide trench across the low circular mound of pure white beach sand. It did not look like a hawitta, nor did the islanders refer to it as such. To them it was just *Fua Mathi*, the Testicle Height.

After less than two hours' careful digging and scraping without encountering anything but pure white sand, Skjölsvold yelled. He had hit a worked stone. It had a dressed and fluted profile on one side. What was more, another of the same kind was adjoining it, and another, and another.

Johansen joined him and, scraping and brushing, they soon uncovered the top of a straight stone wall. Digging further they found another layer of worked stones underneath the first one, and still another. And another again. Johansen brought out his compass and exclaimed with excitement in his voice that this wall was oriented precisely east–west.

The digging was continued along this buried stone wall in each direction until we hit a corner at both ends. At each corner adjoining walls ran due south. We now guessed that the structure had been square, and as the north wall we had uncovered proved to be 10.5 metres (11½ yards) long, we dug a pit 10.5 metres south of the north-west corner, and correctly hit the place where the west wall ended and the south wall began. We had accordingly discovered a perfectly square, sun-oriented structure.

However, this wall had not been built to enclose an interior room; it was not part of any house. While the outside of the wall was beautifully shaped and finished, the inside was rough,

129

irregular and unworked. Obviously the inside of this building was never meant to be seen. It had always been filled with sand, as solid as any Mesopotamian pyramid. This was also evidenced by the fact that inside the wall we found nothing but pure sand, while outside we found all sorts of worked stones that had tumbled down from above.

At this stage, with our previous experience from a similar mound on Gaaf-Gan, I was so convinced that we had hit upon another structure resembling the ziggurat type that I promised 'to eat my hat' if we did not find some kind of ramp entering exactly at the centre of one of the outside walls. We had already started digging along the west wall from the north-west corner, and there we ran into a beautiful secondary wall of large square-cut stones set at right angles to the main wall on the outside. But this wall was only 4 metres from the corner and, accordingly, not centrally placed as I had predicted, since we had found the wall to be 10.5 metres long. Besides it was too narrow to have been a ramp, whereas it could very well be the wall of an adjoining building.

As I was the proud owner of that marvellous blue felt bush-hat from Nepal, given to me by Björn, I had no desire to eat it. I suspected we had found one retaining wall of a broad ceremonial ramp, filled with sand like the building itself. Since this wall was exactly 4 metres from the north-west corner, I marked out the same distance from the south-west corner with a stake set in the ground. Here I was sure we would hit upon the other side of a centrally placed ramp. Twenty minutes later I was shouting that I did not have to eat my hat! As the work proceeded, the second wall of the ramp showed up precisely where I had set the marker.

About the same time, Johansen found a large limestone fragment. 'This is classical architecture,' he shouted. 'This carving resembles what the early Greeks called *triglyf* and *metope*.'

We all admired the fragment. It lay among those that had fallen down from somewhere above and was buried on the outside of the wall. It was indeed decorated in a style the Greeks had borrowed from the ancient Middle East. Below a projecting rim it was crenellated in high relief with alternating rectangular knobs and notches.

'There must have been a temple on top of this mound or pyramid,' said Johansen. '*Triglyf* and *metope* are only found on the upper edges or eaves of structures.'

Loutfi and our liaison officer, Kela Maniku, were visibly impressed by the design of the wall profile we had discovered below the ground. It had come as a great surprise also to the island population.

The front of the wall consisted of nine tiers of worked stones in a complicated arrangement of steps and overhangs. The lowest three tiers projected in steps to form the plinth or supporting base of the entire structure, above which the wall rose vertically. But the four uppermost tiers were intricately chamfered and rounded in various ways, with the top tier projecting as a cornice in front of the one below, like the bow of a boat. The upper surface of this tier was finished smooth and clearly marked the floor of a first terrace, or platform. The total effect was sophisticated and impressive.

When we asked Loutfi and the local islanders what shape they thought the lost upper part of this structure originally had, Loutfi drew in the sand a stepped pyramid with a small domed temple on top. This assumption was clearly based on the stepped remains of ruins these islanders had seen or heard of elsewhere in the Maldives.

All that the archaeologists could confirm from the remaining evidence, however, was that we had uncovered the sun-oriented remains of a square, stepped, stone-lined and sand-filled structure, approached on the west wall by a centrally placed ramp. The polished surface of the upper tier of stones marked the end of the first terrace, but some sand-filled structure must have continued above, to judge from all the stones and sand that had fallen down on all sides. The amount of sand indicated that at least one or more solid terraces had been superimposed on the one still left, and the stone decorated with the *triglyf* and *metope*-like motif suggested that a roofed temple had stood on top, as drawn by Loutfi.

On the fourth day of digging the work began to get monotonous for Loutfi and Kela Maniku, and they spent more time with the men of the village than with us. Suddenly, before noon, they came striding back and headed straight for the exposed stone wall. They took another careful look at the mouldings and then came over to me. Loutfi confided, with a secretive smile, that they had done a lot of thinking since yesterday. They had spent the previous night in the village, and all the old people told them that they had heard from their ancestors, who had heard from *their* ancestors, that there had once been seven pagan temples on this island. And around these seven temples were seven walls with seven gates. The largest of these temples would most likely be the one converted by the first Sultan, Mohammed Ibn Abdullah, into the first mosque. They suggested, therefore, that we all come along to take a new look at the oldest mosque on the island.

Quite correct. We had realised that this mosque had been built from reused slabs. Now Loutfi and Kela Maniku were pointing out that its foundation walls had the very same profile as the foundation walls of the temple we had just dug out of the sand.

The mosque had been built on top of an old base wall that was 12 metres (over 13 yards) long and thus bigger than the foundation we had dug up under the *Fua Mathi* mound, which was 10.5 metres (almost 11½ yards). Our two Maldivian friends were triumphant. The first Sultan had indeed chosen the foundation of the largest of the seven temples as the base for his mosque, and somewhere in the surrounding forest must be the sites of the other five pre-Moslem temples in addition to the one we had found.

We had to give our friends credit for their alertness, and now that we examined the mosque closely we even found evidence on one side of a former ramp. It had been mortised into the foundation wall but later removed when the temple was transformed into a mosque with steps up to a door entrance on the short side. One wall had been entirely rebuilt with small stones, as the original temple had obviously been square and too big for the needs of the Sultan.

We checked the foundations of the mosque with our compass. They ran astronomically correct, north–south, east–west. At the hour of prayer, therefore, we took the liberty of peeping in at the worshippers. It was a comical sight. They were all kneeling diagonally to the rear wall, properly facing Mecca as Moslems should. They had to adjust for the fact that the mosque was not directed towards Mecca as mosques should be.

Having made this strange observation, I asked Loutfi about that first Maldive mosque, which the Sultan had built in Male. Did the worshippers prostrate themselves diagonally to the hind wall in that mosque too?

Loutfi thought only for a second and then he started to laugh. Yes, indeed, it was precisely the same in Male; and in some of the oldest mosques in the Maldives they had even painted lines diagonally on the floor showing the worshippers in which direction to prostrate themselves according to the Koran.

When I asked him why nobody had found this strange before, Loutfi admitted that he had been puzzled himself but he had been told that in ancient times people did not know enough geography to realise precisely in which direction Mecca lay. Obviously, however, they knew enough geography to realise precisely in which direction were east and west. Apparently those who built these first foundation walls were more interested in the sun than in Mecca.

Due east of the mosque a wide clearing had been made through the uninhabited forest down to the beach of the lagoon about 300 metres (328 yards) away. It was wide as an avenue and covered by white beach sand, kept free from any weeds. The purpose of this wide avenue was never explained to us. It seemed to serve for ceremonial processions, if such ever took place, from the mosque to the lagoon. Right in front of the mosque, just where the avenue started, was a small house or pavilion which seemed to block the road until we took a closer look at it and found it to be open at both ends. It was a sort of magnificent gateway built from huge slabs, smooth as table tops. There were stone benches on each side, and the roof was supported by hardwood columns, hard as bone, like the wood carvings inside the mosque, although some of them showed clear signs of burning.

The village elders had told Loutfi that this was the only one left of the seven gates of pre-Moslem times. According to Nilandu tradition all the other gates had not only been burned but also levelled to the ground. This was the only one that remained.

The elders now came to point out where at least some of the seven walls had gone and Loutfi asked if the archaeologists could direct the islanders in digging some test pits to find

133

whether anything remained. By trenching the loose sand we discovered in every case the remains of stone walls where they were said to have been, and inevitably they ran in the directions east–west or north–south. Some of them had obviously been beautifully decorated with mouldings.

We found hundreds of identically shaped stones smaller than a fist, flat on the sides but with the front strongly vaulted over a protruding lip. The rear was unworked. These ornamental bosses had presumably been set their own width apart in a continuous crenellated frieze running along the walls. But some of these buried walls contained fragments of blocks with mouldings from earlier temples that had been torn down, even some carved with *triglyf* and *metope*-like decoration similar to those fallen from the temple of the Testicle Height. The builders of the seven pre-Moslem walls had therefore been preceded by earlier temple architects, presumably with a different religion. Once again we had evidence that the Maldives had a complicated past long before Islam was introduced. Theoretically Buddhist wall builders could have used parts of Hindu temples.

As this vast temple area ended, the terrain dropped down a couple of feet with a marked slope just where the houses of the village started. The whole area was termed *Faru Mathi* by the local people, which Loutfi translated as 'Top of the Wall'.

A constant spectator during our work was Ahmed Moossa Domaniku, a tall, slim man with a sharp face and a thin, strongly beaked nose. Domaniku was the former island chief in Nilandu and himself the son of a chief. He wanted us to dig at a certain place in the wide sandy avenue, right in front of the mosque. His father had once dug there to drain water away from the mosque, and he had hit upon a stone box covered by a lid. It contained ochre colour and some shiny white metal. There was also a piece of what he called lead with inscriptions on it. In those days people believed that black magic was important to the island, explained Domaniku, so his father had reburied the box with all its contents in the same place. Unfortunately Domaniku could only remember the area approximately, so the dig resulted in nothing.

As Loutfi considered this man one of the best informed on Nilandu, I asked him if he had heard of any other people who had lived here in pre-Moslem times. Yes, said Domaniku. He had heard of the Redin and the Holin. Of the Redin he knew nothing but that they were great builders and had been here first. The Holin had been here later, they had even come back by ship to try to conquer the Maldivians and re-enforce their own religion after Nilandu had been converted to Islam. But the Holin had been driven away and had to return to their own land.

I asked where the Holin lived, only to be answered that, since they were Holin, they probably lived in the Land of the Holin. Domaniku had nothing to add except that they worshipped statues and were not Moslem.

According to Domaniku the Holin had been Buddhists, but here Loutfi interrupted and explained that these people called all non-Moslems Buddhists. Domaniku had not heard of cannibals, but he knew that there was some 'business' between the Maldivians and the people of Azékara. Some Maldivians even intermarried with people from Azékara. They came to Nilandu with textiles, pottery, plates and 'food' which they exchanged for cowrie shells, dried fish and coconut rope.

While the island workmen were digging test trenches in search of the remains of the seven walls and the treasures of Domaniku's father, another islander came to us bearing the upper half of a strange tombstone. Moslem tombstones are flat with a rounded top for women and with a sharp central point for men. The one this man brought had three points side by side, however. It was very old and deeply pitted from erosion. Our friends from Male had never seen Moslem tombstones of this shape. Even the local islanders said that this was not a Moslem stone.

The man who brought the carving was willing to show us where he had found it. He took us for a long walk on a wide trail right through an extremely beautiful forest of coconut and *areca* palms mixed with bread-fruit and big jungle trees. We must have been on the opposite side of Nilandu by the time he made us crawl through a thick undergrowth of *ahi* bushes. Loutfi told us that *ahi* was popular for making red dye.

Inside the thickets we entered an area where the upper parts of tombstones barely emerged from the ground wherever we crawled. Some of them had the normal Moslem shapes, but many had three and some even had five points, almost like a

135

crown on the upper end. Nobody could give us any explanation. For the lack of better ideas I wondered if the multiple-pointed tombstones could be those of men grown up with another religion, but converted to Islam before their deaths. This was pure speculation, but the burial ground could well date back to the days when Islam was first introduced.

We were back at our dig next to the Testicle Height, where ever more phalloid stones were brought up from underneath the sand, when word came from the village that the dhoni of the atoll chief had just arrived from Magudu island. The atoll chief was a great man in the Maldive communities, as he was selected by the government in Male. The chief of Nilandu with his little radio station had obviously notified the atoll chief about our findings.

A moment later a broadly built man with a genial face and bowler hat came escorted by the island chief and other men from the village. He had a twinkle in his eye and, with his round red nose, he could have been taken for a disciple of Bacchus were it not for the fact that he was a Moslem and had hardly even tasted a glass of beer all his life. He saluted us with a friendly touch of his finger to his bowler hat.

Skjölsvold had just dug up a big, complete phalloid image which he lifted out and set at the edge of the trench, dusting it with his little brush.

'Do you like it?' he asked politely while looking up at the atoll chief.

The atoll chief rubbed his nose for a moment and then he answered through the interpreter:

'No. But maybe my wife would have liked it.'

From the spontaneous reaction of the crowd, there was no doubt that they understood exactly what the sculpture represented.

From his own island the atoll chief could contact Male with his stronger radio. After he left the island, the message came to us from the village that a fast government vessel had just arrived from Male with the Minister of Atoll Administration on board. He was the brother of the President and one of the fifteen members of the National Council for Linguistic and Historical Research. His Excellency Abdullah Hameed had come to inspect our discoveries, and he was amazed when he saw what we had

136

brought out from the ground. By this time we had uncovered parts of twenty-three different phalloid sculptures in addition to a large number of 'umbrella towers', stone discs with sockets, moulded stones, and slabs with varieties of elegant decoration.

As the Minister left he was visibly pleased with what he had seen. Nothing had been plundered or destroyed, on the contrary what seemed to him to be a completely new hawitta had been added to those they had feared we would destroy.

Before the Minister returned to his ship he told Loutfi that he was free to permit us to dig wherever we cared to.

We had all become so engulfed in our unexpected discoveries at the temple complex in Nilandu that we had almost forgotten we were on our way to the Equatorial Channel. Five days had already been spent on an island where we had never intended to dig, and one month was all the time we could count on for the two archaeologists and the use of the *Golden Ray*. Five teams of archaeologists could dig here for five years and still make new discoveries. The magnitude of this prehistoric cult centre seemed quite out of proportion to the size of the island.

What was so special about Nilandu? Why did the first Moslem Sultan find it important? For even the written record shows that he came straight here to build the large mosque as soon as he had built the one in Male.

And why did the non-Moslem Holin find the same island so essential to them that they came back to it when the Sultan left, and tried to reintroduce their own faith?

When, back on board the *Golden Ray*, I took a fresh look at the navigation map I thought I had found the answer. Nilandu was exactly in the centre of the far-flung archipelago, exactly as far from the northernmost island as it was from Addu atoll in the extreme south. From the days the Maldives had become a single nation this would be the logical centre for the national cult and administration. From the days the sun had lost its importance and the images of human gods were erected in the temples, Nilandu, rather than the Equatorial Channel, would be the natural assembly point for the local hierarchy.

When Islam was introduced and the king became sultan, he would never succeed in introducing the new faith, even by force, unless he first went to Nilandu to level the main pre-

Moslem temples to the ground. This done, he would have to build a mosque to Allah where the main pre-Moslem temple had stood, partly to remove the spell of the demons, but also to remove temptation away from those who had been accustomed to come to this place and worship foreign gods.

Down in the hold of the *Golden Ray*, wrapped in cotton wool and packed in sacks and crates, there lay a heavy cargo of sculptures considered sacred to the people of Nilandu until the Sultan arrived. Who had carved them still remained a riddle to us, although it was the Holin as far as the local population was concerned. But one thing was sure. They had been destroyed and buried by the pious servants of Sultan Mohammed Ibn Abdullah in the middle of the twelfth century AD.

The stones we had secured for the Male Museum this time were so big and numerous that a long line of men had to wade to their chests to bring them to a deeply loaded dhoni waiting off the beach.

As the expedition members climbed on board the dhoni the whole village, large and small, assembled on the beach to wave. It was an exotic spectacle with all the brown faces and the colourful dresses of the women shining warmly in the light of the setting sun.

We waved from the boat and they waved from the beach until the tropical sun sank vertically into the sea and we climbed back on board the *Golden Ray* with all our treasures. We were all sad to be leaving the island, but were looking forward to further adventures on islands we were to visit next.

CHAPTER VII
In the Wake of the Redin
Redin from the North, Buddhists from the East

'*MANGIARE, MANGIARE, MANGIARE*. Food is ready!'

I folded away the map I was studying and jumped up from my berth to join the others at the breakfast table. I had been inhaling the warm aroma of freshly baked Maldive style chapatis ever since being awoken by a sudden change in the ship's rolling. No alarm clock is more effective than the new rhythm of rolling or pitching a ship makes as it starts to move, even if it has been riding at anchor off an unsheltered coast. A quick glance to either side of the vessel showed that we were again right out in the Indian Ocean, with Nilandu and all its nearby islands on the Faaf atoll disappearing behind us.

We were still at the breakfast table when we entered the next lagoon with beautiful little palm islands and frothing reefs all around. Some were inhabited. Loutfi pointed at one of them and, giggling at happy memories, told us how he had spent a year and a half there when he was a prisoner. A Maldive prison term was seldom spent locked up inside four walls in Male. Instead, the criminal was simply expelled from his own island and confined to some other island for a certain length of time. Loutfi had been punished because he was a friend of an outgoing President. It resulted in the finest vacation he ever had. When he was set ashore the sympathetic local population built a little hut for him and beautiful women took turns to serve him morning tea and lunch. The fishermen brought him fresh fish, sometimes even cigars, Loutfi added, and laughed as he puffed on one presented him by Johansen. But a government representative came on inspection and forbade these services. From then on the food was secretly put into his hut while he was away at the mosque for his morning wash.

We passed along a dream island where the early morning sun sent rays low in between the forest of coconut palms, lighting up the red dress of a woman watching us motionless from amongst the greenery. A Gauguin masterpiece brought alive. Johansen said he would do anything to be sent to prison there.

Further away we could just discern some palm tops above the distant starboard horizon.

'Had we time to spare we should have called there,' said Loutfi. 'That is Maadeli, also known as Salazar or Temple Island. It is full of ruins.'

We had no time to spare. This was a pity for, according to Loutfi, this was the next Redin island along our route. That morning I had again been studying Loutfi's marks on my map. After our unexpected visit to the first Redin island, Loutfi had written in green ink on my map the names of all the others where he knew the Redin had lived, according to local traditions. What was more, he had marked with green arrows their legendary migration route.

From old Maldive informants we later learned that the Redin had made their first landfall at Ihavandu island, a tiny speck of land which was the extreme north-western point of Maldive territory. From up north Loutfi drew his arrows straight south to Ari atoll where we, on board the *Golden Ray*, had picked up the Redin's trail southwards at Ariyaddu. From there we followed it to Nilandu. Although now missing Maadeli we would pick up the Redin route again in Kuda Huvadu, which we had to pass anyhow. From there again the Redin had moved southwards from one atoll to the next until reaching the Equatorial Channel. There the last settlement had been one on Addu atoll, the southernmost of all, before they left the Maldives altogether. As far as time permitted we would take a quick look at all the other Redin islands along our route southwards.

I was half dozing in the sun on the foredeck when I sighted the huge, round dorsal fin of a whale-shark with its white dots. Then Björn shouted, calling my attention to a strange fish I had never seen before, although we found it to be common in the Maldives. It shot from the surface of the lagoon as if it were a flying fish ready to take off. But it never did take off. Long and slim as a snake it remained with the tip of its fan-shaped tail in the water while the body stood up vertically with a beaked head pointed forward like the neck and head of a duck without a body. Like a submarine periscope, but with nothing below water except the tiny tailfin bent backwards, it literally flew along on the surface until it decided to dive and swim like a normal fish.

Far away on our port side was a sand bank with two big turtles dozing in the sun.

As we reached the southern end of the sunny lagoon of Dhall atoll, we dropped anchor at Kuda Huvadu. While the others stopped with Loutfi in the village, the archaeologists and I walked into the forest with the chief and some of the village elders to see a man-made mound, not considered to be a hawitta.

We were taken to a huge, low and round mound of pure white sand brought from the beach. The name was *Us Gandu*, translated simply as 'The Mound'. It measured 22 metres (about 24 yards) in diameter, but not a single worked stone was to be seen. I got suspicious when I learned that the oldest mosque on the island was nearby, so we went there. We stood speechless. The rear wall of the mosque was pieced together from the finest 'fingerprint' masonry I ever saw. The best example of fitted stone masonry was supposed to be the famous Inca wall in Cuzco, Peru, where the great tourist attraction is a stone with twelve corners. Here, on a totally insignificant mosque on a tiny islet in the Maldives, was another one. Set in this smooth stone wall was a block, roughly one metre square, with its façade as carefully planed as if cut and polished by machine; but all around the edge, cut into twelve sides with twelve corners, everything fitted so precisely into the complex shapes of the surrounding stones that the fissures would barely show up in a photograph. It was incredible to find such a masterpiece of stone-shaping art here. Everybody has heard of the Incas and of Cuzco in Peru, but who has heard of the Redin or of Kuda Huvadu in the Maldives?

Beside that magnificent wall were the two tombstones of the master mason reputed to have done this job. One tall carved slab was raised at his head and another at his feet, as customary for important Moslem persons. The footstone had beautiful

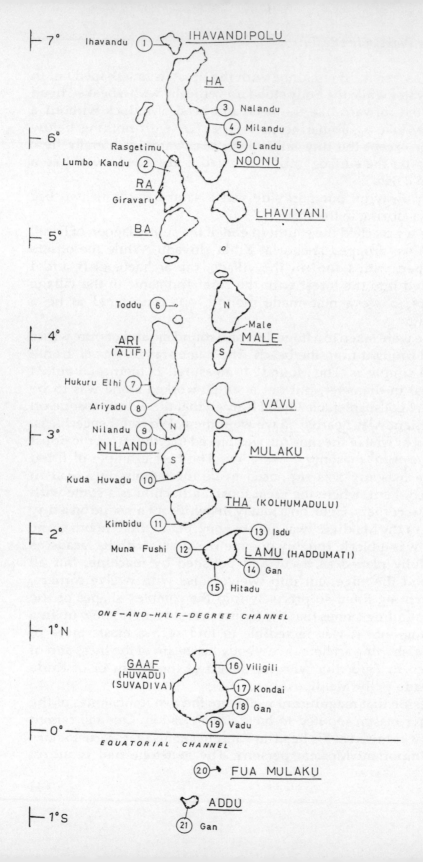

7° — Ihavandu ① IHAVANDIPOLU

HA

③ Nalandu
④ Milandu
6° — ⑤ Landu
Rasgetimu
Lumbo Kandu ② NOONU

RA
Giravaru

BA LHAVIYANI

5° —

Toddu ⑥ N

4° — ARI Male
(ALIF) MALE
S

Hukuru Elhi ⑦

Ariyadu ⑧ VAVU

3° — Nilandu ⑨ N
NILANDU MULAKU

S
Kuda Huvadu ⑩

THA (KOLHUMADULU)

Kimbidu ⑪
2° — ⑬ Isdu
Muna Fushi ⑫ LAMU (HADDUMATI)
⑭ Gan
⑮ Hitadu

ONE—AND—HALF—DEGREE CHANNEL

1°N —

GAAF ⑯ Viligili
(HUVADU)
(SUVADIVA) ⑰ Kondai
⑱ Gan
0° — ⑲ Vadu
EQUATORIAL CHANNEL

⑳ → FUA MULAKU

ADDU

1°S —
㉑ Gan

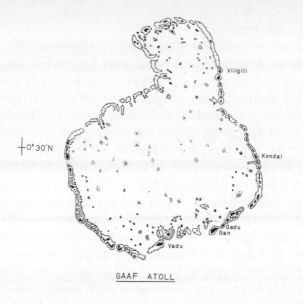

Viligili

+0°30'N

Kondai

Gadu
Gan

Vadu

GAAF ATOLL

+ 0° ─────────────────────────────

THE EQUATORIAL CHANNEL

FUA MULAKU

+0°30'S

ADDU ATOLL

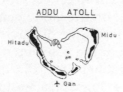

Hitadu

Midu

↑ Gan

REPUBLIC OF MALDIVES

Left: The atolls of the archipelago. The numbers indicate the successive settlements of the legendary Redin. The islands of Rasgetimu, Giravaru, Male and Isdu played important roles in the Hindu and Buddhist periods of the islands before the introduction of Islam in 1153.

Above: The islands of the Equatorial Channel. Enlarged detail showing individual islands (black) and coral reefs.

decoration with bands and scrolls in low relief around the design of an elegant jar. The headstone was equally elaborately ornamented around a frame with inscriptions written in two different types of character. Both scripts were skilfully carved to stand forth from the stone in relief. The one was in the curvilinear Arab letters, the other in some strange rectilinear characters as unknown to our Maldivian friends as to us. Each tombstone had five points on top, rather than a single one. I asked why. Nobody knew. The chief hesitantly suggested that multiple points might possibly have signified that this buried person was a skilled mason. In view of the Nilandu burial place this theory was not convincing, and since this was expressly said to be the first mosque built on the island, the mason who built it must himself have been born with the earlier religion. I held to my suspicion therefore that such untypical tombstones might belong to those who were not born Moslem but were converted later.

If this converted master mason had actually carved the twelve-cornered stone himself and not merely moved the entire wall from an old temple, then we as investigators had an important lesson to bear in mind: in AD 1153, when Islam was introduced, the Maldive religion was changed, but the people and their techniques remained the same. This would explain why the Maldivians, until the present century, were renowned in the Arab world for their skill as stone carvers. They produced the finest Moslem tombstones to be found anywhere.

In front of this little mosque was an outdoor gateway, just like the one in Nilandu. A sophisticated decoration of elegant vases in a row was carved in relief on the stone benches flanking this ceremonial passage. A perfect 'Star of David' could clearly be discerned on the outer wall of the gate and made me wonder if some ancient Jews had come here too. But then I remembered that David was regarded as a common ancestor of both Jews and Arabs. When the chief saw me looking at it he explained that this ancient symbol was *Suleiman modi*, the seal on King Solomon's ring. When the Maldivians start to write charms, he added, they use this sign at the beginning and at the end.

By this time Loutfi had caught up with us and asked if anybody had ever found some buddu on this island.

Yes, indeed. Next to the old mosque they had found the stone head of a man, so big that they could barely reach around it. They had buried it again near the mosque. An eager search for the place was now started, but the underbrush was so thick that they could not recognise the exact spot. Instead they recalled that they had also found a small stone animal. It turned out, to our surprise, that they had sent it to Male.

'When?' asked Loutfi. They figured out it had been in 1942. That was a great pity, according to Loutfi. The museum had not yet been created then, and nobody would ever know the fate of that animal image.

The best description of the large image head was given to us by the atoll chief, Mohammed Kaleyfan, who had come to this island to see it personally before it was buried. A bit of the body was attached to the head. The face resembled a human being and not a demon. The lips were closed with no teeth or tongue showing. There were marks on the sides suggesting very long ears. When we showed him photos of the big Buddha head and the diabolic demon heads from Male Museum he immediately pointed at the Buddha. It was just like that, he said, but more damaged.

Did Kaleyfan know what the Redin looked like? People on this atoll and on Nilandu said that the Redin had red hair, he answered, but they said nothing about the skin colour. The sculptures the Redin had left behind showed, however, that sometimes they looked like people and sometimes they looked like a pudding.

'A pudding?' we queried.

'Yes,' the interpreter repeated. 'He says *badibai* and that is the kind of a pudding he has seen in Male.'

We asked them to draw a pudding in the sand and indicate the size. We were shown a drawing of a vaulted image which indeed resembled a 'pudding' but still more the shape and size of the phalloid sculptures we had excavated in large numbers on Nilandu. The atoll chief had obviously seen some such images among the shattered pagan ruins and assumed that they, as well as the human statues, represented self-portraits carved by the mysterious Redin in the dim Maldive past.

There was nothing more to learn but that the Moslems had long ago broken all such carvings and used them in their own buildings.

As soon as Bengt and Åke had filmed the twelve-cornered stone we had to rush back to the village and the ship. Captain Pakar was already getting worried. There was still a long way to go that day to reach the next safe anchorage. Kuda Huvadu was the last island at the southern extremity of this atoll. Now we had a short stretch of open water ahead until we reached Kulumadulu atoll where we had to enter the lagoon and navigate between all sorts of uncharted reefs and shallows before we could drop anchor off Vilufushi island.

That afternoon we passed the most beautiful palm islands I have ever seen. With the sun low on our starboard side it threw a glowing sidelight on to the tiny islets, which seemed to float by like flower baskets on our opposite side. At the height of the day, when the equatorial sun stood at its zenith, the island would not look this beautiful from the sea. The dense roof of palm crowns would then form a huge parasol, shading everything beneath it, and with the blinding white beach in front, our eyes would not be able to distinguish anything in between the palms. But this late afternoon sidelight lit up the interior of the islands, with their huts and colourfully dressed people amongst a wealth of greenery that formed a park-like landscape which resembled the stage of a theatre more than the real world. Under the spell of this picture of an earthly paradise I made an entry in my notebook that the Maldives are even more beautiful than any of the coral atolls in Polynesia.

Shortly before sunset we dropped anchor in the shelter of Vilufushi island. A number of us were set ashore with Loutfi, who had been asked by his Ministry to discuss a new school building with the chief. Vilufushi was said to have 1,315 inhabitants. The whole island was one big town. No forest, no archaeology. A Taiwan fishing vessel that had come to buy fish lay at anchor next to us, but nobody went ashore. The chief told us that it was eight years since the last foreigners had set foot on the island, and they were Asiatics too. By leaving Male and the tourist islands behind we were really moving in a world all its own.

As the sun rose we were already on the move due south. Loutfi recommended that we make a short-cut from Vilufushi and leave aside for the moment the next Redin island, Kimbidu, on the south-western extremity of the same atoll. According to

Loutfi there was an important hawitta there about 10 metres (33 feet) high, but it had been plundered.

Kulumadulu atoll sank in the sea behind us. Not long afterwards the first palm crowns of Haddummati atoll, also called Laamu atoll, rose up in front. On the north-western extremity of this atoll was the next Redin island, Muna Fushi, but this once important island had been washed away in the last twenty years and the large and beautiful temple ruins which Loutfi remembered had tumbled into the sea. All we could see were some jagged coral rocks projecting above the wild surf.

It was about 10.30 in the morning when we had to change course and steer due east along the reef to round the eastern tip of this atoll.

We were so taken by Loutfi's itinerary of the Redin, which clearly indicated their arrival from the north, that we were puzzled by what he told us next. He pointed ahead to the island that formed the east cape of this atoll, and was in fact the easternmost island of the whole archipelago.

'That island has the largest hawitta now standing in the Maldives,' he said. 'The name of the island is Isdu, which means "the first island sighted".'

'How can it be called "the first island sighted" when the first land seen by the Redin was in the extreme northern tip of the Maldives?' I asked.

Loutfi had no explanation. All he could say was that the hawitta on that island was so high that it could be seen by navigators far out to sea. As he was pointing, we began to discern a big dark hump, as tall as the palm crowns, emerging from the sea far ahead of us.

'Whatever the reason for the name,' said Loutfi, 'Isdu island has been extremely important in the history of the Maldives. It was from this very island that one of the royal families came who went on to Male to rule. Buddha images have been found on Isdu.'

This might explain the name. We knew the Buddhists had been here, and if we could trust local tradition, they had arrived after the Redin. It would have been logical for the Buddhists to have come from the east, and thus sight this easternmost island first, since the Buddhists could have come from Sri Lanka. Sri Lanka was the most important Buddhist centre in this part of

147

the world at the time that the Arabs came to introduce their Moslem faith to the Maldives. There was no reason for the early Redin to have come from the east, they might well have come from the north, as had the Arabs when they, the last arrivals, expelled Buddhism from the Maldives. After all, the Arabs were not the first seafarers to roam the Indian Ocean north of the Maldives. To judge from archaeological evidence in the Indus Valley, the Persian Gulf and the Red Sea, merchant sailors and explorers had travelled in that part of the ocean earlier than anywhere else in the world.

As we drew nearer to Isdu, and could discern the surf breaking from the east, right at the foot of this colossal structure, we marvelled at its dimensions. It rose like a giant black dome above the surrounding palm forest. Another and quite different question now puzzled us. How was it possible that no modern archaeologist had come to investigate these strategically located islands when they contained prehistoric ruins like this man-made mound on Isdu, which could even be detected from far out at sea? There was only one answer. Modern seafarers, who did not set foot ashore, would have taken it for some kind of recent structure, or depot, and never suspect it to be a prehistoric relic.

We rounded the easternmost cape of the Haddummati atoll where the reef was drawn out like a long finger pointing eastwards with Isdu at its extreme tip. And on Isdu again the big hawitta stood with its base almost in the sea on the eastern promontory of the island. Thus we were able to admire it from three sides while we rounded the cape and continued down the opposite side of the reef. Apart from the impressive size, and the location which would have been ideal for a lighthouse, there seemed to be nothing left of interest. Former facing stones were stripped away and there was nothing else to make a visit worthwhile, unless there was a long period of time for properly conducted excavations.

We were soon sailing past the next little island on the same reef. This was Dhambidu and, according to Loutfi, an attempt to re-establish Buddhism had been made here sixty years after the Maldives were converted to Islam. I noted Loutfi's word 're-introduced' with interest. This was the first time I heard a senior Maldivian official openly referring to a Buddhist period ante-dating their own Moslem history.

148

After the two Buddhist islands on the eastern extremity of the atoll, there was a narrow opening in the coral reef where Loutfi and Pakar agreed to turn in across a belt of bright green shallows where we rode over the atoll ring and into the protected lagoon. There we were met by the atoll chief who came on board from a big dhoni to join us as we followed the same reef southwards inside the Laamu lagoon and anchored off Gan island. This was Gan of Laamu atoll, which, like Isdu on the same atoll, was marked by Loutfi as a Redin island. Indeed, there were two more Redin islands with the same name which Björn and I had explored on our last visit. Gan on Addu atoll, and Gan on Gaaf atoll, were separated from each other by the Equatorial Channel, and this Gan on Laamu atoll was only separated from Gaaf atoll by the One-and-Half-Degree Channel. Three Redin islands all named Gan were thus flanking the only two navigation channels that permitted safe passage through the Maldive archipelago.

From now on we were to see so many prehistoric mounds that it would be hard to keep them all separated without reference to our notebooks and diaries that were filled in every day. On this Laamu Gan we were to visit some of the hawittas which, more than any others, had been brutally dug into by Bell, and convinced him that all the hawittas were Buddhist stupas, no matter in what condition he found them. The largest one on this island was measured by Bell to be 35 feet (10.6 metres) high, although even in his time it was pitiably devastated and covered by large trees. Today no trees were left, so that this Gan hawitta now looked like an enormous heap of large lumps of coal, with a huge scar, made by Bell, running down like a valley on one side. With every single facing block long since removed it was impossible to visualise the once elegant temple with a seven-tier pinnacle on top, as reported to Bell. Bell stresses that the structure had been 'most drastically stripped by the islanders', yet he had seen enough to state that the masonry of this building had once consisted of surface-dressed madrepore slabs encasing a rubble core of the same material. He found that the entire superstructure had already disappeared, together with virtually every trace of the base staging, 'nothing but a few yard's width of neck and convex casing of the dome on the South West front has resisted the ravages of man in addition to Nature's corroding forces'.[17]

We were given the same name for this hawitta as recorded by Bell, *Hat-teli*. But sometimes this mound was also referred to as *Hai-tele*. Our informants said that *Teli* was the word for a cooking pot, that *Hate* meant 'seven' and *Hai* was the word for a royal umbrella. It would seem that both these names referred to the former pinnacle which rose like an 'umbrella tower' or seven cooking pots reversed and set on top of each other.

When Bell, with forty Moslem islanders, dug into what their ancestors had left of this once magnificent temple, he made what he termed 'an astounding and portentous discovery'. Directly under the summit they unearthed a huge, broken face of a colossal Buddha, carved from coral stone. Although the rest of this monument could not be found, Bell assumed it to be part of a standing Buddha, and estimated its height to have been about 15 feet (4.5 metres) from head to foot.[18] Below the broken face of this giant lay the mutilated, headless image of a small seated Buddha. Although saved from obscurity in the debris by Bell, their fate was to remain in even deeper obscurity. These discoveries were never mentioned to us in Male, and even when we asked, nobody could tell us how and where they might have disappeared. Nobody could be found who had been present during Bell's dig.

We needed little imagination to understand the solid foothold the Buddhists had established on these oceanic islands before Islam took over. It must have been a stunning sight for seafarers to see a white Buddha standing 15 feet (4.5 metres) tall on the top of this colossal man-made hill, shining like snow in the tropic sun from dressed and moulded coral blocks.

Perhaps the islanders of Gan did not know, or perhaps they were intentionally secretive when they told us that no image had ever been found on the island. It brought to mind Bell's early statement when he stressed that the Gan islanders were doubtless holding back information on Buddhist ruins lest punishment befell them at the hands of His Highness the Sultan's zealous Moslem servants.[19]

Like the huge mound we had seen from the ship on Isdu, this one on Gan lay very close to the sea, so close in fact that strange looking crabs were playing around in the waves which tumbled in over the reef, and right up to the foot of the hawitta. The thickets on the inland side had recently been cleared to some

150

distance from the ruins, and the atoll chief, who had come with us, said it had been done on his order when the Male radio announced that we were travelling in order to see such things. This gave us a clear view of a small hawitta just to the south-west of the big one. It had not been touched by Bell and some fine blocks carved with ornamentation still lay on top. Close by also was the top ring of a large circular bath of which only a few of the upper tiers of squared masonry blocks emerged from the ground. It had been used for normal bathing until only forty years ago. Until then cool, fresh water had seeped in through round holes in the bottom slabs.

A wide road, with the remains of stone walls on each side, ran due west from this temple area through what had once been a big ceremonial gate, now all in ruins. Shaped ornamental stones could be seen here and there in the road walls, but they had possibly been taken from elsewhere and reused.

Skjölsvold came crawling out of the bushes and reported that he had counted six man-made mounds in this area. As we crawled around visiting them we came upon two men with sledge hammers who were breaking up beautifully ornamented facing stones which they then piled up in heaps ready to be carried away on a big raft to a neighbouring island. Loutfi estimated that they had broken up enough hawitta dressing stones to build four houses. The atoll chief put the two men under arrest. At our suggestion the President had already issued a new law forbidding further destruction of ancient monuments of any sort. The two men said in their defence that people had to build houses somehow, and it was forbidden also to cut down the leaves of the palm trees, which were reserved for building tourist houses on the islands around Male. To cut coral from the reef was a much more difficult job than smashing up old pagan ruins. Besides, it was no longer any secret that breaking up the barrier reef had begun to cause havoc on the coast with the loss of breeding grounds of inshore fish. When arrested, the two men showed no sign of either remorse or dismay and Loutfi commented, with a smile, that it was now their turn to benefit from temporary exile on some other island.

The area around the big hawitta, where those two limestone prospectors had made their harvest, was referred to by the islanders as *Ihu Ma-Miskit* which Loutfi translated as the 'Old

Big Mosque'. This name seemed misleading for something which was obviously a Buddhist temple complex. But on re-checking Bell's record the reason became clear. At that time he had seen here the ruins of the island's first mosque, *Ihu Miskit*, which he translated as 'The Former Mosque'. It had rested on the base, still in excellent preservation, of what Bell identified as the priory of the Buddhist monks. During our visit these ruins had either been broken up by limestone hunters or had become totally buried in dense undergrowth. Clearly, however, according to Bell, this first mosque on Gan had been built on foundations already existing from an earlier religious structure, precisely as we had found to be the case with the first mosque on Nilandu.

There was another reason to suspect that the Buddhists had earlier done the same when they arrived, that is, using the groundwork of still earlier builders. In fact, there was a strong parallel with the large hawitta on Fua Mulaku, of which the islanders sang that it had been created by the Redin, and then built by the Buddhist Singalese. Bell had found that this Gan hawitta had carried a Buddhist dome and Buddhist statues, yet he put on record that 'no tradition exists regarding this mound, beyond the attribution of its construction to so-called "Redin" '.[20]

The Redin were not Buddhists. Nobody in the Maldives confused Redin with the Buddhist Singalese. I sat down on the top of this colossal monument and tried to reassess what seemed to be conflicting leads in Maldive prehistory. Redin from the north, or Buddhists from the east? Perhaps both. We knew, from the demonic images and Shiva bronze figurine, that the Buddhists had not been alone in reaching the Maldives before the Moslems came.

From the top of this former stupa I had a wide view over the ocean. The road was open to these islands from any direction. The Redin could indeed have come here from the north, and built this colossal mound as a stone-faced hawitta. The Buddhists could then have come from the east, conquered the islands, and put a stupa dome on the Redin hawitta. Last of all were the Arabs. They came from the north in the Redin's wake. They stripped the stupa to build their mosque on the foundation of the Buddhist monastery, and left the naked rubble fill of the Redin hawitta as the shapeless, man-made hill on which I was sitting.

I scrambled down the steep talus slope to the others who were still exploring the area. We returned to Mukuri Magu village and, with our landing barge, followed the coast of Gan about 1.5 kilometres (1 mile) south-westwards. Then we walked for about ten minutes along a trail between coconut palms and high undergrowth into the Kuruhinna district. Here we came to a small temple mound referred to by our guides as *Bombaro*. *Bombaro* means 'round' and enough was left of this structure for us to see part of a perfectly round base supporting a wall fragment of elegantly shaped stones still standing higher than ourselves.

The whole building had been solid, filled with coral stones. This was easy to detect as Bell had been here before us and had dissected the ancient structure, right into its centre. On the north-west side, opposite Bell's dig, a ramp ran high up the wall. This was a most peculiar structure, and by far the best preserved we had seen. Bell referred to it as '*Mumbaru Sthupa*'.

We cut away enough of the crooked branches and heavy undergrowth to see as much as possible of the remains. I marvelled at seeing such a sophisticated piece of architecture in the Maldive jungle, and recognised some of the fine ornamental carvings we had dug up around our sandy mound on Nilandu.

Here were examples even of the elegant type of *triglyf* and *metope*-like motif. None of us was sufficiently familiar with the various aspects of Buddhist architecture to identify these ruins merely from what we saw, but this had been Bell's own subject. He had come from Sri Lanka as an expert on Buddhist buildings to see if he could find something familiar here. He had found the large Gan hawitta so badly destroyed that there was nothing to identify but a few traces of its former dome. This prompted him to identify the mound as a former stupa, and as the oldest form of stupa known on Sri Lanka. He suggested a period ending about AD 500.

The little structure we were now admiring also had the remains, according to Bell, of a dome which matched the Sri Lanka norm, but this was not true of the well-preserved walls underneath it. This lower part he termed an exceptional construction. In fact, it was not at all the kind of temple Bell anticipated: 'the compact little sthúpa at Kuruhinna belongs architecturally, as a complete structure, to a type apparently unique whether in Ceylon or India'.[21]

If the Buddhists had built no structure like this either in Sri Lanka or in India, who then had designed the plans for this building? Could it be that the big stupa on this same island had been built with a similar unconforming substructure before it was reduced to its present shapeless state? If not, then this was an indication that two distinct architectural types of temple building had reached the Maldives in pre-Moslem times.

It was tempting to ask: was this fine little temple a Buddhist dome built on top of a pre-Buddhist construction?

Filled with fresh food for thought we returned to the launch. On our way back to the *Golden Ray* we passed three boys who were punting along the lagoon with a remarkably fine log raft. The logs were slightly curved up in the bow, with the longest in the middle like the curved fingers of a hand. This was precisely the custom shown in the earliest drawing of a balsa raft from the coast of Peru. This raft was very professionally built with cross beams and ingenious lashings, and clearly it had not been built by the boys who now landed their craft and put it ashore next to a larger one of the very same type which belonged to a fisherman. Such rafts had been very common throughout the Maldives until recent years. They were still preferred to dhonis when it came to crossing reefs and shallows with heavy cargo. They were built from very light wood and were known as *kando fati*, where *kando* simply meant 'log', and *fati* was translated as 'lying one by one'.

When we left next morning, we were never again to see such well-preserved hawittas until we reached the one we were to excavate ourselves on Gaaf-Gan.

From the cluster of former Buddhist centres on the Laamu atoll, which had begun with Isdu in the eastern extremity, we continued with *Golden Ray* southwards inside the same lagoon. Other small islands followed in a close chain on the same reef. First we stopped at Funadu, where Loutfi had to discuss another new school project with some 800–900 inhabitants. There was nothing for us to see on this island, they said, so while waiting we strolled in the clean and well-brushed village streets. On the wall of a woodcarver's tidy house was a sign in Divehi letters which Abdul translated as: 'To spit in front of the house is not a nice thing so for you I inform this. Abdu Rahiim Ali Finihiage.'

Further down the road was the village mosque. Not old. Built about AD 1500, or contemporary with Columbus. But inside the mosque was a corridor surrounding a smaller and older mosque enclosed as a shrine inside the big one. And this was really beautiful. The walls were shining smooth as if composed of large sheets of polished white marble, cut and fitted to perfection. As if the fingerprint fittings of larger and smaller blocks mortised into the edges and corners were not sufficient challenge to the mason, he had in places cut a square hole as big as a postcard into the middle of a block only to patch it up again with a small stone shaped to fit with minute precision.

Had these walls been built by a Moslem who had inherited the skills from his island predecessors? Or was this part of a Buddhist or Redin building converted into what became the first mosque on Funadu island? We could not give the answer. We found several pre-Moslem temple stones with mouldings casually reused in garden walls on this island. But knowing that temple stones were smashed and carried from one Moslem island to the next, we could not tell whether or not they came from former buildings on this same island.

At the southern extremity of the Laamu atoll we reached the exit where the lagoon opened into the One-and-Half-Degree Channel. Two islands flanked this exit, Hitadu to the west, which was a Redin island, and Gaadu to the east. We stopped first at Gaadu. The atoll chief was still with us and he confided that two bronze buddus had been found here by a person digging foundations for a house.

We had tea and turtle egg cake in the island chief's house and were then taken on a walk in the forest. We were shown no less than three different hawittas on this island, all robbed of facing stones and in very poor condition. Worked stones lay scattered about, one of which was beautifully decorated with the lotus motif. Another, carved with horizontal and vertical curves inside and out, precisely like the block of an igloo, had surely to be part of a former dome or beehive-shaped building.

In the spacious and clean village street a boy came out of his home of woven coconut leaves and showed us a basket full of white cowrie shells the size of small birds' eggs. This was the first time we had seen in quantity what used to be the most important trade item of the Maldives in former times. The boy thrust his hands into the contents of his basket and let the little empty mollusc shells fall through his fingers as if they were silver coins. Indeed this is precisely what they had been in the Maldives since before written history.

Although he clearly treasured his basketful of '*boli*', neither he nor his family could imagine how much this little mollusc meant in our efforts to trace the capacity and range of early Maldive voyagers.

We were not to see any more cowrie shells in the Maldives except the handfuls which other little boys picked up for our curiosity along the beaches. But in Bell's time they were still common currency within the group and he mentions that, at the turn of the last century, each man on Isdu had to pay 18,000 cowries in tax to the Sultan for himself and one wife.[22]

Both Bell and Maloney stressed the extreme importance of the cowrie shell in the early economic life of these islanders. The cowries had placed the Maldives on the map of the outside world, even before their own written history began. The fact that this archipelago functioned as a sort of bank or mint for the surrounding continental nations impressed the business oriented Arabs, even before they brought the Moslem faith there.

The Arabs had barely started to take over the ancient trade routes off the coasts of India when Sulaiman the Merchant, in the period AD 850–900, recorded how travellers had visited the Maldives and witnessed the importance of the cowrie shells. He first stated that there was an ocean on either side of India and that between these two oceans lay numerous islands.

They say that their number goes up to 1900. These islands separate two seas. They are governed by a woman . . . In these islands, where a woman rules, cocoanut is cultivated. These islands are separated from one another by a distance of two, three or four parasangs [about six to fourteen miles]. They are all inhabited and they grow the cocoanut-tree in all of them. The wealth of the people is constituted by cowries, their queen amasses large quantities of these cowries in the royal depots. They say that there is not in existence a people more industrious than these islanders.[23]

In the early tenth century we learn from El Mas'udi that cowrie shells were cultivated in the Maldives: and about 1030 Al-Biruni wrote the same, and added that these islands were called the 'Cowrie Islands'. In the twelfth century Al Idrisi remarked that the trade of the Maldives consisted of cowrie shells.[24] By 1343, when the great Arab traveller Ibn Battuta came to spend a long time in the Maldives, he wrote:

> The money of the islanders consists of 'Wada'. This is the name of a mollusc, collected in the sea and placed in pits dug out on the beach. Its flesh decays and only the white shell remains. A hundred of them is called *siya*, and 700 *fal*; 12,000 are called *kotta*, and 100,000 *bostu*. Bargains are struck through the medium of these shells at the rate of 4 *bostu* to a dinar of gold. Often they are of less value, such as 12 *bostu* to a dinar. The islanders sell them for rice to the people of Bengal, where also they are used for money. They are sold in the same way to the people of Yemen, who use them for ballast in their ships in place of sand. These shells serve also as a medium of exchange with the negroes in their native country. I have seen them sold, at *Màli* and at *Jùjù*, at the rate of 1,150 to a dinar.[25]

Ma Huan, a Chinese Moslem who served with Cheng Ho's expedition to the Indian Ocean in 1433, wrote a book on his return to China. He sailed direct from Sumatra to the Maldives in ten days and from there he sailed on to Mogadishu. His map gives an error for Male of only eight seconds, but what is remarkable is his statement that Maldive cowries in heaps are sold to Bengal as well as to Thailand.[26]

At the turn of the fifteenth century, coinciding with the discovery of America, Vasco da Gama and the first Europeans entered the Indian Ocean when the Maldives were still functioning as a cowrie shell bank. The Portuguese now tried to wrest the trade monopoly in the area from the Arabs who had by then held it for half a millennium. During his services in the east between 1501 and 1517, a Portuguese soldier, Duarte Barbosa, wrote about the Maldives: 'At these islands is much dried fish, which is exported; as also some little shells in which is great traffic with Cambay and Bengal, where they are used for petty cash, being considered better than copper.'[27]

Shortly after, in a book published in 1563, J. de Barros, the historian of Portuguese India, also pointed out the great importance of cowrie shells from the Maldives in the maritime commerce of the Indian Ocean:

> With these shells for ballast many ships are laden for Bengal and Siam, where they are used for money, just as we use small copper money for buying things of little value. And even to this kingdom of Portugal, in some years as much as two or three thousand quintals [100–150 tons] are brought by way of ballast; they are then exported to Guinea, and the kingdoms of Benin and Congo, where they are used for money, the Gentiles of the interior in those parts making their treasure of it. Now the manner in which the islanders gather these shells is this: they make large bushes of palm leaves tied together so as not to break, which they cast into the sea. To these the shellfish attach themselves in quest of food; and when the bushes are all covered with them, they are hauled ashore and the creatures collected.[28]

As late as 1611, François Pyrard wrote that he witnessed that thirty to forty ships per year left the Maldives with cowries for Bengal.[29] While early Europeans saw all those ships leaving the Maldives for Bengal on the north-eastern extreme of India, others recorded that they were in demand just as far up on the north-west coast. An early British party thus reported in 1683 that they bought 60 tons of cowries in the Maldives. Only by the force of their guns could they obtain 'permission' to load the cowries and take them on their own ships to the old Maldive market place of Surrat in the Gulf of Cambay.[30] From this time on cowries began to lose their value as a medium of exchange in the Indian Ocean.

The little pale shells which the boy showed us had thus indeed impressed the early merchants. Not for their modest beauty; the large cowries, like the leopard shell and countless other molluscs in this ocean, were far more pretty than these. It was the Maldive monopoly as currency provider that gave the islands their place in early records.

'This is Maldive history,' said Loutfi as he squatted beside the boy and scooped up handfuls of cowrie shells which he poured back into the basket. 'This was the wealth of our nation since the days our civilisation began.'

'Since the days of the Indus Valley civilisation,' I could have added if I had known then what I was to learn a year later. Only then did I revisit the Gulf of Cambay where the early written records told me that cowrie shells were shipped from the Maldives. Only then did I come back to the prehistoric port of Lothal, the harbour city of Mohenjo-Daro, capital of the Indus Valley civilisation. Lothal had been the most active port in the Gulf of Cambay, and probably of all Asia, between about 2500 BC and 1500 BC, when the Indus Valley civilisation collapsed. From then on the port was forgotten, buried in sand and silt, until rediscovered and excavated this century by modern archaeologists.

As I came back to revisit the little museum built at this old port I noticed something in a glass case which I had overlooked before. There, among the treasures excavated at the Lothal wharfs was a hoard of small white cowrie shells, *Cypraea Moneta*, the very species the Maldive boy had shown me in his basket. As Lothal had been a dead port since 1500 BC, this little hoard, if nothing else, showed that the tradition of the value of cowries had survived in the Indian Ocean for more than 3,000 years.

Did the first settlers of the Maldives bring with them some special appreciation for cowrie shells from their former fatherland?

Had the historically recorded import of cowrie shells to the Gulf of Cambay area continued uninterrupted through the subsequent centuries after the fall of the Indus Valley civilisation?

These were questions easier to ask than to answer. Certain was it that the Maldive shipbuilders mastered the art of building seaworthy vessels before they settled these islands. And there was no reason to suspect that the ships that brought them there, as ready developed master architects and temple builders, had been less seaworthy than those which later brought them to

159

the Gulf of Cambay when the early Arabs and Portuguese arrived. Directly or indirectly, the cowrie shells of Lothal had a bearing on the mystery of Maldive prehistory.

I asked the boy what he was going to do with all his cowrie shells. We learned that his father was going to sell them in Male. 'From there they will be exported to merchants in India,' explained Loutfi.

'What for?' I asked, but nobody had the answer.

In the afternoon we moved to anchor off Hitadu, the Redin island across the narrow outlet from the lagoon. From the deck we could see now at least a dozen islands running along the reef until they disappeared on the horizon, while the One-and-Half-Degree Channel lay open outside the lagoon.

Loutfi and the atoll chief confirmed what the local islanders told us, there was no archaeology to be seen on this island, even though it was a Redin island. We therefore spent the afternoon in the village, while Martin took a nap on the ship. When he woke up he decided to join us and was set ashore in the launch where he found nobody but an islander of his own age. Trying to locate us, Martin assumed we were visiting some ruins and by now he had learnt one Maldive word, which he told the islander: 'hawitta'. The islander took him by his hand and with no further conversation the two walked through the village and far into the forest where Martin was shown a hawitta, but without seeing any traces of us. He returned to the village streets where he could not miss us for long, and asked why we had left the ruins so quickly. Ruins? There are no ruins on this island. Martin was triumphant. He had found the ruins, and we all followed him as our guide.

We came to an old burial place closed in by a high stone fence ornamented with a large number of small white flags fluttering in the breeze. Some early Moslem of great importance had been buried here. From this high, white-washed wall a clear open road led directly down to the lagoon, and outside the gate lay two rows of some of the finest carved stones we were ever to see. Some of them were pedestals of large round columns so beautifully ornamented that they could have come from some ancient cathedral except that none had ever existed in the Maldives. Other stones were large cornerpieces of elaborate doorways, everything testifying to the former existence of some magnificent building of which no foundations could be seen.

About 90 metres (100 yards) away, however, hidden in dense undergrowth, the otherwise flat ground surface rose to a sandy hill – the stripped remains of a former hawitta. A central depression on top indicated that the mound had been plundered. Since nobody could give us the name we termed it 'Martin's Hawitta'.

That evening we had a great celebration on board in honour of our intrepid discoverer, but those who tended to feel the sea went to bed early. We had to set out that same night across the wide open One-and-Half-Degree Channel in order to reach the reefs on the other side before sunset the next day.

CHAPTER VIII

Return to the Equatorial Channel

The Lost Inscriptions

BLUE OVER, blue under. Intensive light. The fine line where the blue above met the blue below rose slowly above deck level on one side to sink again and come up as slowly on the other side. Those who were suffering from the gentle rolling fumbled for anything they could hang on to and staggered below. Others blessed the fresh sea breeze in the shade of the canvas. Like a cradle or a rocking chair, a friendly rolling ship allows the mind to relax.

We needed this break away from land. Away from all the stones. We had been overwhelmed by all we had seen in the last few days. Indispensable clues to the riddle of the Maldives were churning about in our minds' computers, requiring time for digestion. Time to draw a deep breath before we dived into more revelations. For we were wasting no time.

We were now sailing into the real realm of the sun-god. It was unbearably hot outside the canvas shade. The sun would be at full power when we landed on the next islands ahead. Just below the horizon in front of us lay the large atoll of Suvadiva, also known as Huvadu, *alias* Gaaf. That is the sun's real domain. That is where it lured the early sun-worshippers to sail into the Equatorial Channel. That was where the unknown architects of the past had quarried limestone blocks to build the big 'sun-temple' on Gaaf-Gan.

We were still on the trail of the Redin. We would actually be calling at two other Redin islands on the north and east side of the Gaaf ring-reef before we reached Gan on its southern

162

extremity. The ring-reef of Gaaf stretched all the way from the One-and-Half-Degree Channel down to the Equatorial Channel. Gaaf-Gan was uninhabited, but the two other Redin islands we would pass on the way were both inhabited. The first had no traces of any earlier population, but the second one had, Loutfi said.

The first was Viringili, or sometimes Viligili. We entered Gaaf lagoon through the northern reef and anchored off that island just as 'Mangiare', as we now called him, cleared the lunch table. This was the present seat of the atoll office, with a population of some 1,200. There had been a big hawitta on this island, said Loutfi, and there was still a street in the village called Hawitta magu, which meant Hawitta road. It ended at the coast where the former hawitta had been lost to the sea.

With some doubt in our minds we accepted Loutfi's assurance that there was nothing of interest left for us to see on this island, and the rest of us remained on board as he and Wahid were set ashore with three of the crew to fetch rainwater, fresh fruit and dried fish.

Because of many coral reefs we left the Gaaf lagoon again only to enter it once more in the late afternoon through another opening near Kondai, the next Redin island. We counted twenty-two low palm islands around us on the horizon as we dropped anchor off Kondai. Nothing could stop us from going ashore here when the island chief came out in his dhoni and told us of a strange bird they had just found in the forest.

'A bird?'

'A bird.'

'With feathers?'

'With feathers. But of stone.'

Full of curiosity and expectation we jumped into the dhoni and landed in Kondai together with the chief.

Ashore was a village of some 250 souls. Many of them had seen the stone bird, but nobody knew where it was now. It was gone. The man who had found it in the forest had already lost it in the village. The stone bird had simply disappeared.

But Redin? Had anybody something to tell us about the Redin?

Redin? They had never heard the word. There had been nothing on this island before the mosque was built.

163

'Patience,' said Loutfi in a low voice. Quietly he offered to guide us into the forest while there was still daylight. We could come back and look for the bird later.

We crossed a field of banana plants and headed for the uncleared jungle. The sun was already low as we left the last hut behind us for a twenty-minute walk through dense tropical forest to reach what Loutfi wanted to show us. Two of the village men with long jungle knives followed silently, no doubt driven more from curiosity than by a desire to clear our path. Thick moss-green limbs of jungle trees stretched above our heads with their burden of parasitic ferns and orchids which tempted even Loutfi to cut off samples for his garden in Male. The trail branched, and branched again, until we entered trackless thickets and, seemingly only by chance, came upon a totally crumbled temple mound. It stood no higher than a man and measured some 10 metres (about 33 feet) across. A crater on top told of a former dig.

The two Kondai islanders had nothing to say. They acted as if they had never been to this site before. But asked if the place had a name, one of them mumbled:

'Hawitta.'

About 90 metres (100 yards) away lay another mound of slightly larger size, also completely covered by jungle. Among the coral rubble a few worked stones could be seen, some even with plaster mouldings, but all black and soft with age.

The name of this place?

Also just 'Hawitta'.

We barely got a glimpse of a third mound when we had to search for a quick way out of the thickets. It had become too dark. The jungle knives came into their own. Loutfi explained that the village people rarely had any reason to come into these thickets, therefore hardly any of them seemed to have known about these things when he himself stumbled upon them twelve years ago. The island settlement had been on the opposite side of the island ever since the people of Kondai embraced Islam. For some reason which we never learned, the entire island had been depopulated about twenty years ago. The present population had returned to the island and resettled in their abandoned homes as recently as 1975.

The sun set and left us in the dark, so we cut our way out to the

164

nearest beach and followed the open sands around the coast back to the village.

There was little to see but stars and silhouettes of roofs as we fumbled our way into the unlit village streets where we stopped among dark walls to give Loutfi a last chance to locate the stone bird. A growing crowd of silent people came slowly out of the huts to stare at us as much as the sparse light from the stars permitted. They seemed to have the night vision of bats and owls, however, unspoiled as they were by sharper lamps than the little flame on their own oil burners. Even Loutfi seemed to have no trouble moving about as he left us in the crowd and disappeared in the dark night.

Somebody had come out with a small oil lamp flickering in the wind. In the faint light I could see a happy flash of triumph in Loutfi's face when he finally came back and grabbed my arm. He whispered that he had found the bird. But perhaps it wasn't a bird. Maybe it was the head of an elephant. I was to follow him.

We sneaked away together. As Loutfi had suspected, he had found the sculpture in the hut of the caller of the mosque. That is where we went. This religious leader confessed that he had hidden the stone figure merely to save it from destruction by the village population who argued that the Prophet forbade pagan images of any kind.

Before I knew it I was holding in my hands a limestone sculpture as big as a cock and black with age. It was a head. I could see an almond-shaped eye staring at me with a devilish expression. It didn't look like a bird. In the dark night it seemed dominated by a coiled up snout that looked more like an elephant's trunk than the hooked beak of a bird of prey. The shrewd expression in the eyes was also that of an elephant, yet there were clearly feathers to be seen on top of the head and all around. But there was also a row of large molar teeth exposed below the coiled up snout. It was some sort of demonic monstrosity, the head of a grotesque monster broken off at the neck.

I could not help feeling that I had seen something like this before. In some museum, perhaps. Loutfi had never seen anything like it in the Maldives. The caller of the mosque had no comment. He was only too pleased when we carried the heathen image away.

165

Björn Bye was soon beside us with matches.

'I have seen many heads just like that!' he exclaimed. 'In Nepal!'

Nepal, the mountain kingdom in the Himalayas, is as far above and distant from an oceanic atoll as anyone could be. It is also the only nation in the world where the state religion is pure and unmixed Hindu.

'Hindu!' The others had now joined us. 'That's a Hindu Makara head!' said Skjölsvold.

We began to perceive what the caller of the mosque had passed into my hands. It was the head of the Hindu water-god Makara, an ever-present demon decorating the entrances to Hindu temples and sculpted as projecting waterspouts in sacred Hindu fountains. For a few days we had been so absorbed by Bell's Buddhist visions and the stupa complex on the last atoll that we had forgotten that Maldive prehistory had room for still other religions. As the Buddhist religion had been replaced by Islam over 800 years ago, this Hindu sculpture could well be 1,000 years old. I held it as tenderly as if it were a baby and did not let it go until the archaeologists wrapped it in cotton wool and stored it safely away, in a case in the hull of *Golden Ray*, for transport to Male Museum.

The Maldive crew on board nodded in agreement when we told them that the stone head was Makara. 'Yes, *makara*,' they confirmed. And yet none of them had ever seen or heard of anything like it. In their own language, however, the word *makara* survived as the term for 'bad' or 'evil'. Even the head of Buddha or of an angel would be *makara* to them since Mohammed had forbidden portraits of any living creature.

The man who had brought this head to the village willingly took us along to the place where he had found it, not far from the village cultivated area. This time we entered the jungle well provided with flashlights and a kerosene lamp. He led us to a spot cleared of undergrowth where we wriggled in between lianas, fallen trees and stems. The deep black forest soil had been freshly dug and thoroughly disturbed. I picked up a beautiful little stone dish once probably used for incense or offerings. The whole area was littered with carved limestone fragments and sherds of hard plaster with parallel imprints from cane walls or roofs. All the big blocks had been dug up and removed, no doubt looted for house building.

There was nothing left to indicate the presence of a former mound. How much havoc the plunderer of this site had accomplished was anybody's guess, but our guide pleaded ignorance of the freshly announced law protecting pre-Moslem ruins. We ought to have denounced him and got him a prison term, Maldive fashion. Instead we gave him a harsh warning. And a recompense for having saved the Makara head.

As the sun rose we were on our way straight south again for Gan. We remained in the sheltered Gaaf lagoon, alert for coral reefs and changing sand-bars, and headed for the southern end of the ring-reef. Two low islands, one short and one long, rose into sight in front of us. Gadu and Gan. Gadu crammed with houses. Gan covered with jungle and coconut palms.

Our binoculars told us that news of our arrival had preceded us. A crowd of people had already come across the narrow channel to Gan from Gadu, and when we got close enough they made signs to direct us to the best spot for anchoring. There was shelter and deep water just off the sandy isthmus where they were standing. Ocean swells came rolling in from the white-capped Equatorial Channel outside, and broke like cascades as they entered the lagoon over the shallow coral reef separating the two islands.

As we jumped ashore from the barge a tall fellow with a familiar face stepped forth from the waiting crowd and greeted us one by one with both hands. It was our old friend, the 'owner' of the island. We were back on familiar ground.

Radio Male had announced our planned return to Gaaf-Gan. Hearing this, the 'owner' had taken matters in his own hands. For three days now he had brought twenty men across from Gadu to clear trails and begin opening up the jungle around the great hawitta.

Not a little uneasy about this unexpected enterprise, we set out on the hour-long walk, eager to see that nothing had been disturbed. The narrow trail had been broadened considerably, but everything was still so familiar to Björn and me that we almost felt like greeting the big flying foxes as they took off from the palms.

The 'owner's' twenty men all carried jungle knives, long-handled axes and spades. One of them even carried a heavy iron pry-bar across his shoulder. This annoyed the archaeologists. Archaeology is always conducted carefully and delicately, with little trowels and brushes, not with brutal iron crowbars. When I tried to tell our Maldive friends that we needed no digging tool as gross as this, it was gently explained to me that the crowbar was not for use on the hawitta. It was brought only to make a hole in the ground for private use. It was a sort of portable toilet for the workmen.

We reached the treeless spot with the stone-lined well where the forest opened up and gave view of the Equatorial Channel. As our trail forked off inland we began to smell the smoke of burning wood. When we approached the site where the jungle hid the sun-temple, fire was crackling and smoke rose above the forest roof. A few of the workmen had rushed ahead of the party. In a small clearing they were throwing trunks and branches on to a camp fire to chase the mosquitos away. Behind them rose the steep hill. I barely had time to get an impression that nothing seemed to be damaged, when Johansen behind me burst out in excitement:

'Ai-ai-ai!'

The two cameramen were straightaway in action – Bengt with his microphone under the noses of the archaeologists to get their first comments, Åke with his camera panning from excited faces up to the summit of the artificial hill.

For some seconds Björn and I remained speechless. Clearly we had not been able to convey the magnitude of this mound to our companions. We had not seen it this way ourselves. The jungle in front of the structure had now been cleared away on the east side, and from there a broad belt had been laid bare up the steep slope of the mound from the base to the top. It was colossal.

Skjölsvold and Johansen now began to grasp the magnitude of the archaeological task awaiting them. Here was a man-made structure of a size comparable to the largest royal tombs of the Vikings. Years would be needed to complete a professional job here, not merely a few days.

'We need not go into the mound now, Arne,' I explained when I read Skjölsvold's mind. 'We have to come back.'

'Yes, but we have time to check the shape of the foundation,' he answered, relieved. It was he who would be in charge of the excavations. 'We may even find some organic material to give us a carbon dating.'

'Sure,' said Johansen optimistically. 'Anything we find will be the first archaeological dates from the Maldives.'

A quick trip around the hill assured us that no harm had been caused by the workmen. They had just cut down trees and cleared vegetation. The last time we came we had merely seen glimpses of dark coral blocks lost in the greenery above our heads. This time we could see the side where we had climbed, right up to the colossal *kandū* tree that still stood untouched on top. There were others somewhat smaller down the slopes, even in the cleared strip, left because it would be quite a job for these people to fell them with their home-made axes. Surely the large roots must have harmed the structure. We had therefore brought with us a long loggers' saw. But the giant on the summit was too magnificent. We gave orders to let it stand. It was too huge to grow any bigger, so the roots down through the coral fill had probably done whatever damage they would do. But surely the colossal dimensions of this tree made the hill look smaller.

As the clearing proceeded all around, the profile of the hill showed up on all sides. Even the men from Gadu were visibly impressed. Their own mosque was dwarfed in comparison to this structure. They made no attempt to give the honour of this work to their own ancestors. This was the work of the Redin, and the Redin to them were a former people with more than ordinary human capacities. Ordinary people, such as those living on these atolls today, they said, had enough to do struggling to wrest a mere living out of fish and coconuts. None of them would find time to collaborate in an enterprise like this.

We agreed. And the first conclusion the archaeologists reached, even before a shovel was put into the ground, was that the builders of this hawitta must have had access to something the present population lacked. They must have had intimate links with the outside world, and support from somewhere abroad. Whoever the immigrant Redin had been, they must have maintained a surplus in their economy permitting such an extravagance as the erection of religious shrines of this magnitude. Stripped of all its former facing stones and elegant decoration, and deprived of either temple or spire on top, the solid edifice still stood as high as any tumulus commemorating the greatest prehistoric kings in Europe, as bulky as an average Mayan pyramid or a ziggurat in Mesopotamia. Yet the area of land supporting it was tiny, and barely rose above sea level. Sand and reefs, deprived of riches of any kind. No metals or precious stones. No fertile fields. Cowrie shells, yes, and the almighty sun. The midday sun beamed from its zenith, and the natural channel linking east to west ran along the shore.

When the hill was laid bare there was still no indication that either Buddhists or Hindus had made use of this mound, although they must have been here as they had been on so many of the other islands nearby. The Moslems had clearly carried away all the fine facing stones visible above ground. As we searched every trace of worked stone among the coral rubble forming the steep talus of the hill, we continued to find some of the squared blocks with sun-reliefs – high reliefs of the sun sometimes with, and sometimes without, wings. Certainly the sun had been the centre of attention among the builders of this hill. We had not seen sun-symbols on the hawitta we dug on Nilandu, nor among the ravaged Buddhist stupas we visited on the various islands on our way down to the Equatorial Channel. Only here on the equator. Here, indeed, where we had first come to look for possible traces of sun-worshippers.

As we extended the clearing and searched all around the hill, we noted that the sun-decorated blocks were present on all slopes except on the northern side. On the side facing north they were conspicuously absent. Johansen attributed this to the fact that people coming from the northern hemisphere associated the sun only with the east, south and west, never with any other direction, although here on the equator the sun seasonally shone even from the north.

It was an interesting observation. If Johansen's reasoning was followed, this would exclude an arrival of these sun-worshippers from any parts of southern Asia, from any part of the tropical belt which extended to 23°28'N. The Indus Valley and Mesopotamia lay beyond this tropical area, however, and any sun-worshippers in these northern culture centres would never see the sun to the north.

At the foot of the hill we knew that straight walls would be preserved under the fallen debris. The archaeologists therefore began their work by carefully lifting up all the loose blocks that had slid down from above and covered the base. Each stone was carefully inspected for evidence of carving before it was carried away and discarded. We had seen a section of a straight wall on our previous visit of discovery. And now others appeared. As we suspected, it was the late Moslem removal of the retaining walls that had caused the core fill to slide down and form a round hill. But before the Moslems arrived the lower part of the temple was already buried in a growing layer of forest soil and wind blown sand.

When we removed the fallen rubble and began excavating the sides of the building, we found the full lengths of the buried base walls were indeed preserved. But to our bewilderment the walls seemed to take unexpected turns. At the first corner which we exposed the wall turned left, and at the next, when we expected it to turn left again to form a square, it turned right. We began to suspect some sort of irregular or star-shaped foundation. But at the end of the first day's work it was clear that the main building was perfectly square and oriented to the sun. What had at first seemed to be irregularities were the adjoining walls of ramps centrally placed on all four sides, just as so commonly seen on Mexican pyramids.

As work began on the second day the outline of the pyramidal structure, with its four ceremonial ramp approaches, was evident. And in the process of clearing we had already sorted out from the fallen rubble a large collection of shaped and decorated blocks. The solar symbol in high relief dominated, but now we had also found suns carved so small that there was room for two on the same stone. One cornerstone had four such suns, two vertically above each other on each side of the corner. Particularly artistic were some stones decorated with pairs of suns intercepted by triple staffs, running as a continuous pattern.

One small limestone corner fragment was so completely covered by a complex design of tiny suns, indentations and rows of miniature columns, that only a highly skilled designer could have composed it and only a master craftsman carved it. The carving went deep into the stone and all the details were so minute that it had to be part of some exceedingly elegant frieze, or perhaps the corner knocked off some small shrine. There were also fallen cornice slabs with different designs. Some had

171

the by now familiar band of lotus petals. Others were deeply indented in the manner resembling the classical Greek type of *triglyf* and *metope*.

Most astonishing was an elaborate building block that began to show itself frequently at the south-eastern corner of the pyramid. The first we noticed of this type had all its deep cavities so thickly clotted with soil and white plaster that, until cleaned with trowel and brush, it seemed to be a plain squared building block. Then we suddenly saw a stylised cranium seemingly staring at us with the hollow eye-sockets of a death skull. The staring impression was caused by ridges running around the eye-sockets like goggles, elegant goggles with a straight upper rim, leaving an eerie expression. The cranial image was compressed from above. It had a pit for the nasal opening and no lower jaw. But if these cornerstones had been placed on top of each other the dense row of square knobs that were carved as a crown on the skull below would become the teeth of the one above.

A short bar ran down below each eye-socket, like a flow of tears, just as the classical tear mark symbolised rain from the sun-god in the ancient art of Mexico and Peru. In the Mayan ruins of Chichen Itza I had seen stylised death skulls carved as building blocks in sun-oriented temple platforms. Pyramids, ramps, stone skulls with tear marks in sun-oriented temple walls: perhaps this was enough to make my imagination run wild. Perhaps these did not symbolise death skulls at all. The way we held these stones they could not represent anything else. And our workmen, who had never seen such carvings before, pointed to their own faces and, eyes closed, made the signs of cutting off their own heads. But when I later showed a photograph of one such stone to an archaeologist whose speciality was the Orient, he turned the photograph upside down and said the goggle-framed concavities did not represent eye-sockets at all, but caves with a vaulted roof and flat floor. Similar motifs were known from religious art in ancient southern Asia and were interpreted by local scholars as being symbolic of the caves in which early monks had taken refuge.

But if caves, why always carved in pairs? And the tear marks? Turned upside down, did each represent a column on top of a cave? None of us had any explanation. Whatever be the case, in reconstructing the forgotten past there is always a danger of being led astray by enthusiasm and preconceived ideas. Certain it is that these and the many other sculpted stones we saved from the rubble were carved from splendid designs, and once upon a time, when all were assembled in the white limestone walls of this colossal edifice, shining in the sun, it must have been a sight for the gods.

Now that it lay before us as a lofty heap of rubble it seemed more a monument to man's eternal egocentricity. Throughout the ages men of all creeds have fought those who thought otherwise. We have always believed, and still do, that *We*, our extended ego, are on the right side. *We* know the only truth. What *We* believe, others should believe too. If not, our god wants us to kill and destroy.

The worshippers of Allah had destroyed what the worshippers of the sun had laboriously built here. But surely the worshippers of Shiva or the worshippers of Buddha must have been here in between. We checked every stone to try to read the full story. Our Maldivian friends were as fascinated as we were by the buried masonry and every sculpted stone that came out of the ground. Each time we lifted up a block with a new ornament, they shouted in delight and speeded up the work with rhythmical Maldive songs. When a small crystal ball turned up in the black soil, the shouting rose to a crescendo. They all assembled in the corner between the ramp and main wall on the east side where the glittering little thing came forth from the ground. When it was lifted up like a glass egg they all began to swing their bodies and sing and clap their hands, imitating an old wrinkled comedian with a single tooth and a huge hat who danced solo up on the slope. It was a wonderful team to work with. Good-humoured, intelligent and effective. They were quick to grasp the fact that crystal was not found naturally in the coral atolls of the Maldives, so that this ball showed contact with the outside world.

'It is a phallus,' exclaimed Johansen, and pointed to the realistic shape with a deep perforation at a flattened base which indicated that the penis-like object had been set on a stick.

Skjölsvold agreed, but later pointed out that miniature stupas were carved more or less with this form in ancient Sri Lanka and on the continent, and used as votive offerings. We all agreed that the stupa itself had a suspiciously phallic form. The stupa was known to symbolise rebirth, so perhaps it represented the male phallus rather than the pregnant female womb as has commonly been suggested.

When we reached the original ground level on which the hawitta had been built, Skjölsvold climbed up to measure the full height. From the top of the mound he took a horizontal sighting to the hand of Johansen who had climbed a nearby jungle tree and let his tape measure hang down straight to the ground. In its present reduced state the remaining structure still rose 8.5 metres (28 feet) above the ground. The original walls now completely exposed at the base measured 23 metres × 23 metres (about 75.5 feet square), which gave a ground area for the pyramid of 529 square metres (5,700 square feet).

During our work we made another interesting discovery. The temple walls had once been covered by white plaster. A thick coat of very hard lime plaster still stuck to the most protected sections. Where the soil had been most humid this covering had softened and come off. A perfectly preserved section was the corner where the east side of the ramp adjoined the south wall. Here the plaster coat was so thick and solid that no contour could be seen of the stones beneath. This helped us to understand why we had found crumbling remains of white plaster plugging up the deep concavities in the 'skull' stones. We also found 'sun-stones' with only a segment of the solar disc visible because plaster still caked the rest. Many building blocks did indeed appear not to be ornamented until we broke off the thick plaster cover which hid the decoration from sight.

Why had the ancient sculptors gone to all the trouble of, first, carving these elaborate motifs, and then hiding them under a cover of plaster so thick that they could not be seen?

The answer seemed obvious. The original artists had not smeared the plaster cover over their own decorations. This had been done by other people with a different creed, who had come subsequently and remodelled the pyramid for their own use. Again we encountered this evidence of two different periods reflected in the religious architecture before the Moslems came and stopped the use of the hawitta. Originally built for sun-worship this pyramidal structure had in its last phase been taken over by people who no longer paid divine honours to the sun. They thus covered up the existing religious symbols to obtain an all-white, unornamented structure. This was in fact what the Buddhists had done when they white-plastered over the whole surface of their large stupas on Sri Lanka.

Important information had been gained merely by clearing the Gan hawitta. But with the old walls exposed Loutfi and our Maldivian workmen expected us to dig into the mound, now that we had the permission to do so. They took it for granted that we had only come to look for the hidden riches in the hawitta. But there is more to archaeology than exposing buried walls and searching for treasures. To their surprise the workmen were told to sharpen some short sticks which Skjölsvold and Johansen then hammered into the level ground outside the hawitta. The sticks were set as corner marks for very precise one metre (3.28 feet) squares, and a string was tied between them. Exactly inside these strings, and nowhere else, digging should begin, the archaeologists explained to the puzzled islanders. It clearly made little sense to them why they should dig on one side of the string and not on the other. Or better still, why not inside the hawitta?

When they came with their picks and shovels to start digging within the strings, they got another surprise. They were told to put their good tools away, and were handed some tiny masons' trowels instead, not much bigger than spoons. And they were not even allowed to shove the pointed end into the ground, only to use the edge to scrape away thin layers of dirt, under rigid supervision. It must have seemed really silly to them.

These people had known Skjölsvold as an amiable person with a friendly smile behind his glasses and mighty beard, and the younger Johansen as a humorist always ready for a joke. But now, if a trowel dug down instead of scraping evenly, or if it passed beyond the string, Skjölsvold would shout at them and Johansen yell in despair. And if someone stepped too close to the strings so that the edge of the dig broke off and fell down in the trench, then these two crazy foreigners would become as upset as if the sand had fallen into their soup. There were neither smiles nor praise unless the sides of the dig were as smooth and exact as the floor.

When the measuring stick showed that 5 centimetres (2

inches) had been scraped away, the archaeologists declared a halt. Much commotion went on before the confused workmen were allowed to go on scraping deeper. Always 5 centimetres at a time. Neither more nor less, although they had to reach the solid island bedrock in the end anyhow.

The eyes of the workmen widened even further when Skjölsvold stooped in front of their noses only to pick up a tiny bit of charcoal. He put it in a labelled plastic bag. Then Johansen picked up some old fish bones and a minute fragment of a broken pot and saved them too. The workmen now laughed openly, but went silent and looked really worried on our behalf when they saw that we were so afraid of missing the smallest bit of this rubbish that we used a screen of chicken netting to filter the dirt they had scraped loose.

For fear that the islanders should lose all respect for us and think we had lost our wits, I called upon Abdul as interpreter to explain what was happening. The workmen listened with surprise and interest and, as they grasped the idea, were visibly impressed.

There were machines in our homeland, we explained to them, that could tell the age of a piece of bone, shell or charcoal if such materials were put inside and burnt. It measured a kind of invisible radiation that came from everything that had once been alive, plants or animals. We called this method C-14 or radio-carbon dating, and the answer given would be approximate, but often less than half a century wrong. The smallest piece of charred wood or a splinter of a chicken bone could tell us roughly when the fire had been lit or the chicken eaten.

From now on our Maldivian workmen became men of the profession, and no piece of organic material the size of a grain of rice would escape their attention.

But why the broken bits of old pots?

Potsherds cannot be dated by machines, but very often they can be by human experts. The type of earthenware and the shape and colour of the pots differ from one part of the world to the other. Even within the same area the type of pottery often changes from one century to the next. Human bones and any parts of beasts and plants may decay and disappear, but potsherds will last forever. They can only be broken into smaller pieces. In many cases a little sherd from a broken pot can tell us where and when the pot had been made. I could have explained that pottery to an archaeologist is what stamps are to a philatelist, identifiable as to place and time, but I realised that our audience had never seen a stamp. Never mind, they all used pottery, imported from India. And they knew potsherds well enough not to let the smallest fragment escape their attention.

They tried to tell us that they would find the buried potsherds and bones much faster if they could dig with their own big tools, like in their taro fields. Why scrape with those little spoons, and only 5 centimetres at a time?

Not only because fragile objects could be broken by picks and shovels before they were seen, but also because it was important to keep a record of how deep everything was found below the surface. Anything found, say, at the depth of 20 centimetres (8 inches) would be older than what was found only 5 centimetres down, and oldest of all would be anything found on the rock bottom. The deeper down the further back in time. As everybody knew, the freshest humus and the most recent human waste would always be on top.

The side walls had to be straight and smooth, so the layers would show up clearly in profile. This would show us if the soil had been disturbed by someone digging in the past; for instance, a hole would be seen filled with soil or sand of a different colour than the ground beside it. Like a wall painting, different types of soil, ashes or sand will show up in layers above each other. They will tell their own story of climatic changes, forest fires, sand storms, floods, or various forms of human activity. If the workmen dug the trench so that the wall became rough and uneven, none of these natural lines of unwritten history would show up.

After these explanations, our Maldive helpers were divided into teams of four, two scraping and two sieving. And no archaeologist could ask for a more eager, attentive and meticulous group of field workers.

Three days allotted to Gaaf-Gan was only enough to whet the appetites of the archaeologists. But we had to move on. And just as sure, we had to come back when we had more time.

As we climbed the hill again and again we did not yet realise that sculptures of both lion and ox lay buried in the rubble under our feet. But we realised we were climbing a monument pointing to the main Maldive mystery. This little island did not offer voyagers an economy permitting such a sophisticated and impressive temple. With whom had the prehistoric Maldivians had their political and religious ties resulting in this cultural extravagance?

As we sat on the top of the hill looking out over the jungle roof and the more distant crowns of coconut palms, Skjölsvold and Johansen both expressed with emphasis the notion I had long nourished. The geography, the location of these Maldive islands, perhaps combined with the cowrie shells, had made them an important port of call or transit station for advanced civilisations navigating the Indian Ocean in pre-Moslem times.

Vadu was another island west of Gaaf-Gan and on the same ring-reef. Like Gadu and Gan it was right on the Equatorial Channel. People were living there, said Loutfi. It was the last of the Redin islands on this atoll, and it was the very island where the plaque with the strange inscriptions had been found.

We weighed anchor by sunrise and, navigating carefully in a curve inside the lagoon, reached Vadu less than two hours later. We had loaded so many heavy stones on the foredeck that we had to spend the time of the crossing restowing them to give even balance to the ship. In Male Museum they would be protected. Not so exposed on Gan now they were known to potential house builders from Gadu.

At Vadu the anchor had no sooner rattled to the bottom when a dhoni came from shore with the island chief. This dark-faced, broad-built man looked more African than anyone we had seen on these islands, and we later learnt he was a distant relative of Loutfi. Yet Loutfi saluted him coldly, and for the first time he did not even introduce us, although we were set ashore with the chief. With the big chief walking amidst us mute and sombre, Loutfi told us bluntly in English that he did not like the man. It was he who had been ordered to send the written tablet complete to Male. It was complete when Loutfi had seen it where it was dug up, but broken, and with parts missing, when a dhoni brought it to Male. The disobedient chief should have been reported and punished, said Loutfi. But he did not deserve a term in exile on another island, he added with a twinkle in his eye.

Loutfi and the chief led us in silence through the main village street. It was the cleanest, most orderly and best swept village street we had ever seen, and that is saying a lot in the Maldives. Well-groomed women sat busy working in front of the picturesque little houses, some white, built from limestone, some tanned and plaited from sun-baked palm leaves. Martin Mehren remarked that we had not seen any foreigner but ourselves since we left Male. No beach on the Riviera was as tidy and well raked as the white sand between the rows of houses where the women, squatting or sitting on low stools, paid little or no notice to us as we passed. Nobody greeted us. Here, as in Male, there is no word for salutation. Not being an expert, I could only see that the women were lacing or somehow weaving or twining together a multitude of brightly coloured yarns with weights on their ends and hanging over a large satin covered ball held on the lap. The result was a broad, curved band more multicoloured than the rainbow, which they attached as a neckpiece on their full-length Victorian style gowns. This was the traditional woman's attire in the Maldives, explained Loutfi. Formerly all women used to wear it. This immediately brought to mind the ancient Egyptian fashion. Nefertiti. Once in a while we even saw a Maldive woman who matched that proud pharaonic beauty in bearing and the refinement of her features.

Where the broad village road ended an equally wide and well-swept street turned right between the low walls of a Moslem cemetery. Sticks with small banners of white cloth fluttered in the wind. Moslem tombstones, old and beautifully carved with scrolls and other artistic decoration, were half hidden in weeds. Abandoned. Many were broken. Loutfi said that the inscriptions were written in the second oldest of the three known kinds of Maldive script, called *dhives akuru*. Like *tana akuru*, the script used today, it was written from right to left. The oldest script known had been *evella akuru*, which had been written from left to right.

At the end of the short road lay a mosque and the large tomb of an important Moslem saint, a gabled hut built of whitewashed stone slabs, and flying white flags. Here rested Vadu Dhanna Kaleyfanu, also known by the Moslem name Mohammed Jamalu Ddeen, perhaps the first person to embrace Islam on this island. This was where the Khanzi people had found

179

refuge after they fled from Gaaf-Gan, according to the old men on Gadu. But the Singalese cat people who drove them away had later come here too and killed them all, according to the same stories. If Singalese they would have been Buddhists. And if the tradition was founded on fact, the saint under these flags might have been a Buddhist who embraced Islam, which was at last triumphant.

The mosque was not big but well built with beautiful wood carvings as full of arabesques as the tombstones. The high window openings looked out over the low stone wall that enclosed the sacred ground, to what seemed like a refuse dump, a long low heap of sand and broken slabs of stone. Loutfi climbed over the wall and stepped on to the rubble. We followed. This was where the inscribed slab had been dug up, he said. He had seen it himself, here, complete.

The archaeologists scratched their heads as we walked back and forth over broken pieces of limestone. Disappointed, they affirmed that there was nothing here that they could do. It was too late. Everything had recently been turned upside down. No possibility for any stratified archaeology. No sense in scraping away 5-centimetre layers where old and new all lay muddled together in complete chaos.

Loutfi regretted this. The local people had dug here recently looking for squared stones which they could re-use for new houses. That was how they had hit upon the plaque. Loutfi had seen it right here. That fellow, he said, pointing at the chief who sat gloomily and with a guilty conscience on the wall, that fellow had promised to send it to Male. And now he could not even remember where the missing fragments were. His people had searched everywhere but found nothing.

'Perhaps there will be other things if we search through this mess,' I suggested.

'It won't be an archaeological dig,' responded Skjölsvold. 'But there could be pieces worth saving.'

The Vadu men were sent by their chief to fetch shovels. Without much enthusiasm they began lifting away stones and digging sand from one end of the long pile. They knew there was nothing of interest to be found for they had already turned everything upside down themselves. But work started. We checked every bit of stone rubble before it was carried aside, while the chief sat morose and motionless on the wall.

We had barely started when Johansen shouted. The mortised base of a round column appeared under the sand and was brushed clean. From previous experience Loutfi suggested it was a pedestal, perhaps of a column mortised together in sections. Gradually we found four more. We had barely pulled part of a beautiful plaque decorated with a band of lotus motifs out of the sand, when all the workmen dropped their shovels and even the archaeologists turned away from the excavations. On the other side of the wall came a long column of women, dressed in green, red and other bright colours, some of them very pretty. Many wore the Egyptian-style rainbow band as collar and cuffs. They carried mugs and glasses with sweet rosewater for us and the workmen to drink. Even though the sullen chief sat undisturbed on the wall and refused to drink, there was a trace of satisfaction in his face when he saw the way we all rose and enjoyed the refreshments. He had organised it himself, wishing to make up for his previous misdemeanour.

The visiting ladies were neither timid nor frivolous, but so charming and gentle that their presence with the rosewater was like a merry cocktail party being celebrated on a rubbish dump. How different these women were from their shy and secluded sisters in other Moslem countries. Here, as elsewhere in the Maldives, was a clear survival of a pre-Arab society where women were not only the men's equal in privilege, but where all existing records from foreign visitors state that the ruler of these cowrie islands was customarily a queen. Even the legendary Khanzi ruler of Gaaf-Gan had been a queen.

The work of checking the limestone rubble was now resumed with greater enthusiasm, but the schemes of the repentant chief were not exhausted. The equatorial sun was scorching and we were again parched with thirst when another procession of different women appeared with fresh supplies of the same cool drink.

In spite of these delightful interruptions, or perhaps because of them, work went on at full speed with singing and laughing. Stones rejected or overlooked by those who had dug here before us were hauled out of the sand and placed in the shade of nearby trees. There we brushed them clean and could inspect them, undisturbed by the clouds of mosquitos which had dived upon us in the jungle of Gaaf-Gan.

Skjölsvold was brushing a broken piece of worked stone incised with a strange symbol. It looked like a pear-shaped hammer head set on a handle. The rest was broken away. I was checking a stone on which a human foot had been pecked out, as if a sandal had stepped in molten lava. Then Björn Bye shouted in triumph; he had found a long stone covered by lime plaster just as on Gaaf-Gan. Picking off part of the plaster he had found what I had silently hoped for but never dared expect: a row of sun-symbols. Here, as on Gaaf-Gan, we were right on the Equatorial Channel. And here was the sun-ornament again, which we had found on none of the other islands except Gaaf-Gan.

Carefully we broke off the thick lime cover from the stone surface. The full length of one side was found to be covered by a most decorative pattern of little suns. The design of the stone was divided into vertical frames surrounding alternating groups of three small, or two large, sun-reliefs set above each other and carved in different forms.

We had found a considerable number of these magnificent sun-stones, all covered by plaster, before we noticed evidence of paint on some of the hidden surfaces. The sun-covered building blocks of white limestone had originally been coloured red.

The refined taste and great skill of the stone carvers was revealed when we began to find fragments where the concentric rings of the sun-disc were surrounded so artistically with flower petals that the corolla of the flower became the rays of the sun. All were painted red. Realistically carved in high relief, each sunflower was the size of a marigold. Only religious fanatics would have covered up these masterpieces of art with a plain coat of plaster. Whoever had laboriously concealed these solar motifs had in turn been overcome by others who objected equally strongly to their taste and faith. Later the Moslems had smashed the stones to bits and thrown them on the refuse heap.

The people of the island were well aware of what their ancestors had done when they embraced Islam. The *mudimmu*, or caller of the mosque, did not hesitate to tell us that the refuse heap we had dug was filled with sand and building blocks from the pagan temple that had once stood where the mosque was now, just on the other side of the stone fence.

A visit to the mosque convinced us that local memories were right. The mosque stood on the beautifully shaped foundation wall of an earlier temple. Now this foundation was covered up with plaster like the sun-stones, but where the plaster had peeled off we found the same classical mouldings we had first seen when we dug the buried temple in Nilandu. The people told us there were also the remains of a low mound on the opposite side of the mosque. A man had found decorated plaques there too when he dug to plant maize but nobody knew the fate of those plaques.

Searching the brush-covered neighbourhood in vain for other ruins, I came back to find Skjölsvold and Johansen very excited. They had found the fragment of a plaque with incised but nondescript symbols, and a thick block with one broken sun-wheel and one engraving of a sign resembling the Buddhist symbol for the baby Buddha. While admiring these discoveries we had to give way to Johansen who was carrying a large and heavy block. A huge sunflower with a pattern of rays which spread out over its eight petals stood out in high relief from a slightly larger, decorated disc which again rose from a cubic base. This magnificent sun must have stood on top of a square post or else projected from the temple wall. One central and four peripheral holes had been drilled straight into the ornamentation as if intended to hold pegs.

Just as the *mudimmu* was calling for prayer in the mosque and the workmen were putting down their tools, Wahid bent down and picked up a bead, an ochre-coloured bead of agate, perforated as if part of a necklace. Agate does not occur naturally on coral islands. This bead had made a long sea journey.

Seeing our excitement over the bead, one of the workmen claimed he had found about 200 of them digging in this place. They had been brought to the atoll office. And lost. Two had been saved by the *mudimmu*, and after prayers he willingly passed them on to us. One was of agate but slightly bigger and brighter than the one we had found. The other was of shell, and not round but long and slender, slightly thicker at midpoint and perforated lengthwise. Not long after, one of our workmen picked up one of that same type from our dig. I was sure I had

183

seen necklaces combining these two types of bead – excavated at Lothal, the port of the Indus Valley civilisation. Clearly I had to return there to make a comparison.

Some lumps and big sherds of an extremely hard greyish-white material really confused us as we took them for pieces of modern concrete. As we had never seen concrete anywhere in the villages, why this evidence of modern construction work in an old refuse dump? Loutfi laughed. This was not concrete at all. Cement was not introduced to the Maldives until after the First World War. This was something the Maldive people had known how to make from the earliest times. He showed us that the 'concrete' was full of black dots of crushed charcoal. The Maldivians had always been accustomed to mix ash and charcoal powder into their lime, and then add 'honey' from the top of the coconut palm. They drew the juice from the palm and boiled the sap to make what people in India called *jaggery*. This ingenious blend of lime, charcoal powder and *jaggery* made a 'concrete' as hard as flint.

Since the rubble heap had been disturbed, it was impossible to tell in which epoch this invention had been made or adopted. We told the workmen to dig half a metre deeper than what seemed to be the ground level below the refuse mound. A whole series of lime-covered sunflowers appeared, as well as several small fragments of broken tablets or plaques. But no sign of any piece matching the inscribed fragments sent to Male.

We had gone through almost the full length of the heap of rubble and were on the verge of abandoning hope. It remained a mystery how such large pieces, with pictographs, could have disappeared without trace. Yet, although failing to find what we were looking for, we had encountered new evidence supporting our discoveries in Gaaf-Gan. When Islam was introduced to this area Moslem fanatics had broken and destroyed a masonry temple already covered by white plaster. Probably this temple had been a solid structure filled with sand or coral rubble inside the facing walls, like the ones we had dug in Nilandu and Gaaf-Gan. Certainly it had stood on a foundation platform with mouldings like the temple in Nilandu.

When the early Moslems destroyed this already plaster-covered temple, they probably also broke the plaques with pictographs, except the last one left complete until broken in recent months. That was due to the indifference of the chief who now sat on the wall looking down on the havoc. Completely covered by plaster as they were, the beautiful solar discs and sunflowers had probably never been seen by any Moslems, not until we uncovered them from the thick coat of ancient plaster.

An exploring party led by Skjölsvold had returned from the eastern part of the island where they had been shown a large hawitta. The core of coral rubble rising to a hill was now a familiar sight, and as there were no carved facing stones to be seen on the ground, they came back to catalogue the material rescued from the rubble.

This was when Loutfi came slowly striding from the mosque, with a broad smile.

'I have found them,' he said.

'Found what?'

'The missing pieces!' Loutfi laughed in triumph.

We hurried to follow him over the low wall to the well in front of the mosque. Here some men had stripped to the waist to take a shower bath. They dipped a can tied to a long stick into the sacred well and poured the water over head and body, paying particular attention to arms and feet, the Moslem way. They had been standing on some flat and smooth slabs laid as a pavement around the well to avoid stepping in mud.

Giggling with satisfaction, Loutfi now pointed at these slabs. They were still wet from the last shower, shining smooth, but with no decoration. We had all passed them many times. What did Loutfi mean?

'See what I have discovered!' Loutfi bent down and turned three of them over.

There were the missing inscriptions! The lost pieces. They had just been turned upside down for the bathers to stand on. How crazy! There were the pictographic symbols in a row, flanked by swastikas, the big sun-wheel and other strange signs, the same as on the slab fragments found behind the door in the museum closet. But one of the three pieces at least was part of a different plaque. A new discovery.

'Hurrah for Loutfi!'

We all shook him by the hand. He had reason to laugh. We had been digging in the heat a few metres away all day. We all

185

laughed and rejoiced with him. Even the stout chief came down from the wall with his big white teeth exposed in an uncertain smile. The least happy was the *mudimmu* when he came out from the mosque and saw the bare mud around the well as we carried the inscribed plaques away.

There was one more island the archaeologists had to see. We could not leave the equator without showing them Fua Mulaku, the lonely island smack in the middle of the Equatorial Channel.

On our second day on Vadu we were off by midday and steered south into the open Channel. Knowing what to look for as we sat in the stern of the rolling ship and watched the island disappear behind us, we could see the large hawitta on Vadu as a hill higher than the forest. Once upon a time, when it rose white and entire above the island, it must have been a perfect landmark for navigators. Sailing vessels reaching the Maldive archipelago along the equatorial line would either have sighted the hawittas of Vadu and Gaaf-Gan on the northern side of the Channel, or the one on Fua Mulaku in the centre, if not perhaps the now lost 'tower' of Addu marking the southern flank.

Four hours after we left the Gaaf lagoon we passed into the shelter of Fua Mulaku. It was late February, so the seasonal monsoon had turned to north-east since our last visit in November. This time therefore we tied our ship to the thick mooring rope on the exactly opposite side of the island, just where the three cameramen had been caught by the surf last time.

We rode in on the surf without difficulty, and jumped on to the steep boulder beach as our landing barge was grabbed by a group of little men and boys. Appearing as a giant among them was Ibrahim Didi, our host from last time. His house was just behind the broad sand dune, and still vacant for us. With *Golden Ray* moored out at sea beyond the thundering surf we had to operate from a base ashore. Food and equipment were landed with us. Once installed, we set out for the village in search of bicycles.

In a tall palm-thatched shed near the other coast we saw a large sea-going vessel under construction. Broad and tall like a Spanish galleon, it was designed precisely like a child's image of Noah's Ark. The hand-sawn planks of coconut wood were joined together with wooden pegs and adzed and chiselled to such a perfection that it was a pleasure to the eye. This type of tall ship was entirely different from the long and slender open dhoni with its elegant Egyptian–Phoenician curves and prow. Loutfi was less impressed than we were. He told us that three-masters of this type, built and sailed by his family in Addu atoll decades ago, were very much larger. This type was called *vedi*, which offered a clue to its origins because *vedi* was also the word for 'boat' in North Indian languages.[31] Clearly such expert ship builders could have had maritime contact with people in any part of the Indian Ocean.

But these seafaring islanders were not only carpenters. Their naval ropes were second to none. Formerly the planks of their ships were not pegged but sewn together from water resistant cord of coconut husk. We learnt that the very thick, 150-metre-long (nearly 500 foot) cable to which *Golden Ray* was now moored had been made by the people of Fua Mulaku from twisted hibiscus bark.

We first headed for the Kedere mosque to start work in clearing the beautiful half-buried masonry bath. With five islanders I took charge of this operation, while all the others cycled off to the large hawitta. Skjölsvold wanted to look for any trace of the original masonry walls.

The purpose in digging further down the masonry walls of the ceremonial bath was to check if benches were running around the sides, such as in the brick-built bath of Mohenjo-Daro and the slab-lined bath of Bahrain, the Sumerian Dilmun. At present the vertical walls and the broad stairways disappeared down into a fill of dry sand and coral rubble. But the stone-lined well in the centre contained water a little way down. Local people had told us that this well in the middle had been built in very recent Moslem times, when the bath itself had been filled, on orders from the government in Male, with sand and coral pebbles from the beach.

With shovels and bare hands the five workmen dug away sand and gravel and lifted out big chunks of broken Moslem tombstones and lotus-decorated pre-Moslem temple stones. All had been thrown in to cover up the once sacred temple water. Sheltered from the sea breeze it was oppressively hot down inside with the equatorial sun shining right over our heads. As for me I was fully rewarded when broad and well preserved

187

stone benches became revealed and were carefully scraped clean with our hands. Although hoped for and half expected, this seemed a revelation, indeed a direct repetition of the baths in Mohenjo-Daro and on Bahrain.

About the length of a hand further down my toiling helpers got their reward. Cool water began to filter between their bare toes: freshwater, and as cool as in the well. Soon they stood ankle deep and had to give up using spades as the sand was washed off by the water. With both hands they dug deeper and deeper, and faster and faster as they were refreshed by being able to immerse themselves more deeply in the bath.

They were all sitting in water up to their necks, and throwing up pebbles and stones, when a real Methuselah came staggering with his stave and peeped over the edge. Seeing the men in the bath he got such a shock that his knees began to wobble. I rushed up just in time to drag him into the shade of the mosque before he fainted. He came to when one of the workmen climbed a palm, picked a coconut, and poured fresh juice down his throat.

At this point Loutfi came and told us that the old man with the beard and Moslem cap was the *mudimmu* of this tiny mosque. His name was Hussainu and, according to records, he was 104 years old. When we asked about the bath, old Hussainu got talkative. He remembered before it was filled with rubble from the beach. Only clear water then. As clear as in the well now. Many men and women would bath together. There were stone slabs at the bottom as smooth and clean as the walls. Now the water was muddy only because we stirred up the fill. In olden days there had been plugged holes as outlets in the bottom. Only freshwater would run in and out of these holes, as in the well now. It was drinking water, and yet it would rise and sink with the tide of the sea. When the tide was high the water in the bath would reach to his chest, and to the navel when the tide was low.

We checked the water level. As in the round bath we had dug in Nilandu it varied some 20 centimetres (8 inches) with the ocean tide. It always kept slightly below the wall benches, where people could have been sitting on dry stones. We counted the steps down to the stone bench. There were seven. Lying on the bench with my arm in water to the shoulder I could feel the smooth wall blocks running on as perfectly fitted together as the walls we could see. But to dig the bath to its bottom would be a major job without a pump. And as we learnt that Maldive law required the boulders and sand to be thrown in again before we left, we dug no further down than the men could reach sitting head above water.

If the government were to allow an exception to its rules, this prehistoric structure with its magnificent stone work, solar orientation and big basin filled with crystal clear water, would make a unique national monument. To science it would be an undamaged specimen of an architectural feature that was once important in the Maldive archipelago.

Work was still going on lifting stones out of the bath when Martin Mehren arrived on his bicycle, curious to see if we had found the stone benches. He stood balancing on a pile of boulders near one wall when he was stung by something so small and fast that it was gone between the stones before he saw it. He felt little pain, and made no comment, so we noticed nothing. He left unconcerned about an insignificant episode that was almost to bring an end to his life.

Leaving the workmen to enjoy themselves splashing in the bath at the end of their job, I mounted my bicycle to see what was happening at the hawitta. The steep hillock had now been cleared of a dense growth of pandanus palms and other trees. As at the bath, here also, a large crowd of spectators had assembled to watch the work. I wrote in my notebook:

> The men work fast and efficiently. They always learn quickly and demonstrate intelligence. Men and women have a great sense of humour. There seems to be no sex discrimination. The women are completely unafraid and self-confident. Wahid claims that on this island women have more to say than men. The young boys and girls are extremely bright and very good-looking. Some of the young girls on this island are among the prettiest I have seen.

With a large number of men and women helping them, the archaeologists had cleared the seaward side of the hillock of turf and soil, and some well-preserved wall sections of large thick blocks were exposed. This had clearly been a Buddhist *dagoba*, not square but round, without a single wall stone carved with ornaments, but with clear evidence of a former coat of white plaster. A crude stairway of unworked beach boulders curved up the side of the slope. Perhaps this was a secondary feature, since the blocks in the wall were carefully squared, although not flat and smooth like the facing slabs we had seen on this and other islands.

Skjölsvold pointed out traces of four walls above each other in terraces, each one stepped in from the wall below. An old man claimed to have seen six such tiers when the hawitta was still in its proper shape.

It was impossible to say from surface observation whether or not this Buddhist dagoba had been shaped around the core of an earlier structure. When the Moslems came it must have looked like a terraced conical pyramid, plastered white and dominating the island and the surrounding sea.

Loutfi was missing from the dig. He had been limping for a few days since scratching his leg and getting an infection. Now I learned to my dismay that he felt ill and had gone to see the 'doctor'. Everybody in the expedition had bandages around their legs because of small cuts and scratches. Everybody but me. I instead had my head bandaged because of running into a broken branch in the jungle. Luckily these jungle germs never seemed to climb higher from the ground than to infect grazes and cuts below the knees.

The 'doctor' proved to be the only island health worker, a fine young Maldivian of 19 years with two weeks training at the hospital in Male. We found him with his patients on a sort of verandah at the entrance to the atoll office. In a wooden hammock Loutfi lay wrapped up to his nose in stacks of thick blankets, shivering with cold. On a camp-bed beside him lay, to my great surprise, an elderly gentleman. Martin! One of his legs was swollen like a melon with two tiny stings side by side, rubbed by the young man with a grey piece of cotton wool. Martin was not happy at all. He had taken his own snake medicine, had vomited, and now had pains in both leg and stomach. Seeing Martin's foot I could not help thinking of six of our workmen on Gaaf-Gan, six out of sixty, who had elephantiasis in one or both legs. Some tropical mosquitos spread the microscopic worm that causes elephantiasis, but the growth is always a very slow process. The marks on Martin's leg looked suspiciously like those of two snake teeth. But everybody swore there were no snakes in the Maldives, so perhaps it was one of the large centipedes I had seen among the boulders. Their sharp pincers are as poisonous as the tail of a small scorpion and, perhaps aided by germs on the dirty piece of cotton wool, sufficed to start the complications that followed. Martin became seriously ill.

Both the health worker and Björn, our own excellent first-aid man, ran out of bandages and medicine, so Wahid rounded up four islanders willing to take him through the surf to fetch our medical chest from the *Golden Ray*.

It was dark when they left and close to midnight as they came back, all five bruised and beaten, dripping wet. But Wahid was proudly bearing the medical chest. When we opened it, sea water poured out as from a mug. Coming back from the ship the little dhoni had been capsized by the surf and all five men thrown into the frothing sea. But it was near land and, miraculously, they had all managed to struggle ashore with the dhoni upside down.

'I never let go the chest,' said Wahid with modest pride, and apologised for the soup of medicine and water inside.

This was when we first heard of a team of Japanese cameramen who had come here last month by dhoni from the airport island of Addu-Gan. They had read a press report about our observations on Fua Mulaku last year and had come ashore on a one-day visit to film the hawitta and local life. As they left, the dhoni had capsized at this very same place. All lives were saved but, according to the islanders, the heartbroken Japanese had lost two film cameras and all the 160 rolls of new and exposed films they had brought to the Maldives. This, however, was not to be their last effort to film in our wake.

Next morning we had to get out to our ship from that same place ourselves. Martin was so ill that we had to deliver him to the airport on Addu-Gan before we started the long leg northbound with *Golden Ray*.

Not only Åke, with his precious cameras, was tense after a sleepless night thinking of this moment. We assembled on the beach with the red sunrise over the sea, ready to depart. We were watching the wild surf, prepared to jump into the dhoni at the right moment. Four towering waves rose behind each other, tumbling in across the reef, followed by an interval of smaller breakers when we had to hurry out to the open sea as fast as our four island experts could swing their oars. At a sign from the helmsman, who jumped on board first, the oarsmen pushed off while big Loutfi, wise from experience, let himself be carried

Page 1: Happily heading for adventure on unexplored islands at the equator, the author *(left)* and Åke Karlson are passengers in a Maldive *dhoni*. Behind Åke is the detached bow piece of the vessel lifted off by the crew as it serves no practical purpose. Since time immemorial it has been a traditional ornament in Maldive boatbuilding which shipbuilding experts have found remarkably suggestive of the papyriform bow of the wooden Egyptian and Phoenician ships.

Page 2: The atolls of the Maldive archipelago stretch for 900 km as a semi-submerged barrier dotted with islands and blocking maritime traffic around the southern tip of India. From the sea voyagers cannot detect the islands until the palm crowns emerge above the horizon as the ground surface never rises more than about 2 metres above sea level.

Page 3: Above: The low atolls of the Maldives are rich in archaeological remains of great antiquity, many of them visible from far out at sea. Yet archaeologists have overlooked the islands because of the widespread feeling that ocean navigation began with Columbus, so nobody could have reached the Maldives in prehistoric times.

Below: As we cleared the jungle and dug around the base of a large mound we found it had been built by man. Below ground we discovered astronomically oriented walls which had once been part of a pyramidal structure faced with ornamented limestone blocks and filled with coral rubble. The archaeologists are checking the excavated soil and Mikkelsen is picking potsherds from the sieve.

Page 4: Above: Cleared of jungle the pyramidal mound of Gaaf-Gan appears like a giant ant-hill with the workmen and only one giant tree left on top. Stripped eight centuries ago for the sculptured facing slabs, only the coral rubble fill was left above ground.

Below: On Nilandu island the hidden walls of an unknown temple appeared as Skjölsvold and Johansen were working with trowel and brush.

dry-foot into the dhoni. Too proud, Martin waded, and was pulled into the little boat which met the first surf with a leap, and leap by leap carried them all to safety in the open rolling waters. It was a relief to see them and all our equipment safe up the ladder of *Golden Ray*. Two more trips and we were all back

Page 5: Above: The preserved remains of the Nilandu temple, which were found protected below ground level, proved that it had been an elegant structure. A compact core of beach sand had originally been retained with classically profiled facing stones to form a sort of pyramidal structure oriented to the sun and with a walled ramp approach on one side. Carbon datings from the interior fill, as well as from a buried wall surrounding the entire temple area, disclosed that this religious complex had been rebuilt about AD 550, as elegantly carved stones from some earlier structure lay thrown in among the fill.
Below: Completely buried in the sand we discovered the ceremonial stairway leading down to a large circular bath with beautifully fitted stone walls. Fresh water rose from the buried bottom to stone benches running around the sides.
Page 6: A lion sculpture found on an oceanic island. Only the forepart with head and flexed front legs had been sculptured, whereas the hind parts were shaped as a square block, showing that these felines had once been set like decorative gargoyles into the facing walls.
Page 7: Self-sustained until present generations, the Maldive islanders have a staple diet of fish and coconuts and they can draw fresh water everywhere by digging wells into the limestone bedrock. Village homes were built from palm leaves, but houses built from coral rubble and lime are now becoming more common.
Page 8: A modest modern mosque of palm leaves beside an impressive prehistoric ceremonial bath. The first Moslems had destroyed what to them was a pagan temple and reused the dressed slabs as tombstones. But, rather than destroy the prehistoric bath they filled it up and built a round well in the middle to serve the mosque. A megalithic stairway and smooth, beautifully fitted slab walls of pre-Islamic origin rose above the well, and as our excavations began, wide stone benches appeared around the walls. Fresh water came up to the level of the benches where the bathers had once been seated. The workmen were delighted to get a refreshing bath under the scorching equatorial sun as the clearing of the loose fill went on inside the old ceremonial basin.

on the fine little hospital ship, southward bound for Addu atoll
with the airport.

Martin was still on his feet when we parted from him and
Wahid on Addu-Gan. Next morning the little plane was due in
for its flight back to Male, while we began our cruise back there
by sea. We were later to learn that our unfortunate friend
reached Male in desperate condition. He was saved by a visiting
lady doctor from India who arranged for an emergency seat on a
full plane to Germany where he was rushed to the tropical
department of a Frankfurt hospital. And from there to quaran-
tine for unidentified diseases in Oslo. The source of his infection
was never in fact identified, and although he recovered he never
quite cleared the trouble out of his leg. The old Arctic explorer
had never thought he was risking his life by stepping down the
broad stairways to a swimming pool.

Our own voyage northwards went smoothly, with only one
unforeseen event. We crossed the Equatorial Channel and most
of Gaaf lagoon on the first day and, after a night at anchor off
Kondai island, we reached Viringili in the same lagoon late the
next morning. We anchored again because the captain was afraid
of reaching land and reefs on the other side of the One-and-Half-
Degree Channel before daylight broke the morning after.

Some distance from our ship lay a strange kind of watercraft
full of children playing and diving. It looked like a huge raft
with a hut on it. Not the type of log raft we use in the Maldives,
said Loutfi. He shouted a question to two men in a passing
dhoni, and we learned that the mysterious craft had been found
on the outer reef off the east coast of Viringili yesterday. Some
fishermen had found it and, perhaps from superstition since
they saw no crew on board, they had set it on fire. Then they
towed it into the lagoon. Nobody wanted it until the children
had pulled it to pieces, then the separate parts would be sold at
auction in the village tomorrow.

We launched our barge and hurried over before the strange
craft was completely destroyed. Little boys were busy tearing
down parts of the cabin wall, but as we approached they dived
overboard and swam ashore.

It was a raft indeed: large, and built from giant bamboo. I had
never seen bamboo as thick as this. Thick as telegraph poles and
tied together in three layers under eight cross beams of wood

with another layer of thick bamboo as a deck well above the water.

We climbed on board the craft which maintained a perfect stability.

'This is not Maldivian,' said Loutfi. 'We have no bamboo.'

'Bamboo this size does not exist in Sri Lanka either,' commented Björn. 'It must have come from some jungle country on the continent.'

'Perhaps Bangladesh or Burma,' suggested Bengt. He was sure he had seen similar rafts of giant bamboo in the Ganges delta.

Twelve metres long and three wide (39 feet by 10 feet approximately) with a freeboard of 40 centimetres (16 inches), the whole structure recalled the balsa raft *Kon-Tiki* which had been large enough to carry me and five companions across the Pacific. The bamboo cabin had been scorched by fire and partly destroyed by the boys, but it was still well enough preserved to bring to mind the bamboo hut on *Kon-Tiki* in size and cosy atmosphere. The cabin floor was stepped up another 20 centimetres (8 inches) from the main bamboo deck, and in one corner there was a raised cooking place with a floor of baked clay, still full of ashes. Above the fireplace was a rack of split bamboo for smoking fish. The gabled roof with watertight coconut thatch had a comfortable flat terrace above it just as we had built on the reed ship *Tigris*. And like us on *Kon-Tiki* they had a storage room under the cabin floor.

We searched the raft and found a few tiny bone-dry fish, but they had probably jumped on board by themselves. In the storage room lay two small pieces of paper. Labels fallen off some can or jar, covered by the scrolls of an exotic kind of script.

'Not our kind of written characters,' said Loutfi.

'Not even Singalese,' said Björn. 'They don't write like that on Sri Lanka.'

'This looks like Burmese,' said Bengt with conviction. He and Åke had just come from Burma, filming the fabulous assembly of 8,000 Buddhist temples standing in Pagán.

'Just a minute,' he added and pulled out his wallet, where he had a stack of visiting cards from his recent journey. 'Look at this!'

We all looked. There was a whole series of scrolls identical with those on the two labels.

Only on our return to the continent did we get help to read the labels. The first line said: *'Buddham Dhammam Sangham'* – that is, 'To Buddha, to the Teaching, to the Monks.' The second line said: 'Tasty and replete with good flavour.' Underneath was the brand name of a Burmese coconut candy!

This raft had come by sea from distant Burma, and had passed Bangladesh, India and Sri Lanka on its 3,000-kilometre (nearly 2000-mile) voyage to Viringili in the Maldives. It was completely covered by barnacles, and with experience of four lengthy raft voyages I could tell from their size that this craft had been floating at sea for less than two months.

Even if Buddha in person had been sitting in the cabin, he could not have told us much more about the route than these two labels inscribed in his honour. The teachings of Buddha's monks had spread fast from the first source in Nepal down the river Ganges to the Bay of Bengal, and Burma. Nowhere in the world had Buddha been venerated with more golden statues and with costlier pagodas and stupa towers than in Burma, which has remained a Buddhist nation in spite of its present left-wing rule. The simplest and most logical route for the spread of Buddhism to the island of Sri Lanka and the Maldive archipelago beyond was the route that this raft had taken, with the north-east monsoon straight across the open Bay of Bengal. Whether manned or drifting away alone when it left the coast of Burma, this raft had shown that seafaring Buddhists might well have by-passed Sri Lanka and come directly from the continent behind these hidden atolls in the open Indian Ocean.

We left the Maldives on this second visit well aware that the mystery we had hoped to solve became more complicated the more we learnt. It was clear enough that Buddhists from Sri Lanka or the continent beyond had a firm hold on this oceanic archipelago before the Moslems arrived, and yet others had been here before them. But one new question that gradually emerged was not easy to answer. With Buddhism so well established throughout the Maldive territory, and with the mighty Buddhist nation of Sri Lanka, with powerful kings and armies, as their nearest neighbour, how could a handful of Moslems from distant Arabia come sailing here to tear down all the beautiful temples and succeed so thoroughly in converting the entire population to Islam?

196

CHAPTER IX
The Maldives, a Crossroad in Antiquity
The Pre-European Epoch of Free Trade

MALDIVE HISTORY is a lesson in religion. Hardly any other nation with such a restricted area and so distant from outside influence has felt the imprint of so many different faiths – ranging from solar cult, the oldest worship of civilised nations, to Islam, the youngest of the main creeds.

The known chapter of Maldive history begins with the hero who brought the Moslem faith. Earlier memories have been systematically erased. The known chapter is mainly of local interest. The earlier chapters, if only partly recovered, would fill in important pages missing in world history.

How little we know about the unwritten epochs of the human past. A voyage may have been put on lasting record when Queen Hatshepsut of Egypt sent her expedition down the Red Sea to Punt, or when Alexander the Great marched to the Indus Valley and sent his troops back to Mesopotamia by sea. But we know nothing about the vast number of adventurers and merchants who made similar journeys before them. We know nothing of what happened in the Indian Ocean in the earliest millennia long before the Arabs and Portuguese came; when the first maritime civilisations grew up along all the coasts of Asia; when global trade began with merchant ships which succeeded in linking East and West together.

Usually the history of a nation begins with a potent king founding a dynasty. The Maldives is a definite exception. A long dynasty of kings was already there before known Maldive history started. This kingdom ended when Maldive history began. The last king was made a sultan by a pious foreigner who came by sea and started local history. He caused all the kings to disappear into oblivion, except one, the one he himself converted. With neither arms, nor with any Maldive blood in his veins, he introduced a new faith, new laws, and founded the present Moslem Maldive state.

In the great Friday Mosque in Male hangs a long board, beautifully sculpted, with entwining Arab letters raised in relief. Carved in the century after the event, it commemorates the arrival of Abu al Barakat, the intrepid Arab voyager who brought Islam to the Maldives and built this mosque. The mosque itself, the oldest in the nation, is one of those where the worshipper must kneel obliquely to the corner because the older foundation is facing the sun instead of Mecca.

The board with its Arab inscriptions probably made no impression on foreign visitors until seen and described by the famous Moorish Arab traveller and author, Ibn Battuta, who came to the Maldives in 1343. Two centuries had then passed since the local people had embraced Islam. Ibn Battuta was one of the many great Arab globe-trotters of his day, and yet his journeys are among the few known to us, thanks to his own pen. He came to the Maldives from his home in Tangiers. That is, long before Vasco da Gama, he had come from his home on the Atlantic coast to undertake extensive voyages in the Indian Ocean and reach Cambay in north-west India. It was from this port area of the former Indus Valley civilisation that he ended up in the Maldives on his way around the southern tip of India. Before he continued to China he made a long sojourn in the Maldives. These islands were known to him before he left the continent, because he wrote: 'I resolved to go to the *Dhíbat Almahal* [the Arabic name for Maldive Islands], of which I had heard much . . . These islands are among the wonders of the world.'[32]

In the Friday Mosque of Male, Ibn Battuta copied the Arab inscriptions from the carved board, and rendered the name of the historic hero who brought Islam to these islands the way he believed he should read the letters: *Abu al Barakat Yusuf*, with the geographical suffix *al Barbari*, which means 'from Berber land'.

Through this reading he identified the Maldive culture hero as his own fellow countryman, and thereby undoubtedly gained popularity and prestige among his island hosts. Modern historians have quoted and requoted this early reading of Ibn Battuta, which inferred that Islam was brought to the Maldives by a voyager from the Atlantic or Mediterranean shores, who sailed into the Indian Ocean by way of Egypt and the Red Sea.

To my surprise Loutfi said that Ibn Battuta was wrong. Islam had not been brought to the Maldives by a sailor with a home port as vague as 'Berber land'. All North Africa was Berber land. And the route of the historic voyager had not been by way of the Red Sea, but by the Persian Gulf, on the other side of the Arabian Peninsula. The way we ourselves had come with the reed ship *Tigris*.

Loutfi had studied Arabic in Egypt, and he had taken the old board down from the wall in order to read the letters better. He had even compared the text with that of another ancient inscription about the same event, painted on the wall of the same Friday Mosque. There the name of the immigrant hero was unmistakably *Abu al Rikab Yusuf*, with the suffix *al Tabrizi*, which means 'from Tabriz'. Tabriz was an important Arab trading centre in Persia, said Loutfi. It was on the main caravan route from the Orient to Baghdad and the ports on the river Tigris.

Back in Male on our return from the Equatorial Channel, Loutfi showed us the old board which they had now brought from the mosque to the museum.

'See here,' said Loutfi and pointed at some marks where small projecting dots had come off or been removed from the old relief letters.

'The loss of these dots makes all the difference.' He drew two almost identical combinations of Arab characters on a piece of paper. One had the dots, on the other they were omitted. He showed the paper to a bystander who knew Arabic. The man read the one with dots as 'from Tabriz' and the one without as 'from Berber land'. The removal of the dots did indeed make all the difference.

These are the examples that Loutfi drew:

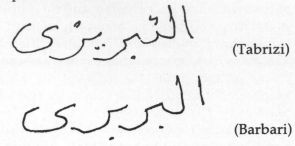

(Tabrizi)

(Barbari)

As is well known to Moslem historians, Tabriz played an important part in the spread of Islam into mainland Asia and down the Mesopotamian waterways to Bahrain in the Persian Gulf and beyond. Even though the globe-trotting Ibn Battuta personally came from Tangiers in the remotest corner of 'Berber land', he too crossed the river Tigris to visit Tabriz, which greatly impressed him. In particular he admired 'an immense bazaar called the Qazan bazaar, one of the finest bazaars I have seen the world over', he wrote. And in a footnote the translator of his travelogue explains: 'Tabriz was at this time at the height of its prosperity as the entrepôt between Europe and the Mongol empire.'[33]

Loutfi was not alone in his revision of Ibn Battuta's reading. He had barely initiated us in the secret of the missing dots when a British expert on Islamic studies, A. D. W. Forbes, published a report on Maldive mosques. Reading the inscriptions on the wall of the Male Friday Mosque, he wrote: 'Lines 2–3 of the inscription read: "Abu'l Barakàt Yùsuf al-Tabrìzì arrived in this country, and the *sultàn* became a Muslim at his hands in the month of Rabì'al-Akhir 548 [i.e. AD 1153]".' He commented: 'The chief difference between this inscription and the abbreviated version recorded by Ibn Battùta lies in the use of the *nisba* «*Tabrizi*» instead of «*Barbari*».'[34]

But this first page of Maldive history was not only carved and painted in Arab letters in the mosque. The Maldivians had short history books written in their own Divehi letters on thin copper strips bound together as proper books. These state chronicles were called *tarikh*, and through them and later paper documents they know the names of all their sultans. The list began with one ruling as a non-Moslem king from 1141 until he was converted to Islam in 1153. It ended with the one ruling until 1968 when the Maldives became a republic.

Bell had studied these old written records and wrote:

The conversion of the Maldive Islanders, according to the Táríkh, came about thus. The Almighty God desiring to free the natives from their slough and ignorance, idolatory, and unbelief, and to lead them into the right path, inspired the Shaikh Yúsúf Shams-ud-din of Tabriz, the most pious saint of the age, 'whose knowledge was as deep as the ocean', to visit the Maldives. The Shaikh there conjured the Islanders to become Muslims, but failed until he had roused them by displaying miraculous powers, such as the raising of a colossal *Jinni*, 'whose head almost reached the sky'. Then the King and all the inhabitants became Muhammadans. . . . Thereafter, emissaries were sent to the different Atols, who converted all the inhabitants without exception, whether willing or unwilling, to the Muslim Faith.

According to Loutfi, the name Shams-ud-din used for Yusuf here is incorrect as Shams-ud-din was a very famous Arab scholar from Tabriz who travelled far and wide but returned to be buried in Tabriz. In fact, throughout the further text of this old *tarikh*, the culture hero who brought Islam is referred to either as *'Tabrizigefánu'*, the Lord from Tabriz, or simply as 'Tabriz': 'Upon the King, who had previously borne the title "Siri Baranáditta", Tabriz bestowed the name "Sultan Muhammad".' And: 'Upon the advice of Tabriz, regulations were instituted for the administration of the Islands, religious laws duly enforced, and knowledge of the new Faith freely disseminated. All traces of idolatory were effaced, and Mosques built everywhere.'[35]

The following *tarikh* translation by Bell leaves no doubt as to the port of departure of this hero:

When God wished to uplift the people of the Máldives from the pit of ignorance, to save them from . . . the worship of idols, and to show them the right path and light of Islám, the most God fearing Chief of Saints of that age . . . *Maulána Shaikh Yúsúf Shams-ud-din of Tabriz* was inspired by God with

201

the desire to visit the Maldives. After that he disappeared from his native town, called Tabriz (in Persia), and appeared at the Maldives.[36]

Clearly the most pious Shaikh Yusuf of Tabriz had not come to Male on a drift voyage, but with the preconceived plan to bring Islam to idolaters in a nation already famous everywhere the Arabs advanced. The Shaikh from Tabriz sailed from Mesopotamia as well informed as did later his Arab compatriot Ibn Battuta from the Indus Valley port of Cambay. In fact, the easiest navigation route for early sailing ships would be that of our first leg with the reed ship *Tigris* from Mesopotamia to the Indus Valley. The next leg would simply be to turn the bow due south to the equator, then to turn for the sunrise, and the Maldive hawittas would show up on the horizon.

Knowing that the devout Shaikh from Tabriz came to the Maldives intent on converting the population, the question is: how did he succeed? Why did the King and all his people so willingly accept the new faith and tear down their splendid ancestral hawittas?

The old Divehi *tarikh* and the later Arab account by Ibn Battuta give two different reasons, both suggesting that the foreigner succeeded through the use of miraculous powers. The *tarikh* has it that he conjured forth a jinni 'whose head almost reached the sky'. Nothing but a kite could have been sent that high at the time, and kites with heads of demons, trailing long streamers behind were a speciality among the early Asiatic peoples. But the sending up of a kite, or any other such trick by a foreign visitor, would hardly suffice to convert the people throughout the Maldives.

Ibn Battuta, on the other hand, from personal experience believed in the local memories of the virgins and the demon from the sea. His version of the legend, written down six and a half centuries ago, was more detailed than the one we heard:

Owing to the demon in question many of the Maldive islands were depopulated before their conversion to Islam. When I reached the country I was not aware of this matter. One night, while I was at one of my occupations, I heard of a sudden people crying with a loud voice the creeds, 'There is no God but Allah', and 'Allah is very great'. I saw children carrying Korans on their heads, and women rapping the inside of basins and vessels of copper. I was astonished at their conduct, and asked, 'What is happening?' to which they replied, 'Do you not see the sea?' Whereupon I looked, and saw, as it were, a kind of large ship, seemingly full of lamps and chafing-dishes. 'That is the demon,' said they to me; 'he is wont to show himself once a month; but when once we have done as you have seen, he turns back and does us no harm.'

Memories of how this demon from the sea was first scared away were still fresh in Male when recorded by Ibn Battuta:

The story and the motive for the conversion of the Inhabitants of these Islands to Islam . . . Trustworthy men among the inhabitants, such as the lawyer *Isa al-Yamani*, the lawyer and schoolmaster *Ali*, the *Kází Abd Allah*, and others, related to me that the people of these islands used to be idolaters, and that there appeared to them every month an evil spirit, one of the Jinn, who came from the direction of the sea. He resembled a ship full of lamps. The custom of the natives, as soon as they perceived him, was to take a young virgin, to adorn her, and to conduct her to the *budkhána*, that is to say, an idol temple, which was built on the sea-shore and had a window by which she was visible. They left her there during the night and returned in the morning, at which time they were wont to find the young girl dishonoured and dead. Every month they drew lots, and he upon whom the lot fell gave up his daughter. At length arrived among them a Maghrabin Berber, called *Abú'l-barakát*, who knew by heart the glorious Koran. He was lodged in the house of an old woman of the island *Mahal* [Male]. One day he visited his hostess and found that she had assembled her relatives, and that the women were weeping as at a funeral. He questioned them upon the subject of their affliction, but they could not make him understand the cause, until an interpreter, who chanced to come in, informed him that the lot had fallen upon the old woman, and that she had an only daughter, who was now about to be slain by the evil Jinni. *Abú'l-barakát* said to the woman: 'I will go to-night in thy daughter's stead.' At that time he was entirely beardless. So,

203

on the night following, after he had completed his ablutions, he was conducted to the idol temple. On arrival there he set himself to recite the Koran. Presently, through the window, beholding the demon to approach, he continued his recitation. The Jinni, as soon as he came within hearing of the Koran, plunged into the sea and disappeared; and so it was that, when the dawn was come, the Maghrabin was still occupied in reciting the Koran. When the old woman, her relatives, and the people of the island, according to their custom, came to take away the girl and burn the corpse, they found the stranger reciting the Koran. They conducted him to their King, by name *Shanúrdza*, whom they informed of this adventure. The King was astonished; and the Maghrabin both proposed to him to embrace the true faith, and inspired him with a desire for it. Then said *Shanúrdza* to him: 'Remain with us until next month, and if you do again as you have now done and escape the evil Jinni, I will be converted'. Wherefore the stranger remained with the idolaters, and God disposed the heart of the King to receive the true faith. He became Musalmán before the end of the month, as well as his wives, children, and courtiers. At the beginning of the following month the Maghrabin was conducted again to the idol temple; but the Jinni came not, and the Berber recited the Koran till the morning, when the Sultan and his subjects arrived and found him so employed. Then they broke the idols, and razed the temple to the ground. The people of the island embraced Islam, and sent messengers to the other islands, whose inhabitants were also converted.[37]

When we combine the national memory of this event, still young during Ibn Battuta's visit, with our own observations, the jinni from the sea begins to take on human characteristics. His desire to have the virgins delivered to the idol temple suggests that the terrible visitor was a performer of religious rites rather than a common sex maniac. Buddhists do not perform this kind of religious act, but certain forms of early Hinduism did. And the demonic images we had seen recently dug up at the former temple site were of Hindu type. The young woman's skull found on top of one of these idols seemed to tie in well with the Male tradition about this very site. What looked like a ship full of lamps whenever the jinni came, was probably just what it looked like: a ship full of lamps. The fiend from the sea and the fear-stricken population ashore hardly shared the same faith. This would indicate that the people ashore, at the advent of Islam from the Arab world, were no longer Hindus, but Buddhists.

The modern Maldive nation was not fond of admitting the evidence for the Buddhist substratum, which had been so systematically erased in the long centuries of sultanic rule. When Bell had bravely pointed to his evidence of a former Buddhist influence, his claims were like seeds falling on rock. But the modern President Gayoom, Maniku, Loutfi and many others of our Maldive friends were open for a revision of their own history, which began from a total blank with the first sultan. No sooner had we brought to Male the sculpted stones from the sun-temple on Gaaf-Gan, than President Gayoom referred to our discovery in his foreword to a remarkable historical document, hitherto unpublished. It was a booklet which, for the first time, revealed the Divehi text and the English translation of an 800-year-old Maldive copper-strip book, the so-called *loamaafaanu*. Though the existence of this book had been known for quite some time, wrote the President, this was the first time that any light had been thrown on its contents, thanks to the painstaking work by Maldivian scholars supervised by Hassan Maniku and aided by script experts from Sri Lanka. Written in the most ancient Maldivian characters known as *evella akuru* ('old script'), this book is unique in including the genealogy of some Maldive rulers from pre-Moslem times. It begins in the year 505 after the death of the Prophet (AD 1105) when 'the great King, *Sri Maanaabarana* of the house of *Thiimuge*, the Lord of the Lunar Dynasty became the King of this country'. It then lists the names and length of reign of four succeeding kings until the one ruling from AD 1179, in the early decades of Islam:

The Great King *Srimat Gadanaditya*, an ornament to the Lunar Dynasty, resplendent as gold, firm as an *Asala* ['stone'] pillar, defender of the entire hundred thousand of islands, brilliant as the sun, moon and stars, virtuous in every manner, lord of

205

love, mine of jewels, adorned with a crown set with gems, –
On the fourth year of his becoming the sole monarch he,
having destroyed the shrine erected previously by the infidel
Kings of Dabuduv, uprooted the Buddha images, and caused
the infidel Kings to read the Shadat [a Moslem creed].[38]

Here was a clear reference to twelfth-century Buddha images
and a shrine on Dabuduv. Dabuduv, according to Loutfi, was
Dabidu, the island next to Isdu, 'The First Island Sighted',
where we had seen the huge hawitta from the sea. This was in
the compact string of islands on the eastern reef of Laamu atoll
where we had followed in Bell's tracks, and where we had seen
ruins of Buddhist stupas resting on substructures of a type Bell
said he had never seen in the Buddhist world. Now we learnt
from the hitherto undeciphered text of the *loamaafaanu* copper
book that this was where Buddhism either lingered on or was
reintroduced.

No wonder that Laamu atoll – with the islands of Isdu,
Dabidu and Laamu-Gan pointing like fingers eastwards towards the Buddhist domain – was most exposed to Buddhist
influence. Although the Maldives clearly was a politically independent nation with its own sovereign kings, certain religious
ties must have been maintained between the Buddhist priesthood on these islands and the high priests in the part of the
world from where the religion had come. The hawittas in
Laamu atoll, whatever they had been originally, were rebuilt by
Buddhists as smaller replicas of the colossal stupas of Sri Lanka,
those built by the extremely powerful Singalese kings, the
rulers of the Lion people. The detailed Buddhist chronicles of
Sri Lanka never refer to any dominance over the Maldive group.
But it would be surprising if the mighty Buddhist rulers of that
large nation made no attempt to re-establish their own faith if a
stranger had come and told the people in the Maldives to smash
their Buddhist images and tear down their stupas.

We never went ashore on Dabidu ourselves, but Maniku
assured us that in the centre of that island lay a large but very
low mound called *Bodu Budhu Koalu*, which meant 'Big Image
Temple', with a smaller one to the east of it, *Kuda Budhu Koalu*,
'Little Image Temple'.

Although not meant to deal with the pre-Moslem period,

these old Maldive records still give us some unintended information. First of all it is apparent that the archipelago was one nation ruled from Male even before the sultanic period. When the last of the Buddhist kings was converted, he just sent his emissaries to the other atolls to have his vassal kings, willingly or not, accept the new faith.

Another deduction is no less important. The Maldives were never invaded by the Arabs in force. From the various sources we learn that a single pious Arab voyager left his home in Tabriz, and in Male he went to live at the house of an old lady with a single daughter. Only upon chasing the jinni from the sea away with the Koran was he brought to see the king. This means that the Maldive population did not change; it was the same before and after the conversion to Islam. The faith changed, but not the nation. Nothing changed except the customs, laws and rites enforced by the new religion.

'Why do you think our ancestors at that time were so willing to embrace Islam?' asked Hassan Maniku and fixed me with his sharp brown eyes as we were chatting one day in his office.

'Probably an invisible creator god made more sense to them than the limestone statues,' I suggested, unable to think of any better reason.

'No,' said Maniku. 'It was politics. Pure politics.'

'How?' I was surprised. Politics have become a substitute religion for many in the twentieth century, but this happened over six centuries ago.

'You know these islands were easy to reach by ship at that time,' said Maniku. 'Sri Lanka and most nations around us had regular navies then. Sri Lanka was tremendously powerful and too close for the comfort of the Maldive kings. If the Maldives were to change to Islam we would get Arab protection in the event that the Buddhists from Sri Lanka tried to conquer us. Our ancestors figured that the Arabs lived too far away to bother interfering with our internal affairs, yet they would protect us if Sri Lanka tried to impose their religious sovereignty on us.'

Maniku was as realistic as his own early ancestors. No miracles, no magic. Sheer political convenience. The behaviour of men has not changed much during recent millennia. It is easier to understand the people of the past if we judge them as our contemporaries. There was no reason to doubt Maniku's verdict of how the last chapter of local history began.

The converted Moslem kings inherited a well organised community from their predecessors. The copper book of *loamaafaanu* which listed the last kings of the Lunar Dynasty and all the new laws and regulations, was written by a professional scribe, Padiata, whose last sentence read: 'As great King Gadanaditya spoke thus, Padiata ... wrote this.' And then twelve of the King's ministers, including the Commander-in-Chief and the Treasurer, signed the last two copper pages of the book.

Although familiarity with Arab letters was introduced with the Koran, the Maldivians went on using their own old Divehi script. They were accordingly a literate nation even before the Arabs came. The earliest local type of letters, those used in the oldest copper books, resemble the characters in the oldest known writing system of Sri Lanka. Yet since they seem even closer to the inscriptions carved on the diabolic images of Hindu type dug up at the pagan temple in Male, they were probably in use in the Maldives even earlier than the Buddhist dominance.

In knowing that an organised kingdom, with literacy and an advanced degree of art and architecture, was active in the Maldives before the Moslem period, we have taken one step further back into the lost chapters of national history. To gain further information we may assume that Ibn Battuta arrived in time to witness many of the old customs from pre-Moslem time. As an Arab himself he would be inclined to write primarily about anything curious to a Moslem visitor, and thus less about Arab influence. For instance, Islamic society was a man's world, whereas Battuta noted a difference in the Maldives: 'One of the marvels of the Maldives is that they have for their Sovereign a woman.'

This was not an isolated instance during Ibn Battuta's visit, for Abu'l Hasan Ali, another seafaring Arab, wrote about the Maldives as early as about AD 916: 'They are all very well peopled, and are subject to a queen: for from the most ancient times the inhabitants have a rule never to allow themselves to be governed by a man.'

If we trust the legends we ourselves heard in Gadu, Gaaf-Gan had also originally been ruled by a queen, and this in a period so early that she was expelled when the cat people, *alias* the Singalese, arrived.

Ibn Battuta tells us that the Queen, then Sultana, was married to her own Chief Justice. Every day he and the other Ministers had to present themselves in her audience hall. There they made a salutation, and when the eunuchs had transmitted their respects to Her Majesty, they retired. 'The army of this Queen consists of about a thousand men of foreign birth, though some of them are natives. They come every day to the hall of audience to salute her and then go home. Their pay is in rice.'

This number of foreign soldiers, paid in rice imported from Bengal according to Battuta, reflects the habits of a nation with ample contact with the outside world. Loutfi's descent from some early royal bodyguard of tall black slaves brought from Yemen shows that this custom of importing warriors for protection was no isolated phenomenon. And the reason seems clear. Ibn Battuta describes the local islanders thus:

The inhabitants of the Maldive islands are honest and pious people, sincere in good faith and of a strong will. They eat only what is lawful, and their prayers are granted . . . In body they are weak and have no aptitude for combat or for war, and their arms are prayers. One day in that country, I ordered the right hand of a robber to be cut off; whereupon many of the natives in the audience-hall fainted away. The Indian pirates do not attack them, and cause them no alarm, for they have found that whoever takes anything of theirs is struck with a sudden calamity. When a hostile fleet comes to their shores, the marauders seize what strangers they find, but do no harm to the natives. If an idolater appropriates anything, if it be but a lime, the captain of the idolaters punishes him and beats him severely, so much does he fear the results of such an action. Were it otherwise, certainly these people would be a most contemptible foe in the eyes of their enemies, because of the weakness of their bodies . . . The islanders are good people: they abstain from what is foul, and most of them bathe twice a day, and properly too, on account of the extreme heat of the climate and the abundance of perspiration. They use a large quantity of scented oils, such as sandalwood oil, etc., and they anoint themselves with musk from *Makdashau*. It is one of their customs, when they have said the morning prayer, for every woman to go to meet her husband or son with the collyrium [eye-salve] box, rose-water, and musk oil. He smears his eye-lashes with collyrium, and rubs himself with rose-water and musk oil, and so polishes the skin and removes from his face all trace of fatigue. The clothing of these people consists of cloths. They wrap one round their loins in place of drawers, while on their backs they wear the stuffs called *wilyan* [Maldive cloak], which resembles the ihrám [Arab pilgrim's attire] . . .

When one of them marries, and goes to the house of his wife, she spreads cotton-cloths from the house-door to that of the nuptial chamber: on these cloths she places handfuls of cowries on the right and left of the path he has to follow, while she herself stands awaiting him at the door of the apart- ment . . . Their buildings are of wood, and they take care to raise the floor of the houses some height above the ground, by way of precaution against damp, owing to the humidity of the soil. This is the method they adopt: They dress the stones, each of which is of two or three cubits long, and place them in piles; across these they lay beams of the coco-tree, and after- wards raise the walls with boards. In this work they show marvellous skill. In the vestibule of the house they construct an apartment which they call *málam*, and there the master of the house sits with his friends . . .

All the inhabitants of the Maldives, be they nobles or the common folk, keep their feet bare. The streets are swept and well kept; they are shaded by trees, and the passenger walks as it were in an orchard. Albeit every person who enters a house is obliged to wash his feet with water from the jar placed near the *málam*, and rub them with a coarse fabric of *lif* [a natural web from palm crowns] placed there, after which he enters the house . . . Any newcomer who wishes to marry is at liberty to do so. When the time comes for his departure he repudiates his wife, for the people of the Maldives do not leave their country . . .

The women of these islands do not cover the head: the sovereign herself does not so. They comb the hair and tie it up on one side. Most of them wear only a cloth, covering them from the navel to the ground: the rest of the body remains uncovered. Thus attired, they promenade the markets and elsewhere. While I was invested with the dignity of *Kazí*

[Chief Justice] in these islands, I made efforts to put an end to this custom, and compel the women to clothe themselves: but I could not succeed . . . The ornaments of the Maldive women consist of bracelets: each has a certain number on both arms, indeed, so that the whole of the arm from the wrist to the elbow is covered. These trinkets are of silver: only the wives of the Sultan and his nearest relatives wear bracelets of gold. The Maldive women have also anklets, called by them *báil*, and collars of gold round the neck, called *basdarad*.[39]

Extensive overseas contacts with the outside world can be inferred from this account. Neither gold nor silver can be extracted from rocks of coral origin, there was no local clay for making the jars at the doorways, rice was not grown on these atolls, and hardly enough cotton for spreading cloth to walk on. Indeed, Ibn Battuta states that the natives barter chickens against pottery brought as cargo on ships, and he adds:

Ships export from the islands the [smoked] fish of which I have spoken, coconuts, fabrics, the *wilyan* and turbans; these last are of cotton. They export also vessels of copper, which are very common there, cowries (*wada*), and coir (*kanbar*); such is the name of the fibrous husk which envelopes the coconut . . . This cordage is used for joining the boards of their ships, and is also exported to China, India, and Yemen.

It is clear that the export of cotton turbans and copper kettles was based on local industry with imported raw materials, or perhaps in some cases a simple reshipping of ready-made goods coming from one side of the Indian Ocean and intended for re-sale on the other. Indeed, ships carrying cargo back and forth between ports in China, India and Yemen, could load and unload in the Maldives almost any merchandise from all over the world. No wonder Ibn Battuta could eat butter in the Maldive Islands in those days, that the Sultana's lieutenant gave him the choice of moving about in Male by litter or by horse, while the official himself, preceded by trumpeters and shaded by four umbrellas, walked about with pieces of silk thrown for him to step on, and covered with 'an ample robe of goat's hair of Egyptian manufacture'.

211

Ibn Battuta himself even became personally engaged in the flourishing cowrie shell trade. He sent two Maldivians with his own hoard of cowries to be sold in Bengal, but in a storm the ship lost rudder, mast, and cargo, and after much endurance they landed instead in Sri Lanka sixteen days later. Battuta subsequently left for Bengal himself, but before that he made a round trip to Sri Lanka and the west coast of India. He was under sail for nine days from the Maldives to Sri Lanka; ten days were spent sailing from Calicut on the south-west coast of India back to the Maldives; and forty-three days from the Maldives to Bengal.

All this recorded contact with other lands was taking place before Ibn Battuta's visit in AD 1344, and it reflects a long tradition of trade and seafaring by Afro-Asiatic nations in the Indian Ocean, in the centuries when mediaeval Europe believed there was an abyss at the world's end. This was a period when the Aztecs and Incas were still masters of their own domains in America.

In 1498, when Vasco da Gama sailed into the Indian Ocean and Christopher Columbus had just crossed the Atlantic, a new era began for Europe. As a result, an old era ended for both Asia and America. This had its impact even on the Maldives. The trade which had flourished freely all around the Indian Ocean since the days of the Indus Valley civilisation, became strangled by European monopoly. This is simple history, but if we look at what we Europeans changed, we will better understand what local conditions had been before.

The historian A. Gray, reviewing records of early visits to the Maldives, points out how all the lines of maritime commerce from China, Indonesia and Further India drew together until the tip of South India was rounded and the Maldives were passed. Then they diverged again with different destinations. Most ships from the east, however, upon passing the Maldives, would first call at the important harbour of Calicut in south-west India. From there they would either strike westwards across the Indian Ocean for Yemen and the Red Sea, or call at the other flourishing ports northwards to Cambay and the Indus Valley, and thence across to the Hormuz Straits. What was landed at Aden in Yemen was carried up the Red Sea for delivery to merchants in Jeddah or Cairo. What was brought to the then flourishing trading centre of Hormuz was reshipped up the Persian Gulf and the Mesopotamian rivers to Baghdad for the caravan routes to Europe.

Clearly the people of the Maldives, with their peaceful disposition and their favourable location as a midway station able to furnish water and fresh provisions, benefited greatly from this intercontinental trade in which they took a personal part. They brought their own cowries and smoked fish to ports as far apart as Bengal and Yemen. Gray shows that one of the most important itineraries for long-range Maldive merchant vessels was the route by way of Calicut to the Indus Valley and Hormuz. This would involve the unarmed Maldivians sailing into the ports of a wide variety of nations with different political systems and different religious creeds. How was that possible?

Gray gives the answer: 'A first preliminary observation is that free trade prevailed: a second, that all nations seem to have had a hand in it, no one race, as in later days, doing a disproportionate share of the carrying trade.'

He quotes the Arab traveller Abd-er-Razzak who recorded Maldive merchants among those who visited the important port of Calicut and the great emporium of Ormuz (Hormuz) during his visit in 1442:

Calicut is a perfectly secure harbour which, like that of Ormuz, brings together merchants from every city and from every country . . . Security and justice are so firmly established in this city, that the most wealthy merchants bring thither from maritime countries considerable cargoes, which they unload, and unhesitatingly send into the markets and the bazaars, without thinking in the meantime of any necessity of checking the account or of keeping watch over the goods . . . At Calicut every ship, whatever place it may come from, or wherever it may be bound, when it puts into this port is treated like other vessels, and has no trouble of any kind to put up with.

Of Ormuz (Hormuz) the same early Arab wrote that it has not its equal on the surface of the globe. Merchants from all climates make their way to this port, he says, and he mentions Egypt, Syria, Turkistan, China, Java, Pegu (Burma), Bengal, the

Maldives, Malabar, Cambay, and Zanzibar. 'Persons of all religions, and even idolaters, are found in great numbers in this city, and no injustice is permitted towards any person whatsoever.'[40]

Fifty-six years later, in 1498, Vasco da Gama arrived and he also landed in Calicut. The old Asiatic trade routes were immediately thwarted by the Portuguese blockade of that and all other ports on the coast of West India. Next Hormuz was also closed when this port was captured. Gray comments:

The Maldivians got their first practical information of the new *régime* when, in the year 1503, four of their ships had the misfortune to be sighted by Chief Captain Vicente Sodré [Vasco da Gama's Commander], then cruising off Calicut. 'When he (Sodré) was off Calicut,' Correa relates, 'he sighted four sails, which he overhauled and took. They proved to be *gundras*, barques of the Maldive Islands . . . *Gundras* are built of palm-timber, joined and fastened with pegs of wood without any bolts. The sails are made of mats of the dry leaves of the palm. These vessels were laden with cairo and *caury* . . . These vessels also carried good store of silks, both coloured and white, of divers fabrics and qualities, and many brilliant tissues of gold, made by the islanders themselves, who get the silk, gold, and cotton-thread from the numerous ships that pass among the islands on their way from the coast of Bengal to the Straits of Meca. There ships buy these stuffs from the islanders, supplying them in exchange with the materials whereof they are made. Thus are these islands a great emporium for all parts, and the Moors of India frequent them, bartering their salt and earthenware, which are not made at the islands, and also rice and silver.'[41]

On these four Maldive ships there were also about a hundred Arab passengers on their way back to Calicut with their purchases. The Portuguese emptied one of the Maldive ships, placed all the Arabs on board, covered them with dry palm leaves used as packing material for the cargo, and burnt the Arabs alive.

While the Portuguese continued their blockade of Calicut, ships from Bengal and beyond, upon leaving the Maldives,

214

avoided India and headed with their cargo direct to the Red Sea. When this became known to the Portuguese viceroy he gave orders that his son 'should proceed with the armada, and see what was going on at these islands, and whether ships could be seized'. The armada set sail for the Maldives but, trapped by the current, they ended up on Sri Lanka, where the Portuguese established themselves ashore instead. The Maldives were left in peace a few years more. But soon Portuguese pirates from India and Sri Lanka began to raid these islands, where one record shows that they seized two rich ships from Cambay. In 1519, the Portuguese despatched an armada intent on conquering the Maldives also. This fleet reached Male where the Portuguese built a fort and the commander compelled the islanders to deliver their products, 'paying for it according to his pleasure'.

Some Maldivians stole away in a boat to fetch a noted Indian corsair from the Malabar coast. They came back escorted by twelve Malabar vessels, seized the Portuguese ships which lay unmanned in Male harbour, and joined by the other islanders they entered the fort from the unprotected water-side. Thanks to the battle experience of the Indian corsairs all the Portuguese were put to the sword, and the corsairs and the islanders divided a rich booty.

Although the Portuguese continued sporadic piracy in the Maldives, real trouble began for the islanders in 1550 when their Sultan, Hassan IX, left the archipelago to join the Portuguese in India where he was converted to Christianity. This encouraged the Portuguese to come back and attempt to take over the Maldives. They failed twice, but in 1558 they succeeded in conquering Male and for fifteen years the Maldivians were under foreign rule, the only dark period in their history. This rule was granted to a hated local traitor, a Portuguese Christian with a Maldive mother, Andreas Andre, locally known as *Adiri Adiri*. The *tarikh* says:

The Maldivians then submitted to Captain Adiri Adiri, who proclaimed himself 'Sultan'. He sent Christians to take charge in all parts of the Maldives, and enforced submission. The Portuguese ruled most cruelly for several years, committing intolerable enormities. The sea grew red with Muslim blood, the people were sunk in despair. At this juncture God Almighty moved the heart of Khatib Muhammad, son of Khatib Hussain of Utimu [northernmost group] . . . to fight with the Infidels and to end the crying wrongs. Praying to God for wisdom to conquer, he took council with his younger brothers.

The *tarikh*, full of names of those who joined the revolt, tells of how a little group of sworn freedom fighters started nightly guerilla warfare throughout the archipelago until all foreigners were restricted to Male. Joined once more by volunteers from the Malabar coast, the guerilla force, under cover of night, stole into Male harbour. The next day had been fixed by the Portuguese garrison for the execution of all those who refused conversion to Christianity. But before sunrise it was Adiri Adiri who died, together with the entire Portuguese garrison.[42]

As the modern Maldive historian, our friend Hassan Maniku, expressed it: 'Every Portuguese colonist departed our shores through the portals of death, never to return to disturb the tranquillity of our independence.'[43]

'Later nobody has interfered in our internal affairs, although we were a British protectorate from 1887 to 1965,' added Maniku, and he showed me his impressive list of close to one hundred sultans and sultanas who had succeeded each other through six dynasties of Moslem history.

We, of course, had been digging in the Maldives to find out what had happened before them. A modern-day President had requested us to look for anything that would reveal what this long line of sultans had wanted their subjects to forget.

CHAPTER X

A Lost Chapter in World History

The Lions and the Bull in the Sun-temple

'THE CLIMATE is changing.'

I have heard this remark everywhere I have been on my travels around the world in the last few years. The monsoon is blowing in the wrong direction. It is raining in the dry season. And now, in the rainy season, as I returned to the Maldives for the third time, the sun was actually beaming from a blue sky. It was November. We had left here in March after our first test excavations. Now I was back in Male alone to arrange for a possible second term of archaeological work.

I was back among friends and could feel it. Maniku was still out of office, but the President had appointed Loutfi as Acting Director of the new National Council for Linguistic and Historical Research. The Chairman was the old, solemn Chief Justice who this time met me with a handshake and a smile at the door of Loutfi's new office.

In Loutfi's office an extra desk and chair had been provided for my use, and on the desk lay a stack of booklets, papers and unpublished manuscripts for me to study. The National Library was in the next door room. Now accepted as having collaborated with the former Moslem Committee, I was being given full access to all information pertaining to the Maldive past. To my surprise, a bright and beautiful little Maldive lady who spoke perfect English was brought in to serve as my translator for the Arab and Divehi texts. I was even more surprised when she told me her mother was one of the members of this Moslem Council for Research. The old Maldive respect for the other sex was certainly surviving. The young lady was married to a German husband who had accepted the Moslem faith, and he had just built a fine Maldive vessel called *Shadas* after her. It was strong, with a shallow draft for the island reefs, and he was now ready to take us anywhere within the archipelago when we resumed our digs.

My next experience was less comforting. Happy at all these promising arrangements I walked over to the National Museum to inspect the sculpted stones we had brought to Male in the *Golden Ray*. For lack of other space we had temporarily put them one by one all over the bare floor with only a narrow trail left for passage. They were still in the same room, but now haphazardly piled in towering stacks up to the windows and under the stairs. Some were broken, many had bad scratches, and crushed stone had filtered down through the pile.

I made no attempt to conceal my anguish. What had been carved at least 1,000 years ago and had survived eight centuries of deliberate destruction, had now been damaged inside the doors of a museum. When the friendly old custodian saw my despair, he explained that because the Prime Minister of Malaysia had been on a visit it had been necessary to tuck away all these 'old stones'.

Mixed in with our own stones were some large slabs of fine white marble, which were splendidly carved in relief. The style, motifs and material differed from anything we had found. Marble. There was no marble to be quarried in the Maldives. The central motif on the largest slab was the 'Tree of Life', well known from the oldest Mesopotamian religious art; but here it was flanked by reliefs of lofty temples with rows of tall windows and with stupa-like roofs. Certainly not Moslem art.

'Just been dug up,' explained the old man with visible contempt. 'In Male.' It turned out that workmen had hit upon these pieces when digging a new foundation under the old *Ma-á* mosque. They had notified Loutfi.

'We do not destroy old things any more,' said the custodian solemnly and opened the doors to the closet where we had first seen the big heads. On top of one of them now lay a tiny stone lion, the size of a fist. It had a goatee beard like the Egyptian

Sphinx, and on its back was a round depression as if intended to hold ointment or powder for ceremonial rites.

A lion! In the Maldives!

This was truly exciting.

'A man brought it from Dhigu Ra, an island in Ari atoll. He found it last week when digging a well.'

I begged the good old man to take great care of the lion, which could disappear into anybody's pocket, and hurried back to Loutfi's office. On a borrowed typewriter I hammered out a memorandum which I gave to Loutfi. It spelt out my conditions for asking Oslo University and the Kon-Tiki Museum to continue excavations in the Maldives. A principal condition was that a new museum should be built in Male to house present and future archaeological finds from the pre-Moslem period. Otherwise it would be absurd to dig up any more from the ground.

Next morning I received my own letter back from Loutfi. Under everything I had requested there were now green lines. Loutfi explained that he had sent a messenger straight to the President's Palace with my letter. It was up to the President to decide, and he agreed to everything he underlined in green. That meant he had agreed to everything. The President had only one question. Abbas Ibrahim, Minister of Presidential Affairs, had called back to Loutfi and said the President wanted to know what the Kon-Tiki Museum could do to aid in the building of the new Male Museum.

I promised to lay the matter before the board of the museum, which at least could assist with building plans and technical advice. That sufficed. Thus we had permission to come back and resume excavations once the rainy season was supposed to be over. In January.

'Come in late February,' suggested Loutfi. 'Recently the seasons seem to be delayed.'

It so happened that President Maumoon Abdul Gayoom had just been re-elected for a second term in office, and while still in Male I was invited to his inauguration ceremony. Never, except at the UN, have I seen such a gathering of diplomats from all over the world. Under a huge canvas cover at the edge of a sports field the President with his government and guests were seated to watch the Maldive guards parade in honour of their re-elected leader. The United States President had sent, in addition to the ambassador, his own personal envoy. The Russian, Chinese and Cuban ambassadors were there too. And representatives from all of the large and most of the small nations in Europe, Asia, Africa, Latin America, not to mention the brother nations of the Arab world. The young Republic has little to offer but fish and sunshine, but it is prepared as always to benefit from unrestricted friendly relations with the outside world. Throughout their history, Maldive culture has survived through business with the outside world. And, to the outside world the habitat of the 160,000 Maldive islanders still has a strategic position. It is a sort of Gibraltar between East and West.

To this gathering of representatives from the many foreign nations were also invited the chiefs from all the atolls in the archipelago. This offered a unique opportunity for me to meet, one by one, all those whom Loutfi invited to his office because he thought they might be knowledgeable about the Redin or other unpublished legends and traditions. The Redin were as real to some of these chiefs as the rubble-piles of former hawittas that lay hidden in their jungles.

Loutfi's version of history was confirmed. The Redin had first arrived at Ihavandu, the northernmost of all the Maldive islands. Ahmed Saib, chief of Ra atoll in the far north, said that people in his area were still full of Redin stories. From Ihavandu the Redin had next come to settle on Lumbo Kandu in his atoll, and from here spread to Nalandu, Milandu and Landu, all up in the northern extremity of the Maldives.

The Redin came long before any other Maldivians. Between them and the present population other people had also come, but none were as potent as the Redin, and there were many of them. They not only used sail but also oars, and therefore moved with great speed at sea. Because of this they might sleep on one island, go and pick fruit on another, and cook the meal on a third.

In some islands there were still tales of how the Redin left when the first Maldive families came, because they disliked having commerce with common people. But they came back to pick limes at night. Limes (*lumbo*) seem to have played an important part in the Redin kitchen, and the lime stories con-

220

centrate about their settlements on Lumbo Kandu and the island of Rasgetimu in the northern end of Ra atoll. Legend has it that an early ancestor from Rasgetimu had once, as a stow-away under deck, taken a quick voyage with some Redin to Lumbo Kando for limes. On return to Rasgetimu he revealed his presence without punishment and the Redin even gave him a share in their harvest. Since that time voyagers from Rasgetimu have always maintained the habit of leaving two limes on the aft deck of their dhonis. Perhaps for some such reason, Rasgetimu was considered to be a 'good luck island'. Maavadi Tuttu Be, an old shipwright from that same area who had built 150 dhonis, said that each new boat should go to be beached at Rasgetimu first, in commemoration of the Redin.[44]

There were references to Redin tombstones buried deep in the island bedrock on Alifushi island, and to other stone slabs with carvings of unknown origin on Baara island where there were still people known for their blue eyes, red hair and sharp noses. But in this northern cluster of Redin islands, Nalandu, Milandu and Landu showed the most visible remains from Redin times, said the chief from Ra. Nalandu is actually a cluster of uninhabited isles in a shallow lagoon, full of large heaps of big shells, shells like oysters, which had been cooked over fires and left by the Redin. On Milandu they had also left a very large mound of stones. Bell had heard of that mound which his informant called *Redinge Funi*, or Redin Hill, and which people were afraid to dig into because of superstition. But on Landu, I now learnt, was the biggest of all Redin mounds, the *Maabadhigé*, or 'Great Cooking Place'. It was also known to people on the neighbouring islands as the Great *Hachcha* or *Haikka*.

Only quite recently had Maldivians settled on Landu, for the first time since the Redin left. Hardly anybody else came to Landu because of the very rough anchorage and difficult land-ing. But five years ago two young Americans had been ashore and experienced how the spirits of the Redin still dominated the island. They had first visited another island in the same northern atoll and there heard of Landu where jinnis came every day for dinner and where there was a huge mound. A Maldivian took them to that island in his dhoni. One of these Americans was nearly 2 metres (over 6 feet) tall and the other, Dave Doppler,

221

who came to tell me the story in Loutfi's office, was a giant too by Maldive standards.

When these two fair strangers and their dark little Maldive companion beached on the former Redin island of Landu, all the people ran away. From their stature and colouring the unexpected visitors must have looked like the legendary idea of the Redin. As they walked up the empty village street they saw people peeping through the door cracks. They entered the unlocked island office to spend the night there. When the chief at last came out the others followed and the old people kept on pointing at the tall blond men. They were shown the house where food was left every night for the jinnis. Every morning it was gone.

Next day they went to see the great Redin mound which Dave estimated to be 15 metres (50 feet) high, in the midst of marshy land. There was no trail or track near the mound, and nobody from the village dared to follow the three visitors there. A huge banyan tree grew on top and other trees and bushes covered the slopes. There was a temple inside, Dave had been told, but he had seen nothing except big crude blocks scattered about. I met nobody else who had seen this 'Great Cooking Place' where the Redin were supposed to have lit their kitchen fires.

From these northern atolls the Redin had established themselves along the whole chain of Maldive islands right down to Addu atoll south of the Equatorial Channel. One of their last hold-outs had been Addu-Gan, where the airport engineers had now destroyed their large hawitta. But when the new inhabitants of the Maldives had come there too, the Redin had retreated for a while to Hitadu in the same atoll but right on the Equatorial Channel. Disturbed by the arrival of the new immigrants there also, they had in the end gone to live on a small islet off Hitadu, called Kabo-Hura. Here the Redin continued to perform their own rites. They danced. The people of Hitadu could hear the sound of their *dumari* trumpets when they danced. The Redin were normally peaceful, but not when they danced. When the people of Hitadu heard the trumpets some were irresistibly drawn to that place because of the sound of the ritual. When they saw the performers they became spellbound and were unable to return to their own homes. They died on Kabo-Hura. Their bones were found there when the Redin left. For the Redin did leave, they did not all die in the

Maldives. They went away in the end, but nobody knew where.

The dance the Redin performed was called *deo*. This meant 'demon' to the Maldivians although it meant 'god' to the Hindu, and old folks in Addu said that many of their ancestors died from the *deo* dance. Not only people in Hitadu but in all parts of the Maldives had died from the *deo* dance. They were naked when they danced this dance, men and women, for it was a sexual dance. They 'did things connected with sex' during this performance. The *deo* dance was prohibited now. About twenty years ago a letter was sent from Male to all the islands saying that this dance was forbidden, like alcohol and adultery.

Loutfi was born on Hitadu. He recalled from his own boyhood that there had been a small stone house with a corbel-vaulted roof left by the Redin on Kabo-Hura islet. The islet and the view from there was so beautiful that the British commander had destroyed the Redin house and built his own bungalow on the site during the Second World War.

Nobody knew how people used to die during the Redin dance, but in his book Maloney describes a traditional Maldive dance which he believes to be of Persian or West Asiatic origin. A prayer is said and incense is burnt before the drummer begins. As the music warms up and frenzy mounts, the dancer begins stabbing his own skull repeatedly with an iron spike and the blood runs. This *tára* dance may well be some remnant of the Redin *deo* dance.

Blood sacrifice, although not of human beings, was once common in the Maldives, but it was certainly of neither Moslem nor Buddhist origin. Many of our dependable informants insisted that blood sacrifice to the god of the sea, *Rannamaari*, still occasionally took place all over the archipelago. In the northern atolls strange masked dances are still performed where words from a forgotten language are used to summon supernatural beings.[45]

The blend of cultures behind the old Maldive nation became even more apparent when the chiefs explained that they followed three different calendar systems on their islands. They had the modern year divided into January, February, etc. Then they used the Islamic lunar calendar. But their own old one was the solar year of 27 months with the interpolation of an extra month every eleven years. This solar calendar year was used for

223

agriculture and by the fishermen. The astrologers who gave advice to their rulers in former times used these solar months, and many of the months were named after stars that came directly overhead during that period.

Maloney had actually been told about five Maldive calendar systems, three of which were solar. The most important he also found to be that of 27 months. He shows how this system must have come to the Maldives from the Sanskrit-speaking area of north-west India where it was originally a zodiacal system for astrology. The heavens were divided into 27 segments, each named after a particular star. Even the Maldive names for each of the 27 months were clearly derived from the Sanskrit names for the same 27 months.[46]

'What about the dhonis?' I asked the chiefs.

One observation that had puzzled me and a great many others was the standard shape of the Maldive dhonis. They had a marked 'Egyptian' form with the tall, arched and incurved bow ending as if it were in a fan-shaped papyrus blossom. This was the typical shape of the elegant reed-bundle ships shared by the world's three oldest known civilisations; in Egypt, Mesopotamia and the Indus Valley. Actually, the Maldive dhoni had even more in common with the Phoenician sailing ships which were built from planks and only retained the papyrus form of the older mother civilisations. Until very few years ago all Maldive vessels had square sails, like the ships of these earliest seafarers. We could see these square sails hoisted on some of the dhonis in the southern atolls. When, at sunrise, they sailed out of the lagoon with their lofty papyriform bows against the morning sky, it was like seeing a Phoenician fleet heading out into the ocean waves.

'Why do you have that strange bow on all your dhonis?' I asked the chiefs and the old shipwright.

'It is only for beauty.' 'It is an old tradition.' 'It has no practical purpose. We call it *moggadu* or *mulahgadu*. It is detachable so we can lift it off when it disturbs our work. It is loose and not part of the keel,' were the answers I was always given.

The ship was the only means that could have brought these people out to their islands. I knew from the beginning therefore that the standard type of dhoni would be yet another jigsaw piece in the Maldive puzzle.

As I once again sat in the airplane and watched the Maldives sliding away like leaves on a pond, I knew from my many informants that, formerly, these islands were a week's sailing away from India for the traditional Maldive ships. Not bad for that period. But today India was little more than one hour away.

Hectic days followed. Back in Oslo I barely had time to organise the return of a new expedition to the Maldives two months later. It would be my fourth visit in fourteen months.

The Kon-Tiki Museum and Oslo University showed a very positive response. Knut Haugland, my companion from the *Kon-Tiki* journey and now running the museum, was given approval by his board to cover all flight tickets to and from Male. Transport and labour inside the archipelago would be covered by the Maldive government. Oslo University gave the archaeologists leave on full pay, and the Department Head, Professor Arne Skjölsvold, agreed to come again. With him once more was his colleague Öystein Johansen, and this time a third archaeologist also, Egil Mikkelsen, the Director of Norway's National Museum of Antiquities.

In mid-February we again landed in Male, following local advice on the timing of the dry season. The rain was still pouring down. In the dry season! The sandy streets of Male were unable to absorb it all. There were more cars there on each visit, and they had to manoeuvre slowly, avoiding the deeper puddles while we ourselves hugged the walls to find patches of dry ground. For millennia the rain clouds had been bound for the dry zones in Africa. Now they had lost their former sense of direction and left the Africans dry and these islanders drenched.

'The sun will shine tomorrow,' said Loutfi, who greeted us with a broad smile. His Minister had instructed him to come with us again. 'We can leave from Male as soon as you approve the expedition ship the government proposes.'

Down in the crowded harbour he pointed out a fine little ship, with both sail and engines, which stood out among the closely packed rows of dhonis and other Maldive-built ships. Indeed, it was built from local wood and in the best of Maldive styles, but with a dash of elegance and as clean as a lady's handkerchief. Her name was on the stern: *Shadas*.

The owner was the young German husband of my Maldivian translator, Shadas. 'He built this vessel himself with the help of a Maldive shipwright and runs it with only an engine-boy and a cook,' said Loutfi.

Shadas was indeed a fine vessel, and ideal for expedition work in these waters.

I met the blue-eyed Moslem owner in Loutfi's office, a wiry and fit little German with an open, friendly face and a Moslem-style moustache as blond as his hair. He spoke to Loutfi in Divehi before he turned to me.

'My name is Muhamed Asim Simon,' he said in good English. 'I would be glad if you call me Asim.'

We agreed everything on the spot. We would pay the daily rent for his ship when we were at anchor and used it as our base; the government would pay their own agreed price for each travelling day. In record time Asim, with his bicycle and his happy Maldive cook Zakkaria, helped us provide for the expedition while his engine-boy Hassan kept watch on all these treasures as they were delivered on board.

Late one evening we were standing on the waterfront among a crowd that represented all of Male to witness Singapore Airlines landing the first Jumbo Jet in transit from the Far East to Europe. It all went well. East and West were now even closer, and the Maldives squeezed ever more in the middle. Then we gathered up our personal belongings to join Captain Asim and his two-man crew on board the *Shadas*.

The stars now began to twinkle between the clouds. High time the weather changed. Loutfi repeated his prophecy. In addition to him, the crew, and the four of us from Norway, an official representative from the Atoll Administration had joined our expedition. A new Maniku: Ibrahim Maniku Don Maniku.

As the morning sun rose above the horizon we thumped out of Male lagoon at good speed, bound south for Nilandu.

In the late afternoon we passed through the Ariyaddu Channel and, as we coasted along the reefs, Hassan pulled in three bonitos and a dolphin. We rounded Nilandu and this time we were able to make our way by lead soundings right into the lagoon. Asim and Hassan rowed in front in our rubber dinghy and Zakkaria, at the tiller of *Shadas*, followed their directions. The draught of *Shadas* was only one metre (about 3 feet). Asim found a passage where the depth was almost 3 metres, and there we floated right across the reef which was 400 metres (about 440 yards) wide. Before the sun set we had followed the inside of the reef back to Nilandu and dropped anchor a few yards away from the piers. Last time we were only able to come in here with the flat-bottomed barge.

Nilandu again.

As darkness fell we were not a little surprised to see a light twinkle rhythmically out on the reef. Two sharp flashes, a long pause, then two flashes again. A light-buoy! It was another sign of how the Maldives were racing into the technological age. We had seen nothing like this, except in Male, on our visit the previous year. And Nilandu was well away from any shipping lane, so this was just marking the reef for the benefit of the local fishermen. The buoy was powered, we learned to our increased amazement when we came ashore, by solar energy. We also learned that, since we last left, a boat from Male had been here with some Japanese visitors. No doubt this explained the miraculous light-buoy.

Ashore we noticed other changes since a year ago. The music from modern Japanese transistor radios blared and screamed at us from a number of huts in violent discord with the rustling of palms and the atmosphere of the village, the stars, the lagoon. Tastes may differ, but this to me was an unhappy blend, like drinking milk with caviar or playing Beethoven at a football match.

Perhaps the sound was set at its loudest to impress and welcome us. As we reached our little sand-filled temple mound among the palms, the noise faded away, but here too things had changed. The mound was untouched, but the sandy area around the trench where we had found the phalloid sculptures had been turned upside down like a potato field.

'They took away only one stone,' said the chief when he saw how upset we were.

'They? Who were *they*?'

'The Japanese. They came to film what you had found. And then dug like you did.'

'Were they archaeologists? Scientists?'

Nobody understood. Loutfi had to intervene. No, we learned. They were film people. They had chartered a Male boat to film what they heard we had seen.

We were not in the best of moods when we saw our 'phallus' site so disturbed. Hoping to make us happier, however, the people showed us where their visitors had buried everything they found. This was of scant service unfortunately to any archaeologist and reminded us of our digging in the Vadu refuse place. The Japanese had struck upon a deep stone-lined pit next to our trench, obviously a square relic chamber under the walls of the former fertility temple. Into that they had thrown all they had found, some phalloid stones and 'umbrella towers' similar to ours.

'A waste of time to dig here any more,' said Skjölsvold and turned to look at the untouched areas. 'What we need now is more material for carbon datings.'

We held a council on the little temple mound. There was no dissent. We all agreed that we needed no more phalloid stones or 'umbrella towers'; what we required was something to give us the date of what we had found.

Skjölsvold stretched ropes north–south across the temple mound where he wanted to trench. Another long trench was marked out by Mikkelsen and Johansen on level ground some 200 metres (220 yards) further north, where legend said the wall had passed which once enclosed the seven former temples. When workmen had been selected, Loutfi wanted to show me a place worth digging in front of the nearby mosque. An old man had told him that a huge swimming pool would be found if we dug at that place.

There was nothing to see, only a broad sandy road leading to the nearby village. But then I got a new shock. We were standing in front of the great old mosque where Loutfi and Waheed had made their interesting discovery last time. They had shown us that the foundation wall under the mosque was precisely like the one on the prehistoric temple wall we had dug up from the ground. But where was that splendid wall now?

It was gone. The beautiful stone work had been covered entirely by modern cement.

I was stunned. Loutfi was furious.

'Fanatics have done this,' he exclaimed. 'They did it because we discovered it was part of a pagan temple.'

The old pre-Moslem wall was gone forever. On one side of the mosque was now a deep pit. Here the masons had recently dug sand for their cement. At the bottom of the pit we could see the top of another buried wall.

The old people were able to tell us that beach sand had been brought in to bury the pagan bath in front of the mosque. We dug a test trench through loose sand and found the upper stone steps of an elegant stairway which led down into the ground. More men were brought with shovels. There was a half-moon shaped stone where the stairs began and a beautifully dressed and fitted line of blocks forming the upper rim of a buried structure. It was large and circular. As we dug our way down through loose sand we found broken bits of limestone, part of a Moslem tombstone and a phalloid sculpture, all thrown in with the sand to fill the structure. From the upper rim a broad flight of stairs with seven steps flanked by vertical stone walls led down to a stone bench 50 centimetres wide (about 20 inches) which ran out in a wide circle in both directions.

Just below the bench we hit water. Freshwater. It sank with the tide as we worked to clear a large segment including half the rim. The perfectly circular bath was 7.2 metres (23 feet 7 inches) in its inside diameter. Where the straight walls of the stairs and the round ones of the bath butted together, the blocks of the former had been shouldered to withstand the water pressure. The large ceremonial bath had been built with the same technical ability and aesthetic perfection as the square bath in Fua Mulaku; but here all the walls and steps had been covered with a coat of lime plaster, almost certainly at a secondary stage since the stones themselves had been smoothly dressed and polished. The compass showed that the stairs entered precisely on the south side, from a former causeway that went from the east wall of the mosque on the now cement-plastered temple foundation, straight eastwards to the nearby lagoon.

A shout from Mikkelsen and Johansen left no doubt about their trench having hit the legendary boundary wall of the former temple complex. There it was indeed. Running exactly east–west. An amusing interlude came when one of the workmen shouted that he had caught a 'modern crab' on his shovel. A hermit-crab, of the kind that normally runs around with its soft body hidden in an empty snail shell, was struggling to get up from the trench with the lid of a plastic bottle on its back.

Bits of carbon appeared. And pieces of thick pottery. '*Rumba moshi'* the workmen called it. This was the kind they used themselves for storing water in their own houses. But deeper down Mikkelsen picked up a piece of a greenish ware. *'Tashi moshi,'* said the workmen. Loutfi translated 'Chinese pottery', and that was indeed what it looked like to us too.

'Barábaro,' said Johansen, and he put the green sherd in its proper plastic bag. That was the Divehi term for 'good, fine'. This was the first Maldive word we learnt, the most useful one, and one that served also as a piece in our detective puzzle, for the Maldivians shared this word and this meaning with old Urdu, the Indo-Aryan language of the Indus Valley region.

Further down the trench the archaeologists hit upon more of the Chinese-type potsherds. It had a very special cracked green glaze and really looked like ancient ware from the Far East. They found it as well as other ware, shell fragments and carbon right down to the ground level of the old wall.

At the depth of 90 centimetres (36 inches), Mikkelsen scraped up a strange bead of red and black mosaic, oblong and perforated lengthwise. It was a delicate composition and a unique piece. Our island friends had never seen anything like it. We had. In some museum. But where?

The buried wall, which proved to be just where the old islanders indicated, enclosed the whole legendary temple area. Test pits showed that it ran in a square covering more than two acres of ground.

The wall itself provided mute information from an epoch unknown to Moslem tradition. It was built with squared stones outside and with coral fill inside, and was as wide as a man could stretch his arms. Way down inside the fill was imbedded a big limestone piece from a cornice decoration of a former temple. It was carved with a pattern of knobs and notches that resembled classic Greek design. A sophisticated temple had been built on this island, and later it had been destroyed or fallen into disuse before this pre-Moslem wall was built. Again, this confirmed our findings on Gan and Gadu.

'Two peoples seem to have succeeded each other as temple builders here,' commented Johansen. 'And both before the mosque was built.'

The temple mound indicated the same to Skjölsvold. His team had trenched the interior fill of coral sand to the bottom. Only sand, some dirt, and an odd lump of coral made up the solid pyramid. No charcoal. No relic chamber. No burial. But right down at ground level, and smack in the centre of the square base, lay a big conch. A complete marine conch placed there on purpose, perhaps for magico-religious reasons, by the architects of the building. Next to the conch lay some unusual reddish or rather ochre-coloured stones, cut to the size and shape of modern bricks. Only one was whole; they all lay tossed in as base fill among loose coral blocks. We had never seen brick-coloured sandstone like this before on these islands.

'We have it, but not much. We call it *rat-ga*, "red-stone",' explained Loutfi.

This was one of three types they could quarry. Most common was *veli-ga*, 'sand-stone', the smoky-white, coarse-grained limestone used as building blocks in the temple and all the walls we had excavated. It formed the foundation of all these islands. Then there was *hiri-ga*, or 'white-stone', which was quarried from the outer reef or the bottom of the lagoon. That was the fine-grained shiny white limestone used as outer dressing stones by the original temple builders and usually removed by the Moslems for use in their own mosques.

The presence of the red-stone, which we had never seen before, was therefore not so surprising. But these discarded red-stones had been carved as part of some decorated temple wall and not for fill where we found them.

'Two temple periods,' concluded Skjölsvold too. 'We cannot say any more until we get the conch carbon-dated.'

Next Gaaf-Gan, for our third time. We could not wait to find out whether the Japanese had also damaged the sun-temple.

Asim had a firm trust in Allah and was not afraid to take calculated risks. In the channel between Gaaf-Gan and Gadu he and Hassan rowed ahead in the dinghy, and dived, until he came back and steered *Shadas* right in over the outer reef.

'It is high tide,' he explained, 'and yet the reef is so shallow outside that the surf breaks before it reaches us.'

Then he and Hassan dived again to fasten a whole array of ropes from the ship along the bottom of the coral formations around us; so that when the tide went out we were left as sheltered as in a swimming pool of calm and crystal clear water, with coral showing above the surface all around and so little water under our keel that the largest of the colourful fishes had to swim around to get past. Porpoises tumbled in through the unsheltered channel next to us, but there was no room for them in our pool.

A boat came out with the 'owner' of Gan on board, and before we had time to ask he told us that the Japanese had been here. They had asked to see what we had found, and were taken to the great hawitta. But they had not been able to dig, said our tall friend with a broad smile, because the people of Gadu had refused to lend them pick and shovel.

The site of the sun-temple was indeed as we had left it. The great hawitta still lay there complete with the giant *kandhù* tree as a spire. Nor did we ourselves intend to open this colossal mound in search of any hidden relic chambers. That needed to be done by a major expedition able to build up walls holding the rubble from caving in when deep trenches or exploring shafts were opened. Looking instead for datable carbon and potsherds, we trenched to the bottom of all four walls outside the pyramid, and ran other trenches at intervals out into the surrounding terrain. Work was repeatedly interrupted by torrential rain which came in true tropical style. We hung a huge canvas sheet up between the trees, and under it sixty of us were cramped together, being entertained by laughter-loving workmen and drinking the water that gushed down from the canvas covering. Then the sun came out again and we were back at work.

The pieces of carbon, bone splinters and potsherds that fascinated the archaeologists did not particularly appeal to Loutfi. He was looking for bigger game, and used all the spare labour to cut trails and clearings in search of more hawittas. And he found them. In the jungle immediately surrounding the large hawitta were six more mounds, low, but some of considerable extent. On top of one of them lay large, long building blocks covered by green moss but revealing a beautiful decorative relief of staffs and concentric rings as the moss was peeled off. Shaped stones lay everywhere, and square blocks with a central pit that looked as if they could have been pedestals for posts. Dead east of the great hawitta, and only some 70 metres (230 feet) away, was a marked depression into which I almost fell. When we pulled away the ferns and branches it proved to be a half-buried ceremonial bath, circular, and built from thick dressed blocks. In addition to the smaller hawitta we had visited last time, our workmen cut a trail to another in the opposite direction, near the southern end of the island and half an hour's walk away. When we asked our friends why one huge hawitta had not sufficed for the former people of this island, they repeated what we had heard before. There had been more than one kind of people living here before the last of them were frightened away by the large cats.

Looking at the faces, and even at the physique of our friends from Gadu as we were crowded together under the canvas shelter, there was no doubt left in our minds. Here was the surviving evidence of a population mixture, from typical Semitic to Malay, from European to Negro.

After we emerged from one thunder shower I noticed something shining like metal in one of the sun-symbols that had just been excavated. The rain had washed away all the dirt, and there was a piece of copper, green with verdigris, inserted right in the centre of the sun-disc. A careful check on the other sun-symbols just brought out of the same trench showed the remains of a thin copper plug rammed in as if to mark the centre. Usually it was so eroded that only an empty pit was discernible. By chance there was one broken piece where only half the sun was left and the whole central cross-section of the stone was visible. There we saw that a pointed copper spike 8 centimetres (3⅕ inches) long and 6 millimetres (¼ inch) thick had been hammered into the stone from the centre of the solar symbol. It took little imagination to deduce that these copper spikes had been inserted in the stone to hold something precious so that it could not be easily removed, very likely a disc of shining metal, perhaps gold, covering the sun-disc inside the concentric rings.

A very tiny bead of reddish-brown colour was detected by a sharp-eyed workman as he helped to sieve the excavated dirt. It was so tiny that it would have been lost through the net of the sieve had he not caught sight of it. It looked like agate. It may have been eroded, but nonetheless it was so minute that nothing much thicker than a hair could pass through the hole. This minuteness, as well as the material, reminded me of the famous miniature beads of Lothal where archaeologists had dug up the remains of a bead factory specialising in just this kind of mini-bead. Thousands of them lay ready for export by sea.

'Moslem girls don't wear beads,' commented Loutfi.

Nor do girls lose their beads by the walls of temples, I thought. This tiny one and the larger one so cleverly composed in mosaic at Nilandu had probably decorated certain images. The images had no doubt been broken up by Moslems or by those before them who had covered the old temple decorations with plaster.

Carved stones of the strangest shapes had fallen down from above and become buried at the foot of the pyramid walls. Nearly all had been broken, and the missing parts thrown elsewhere and lost. When everything had been in its proper place this must indeed have been a most elaborately decorated temple. Some stones were cylindrical and when fitted together formed part of columns. Others were flat and semi-circular, others still were straight with classical profiles like plinths. One was even globular, with a short neck projecting at each pole. There were slabs with an elegant grid pattern, others with square and round perforations, and some had steps and stepped pyramids carved in relief, as well as in three dimensions. There were also more examples of all the types we had found on our previous visits.

Then came a big surprise. Mikkelsen had dug up the bust of a little lion in the corner between the east wall and its ramp. It had clearly been carved to be set, gargoyle-fashion, into the wall as decoration. As he brushed the soil off the lion's head he exposed a round depression carved at the apex, precisely in the manner of some of the stone lions carved in pairs at the foot of the Hittite sun-god. The purpose of this cup-shape is not known. It is one of the puzzling parallels that also found its way to several of the stone pumas carved by the Olmec founders of Mexican civilisation.

Johansen brought up from his trench a broken piece from a small statuette. The five toes of a foot could clearly be seen on it, but represented with the sole turned up and flanked by a bent knee. We turned it round in all directions until it dawned upon me:

'It is a piece of a seated Buddha, for he is sitting cross-legged with his right foot bent up next to his bent left knee. Hindu gods sometimes sit with one foot bent up but then the other hangs down.'

Then we heard a shout of excitement, turning into triumphant singing. It came from a group of workmen who were struggling to tear up the huge stump of a tree still left on one of the ramps. In the deep cavity where the roots had been lay a stone bull facing upwards. The horned animal was carved front view, standing with head, forepart and two legs shown, as if in the process of emerging from the stone. There was a strangely Mesopotamian feel to this particular carving. As a motif, however, the lion and the bull were two main symbols of divinity which ancient Mesopotamia shared with their great neighbours in India.

Next day we went to work after a full night's thunderstorm had passed over. Heavy clouds still hung around. Crazy weather for the dry season! Damp and rheumatic. A number of the workmen were missing, although they never seemed to worry much about getting wet. It was almost noon when Johansen scraped out what looked like a stone phallus but, when brushed clean, resembled more the bud of a large lotus flower. A moment later he began to yell, and his Maldive team jumped and danced around him.

It was another lion, this time a complete one with the front paws bent forwards under the head. It was roughly 40 centimetres long and 21 centimetres high (16 inches by 8¼ inches), carved as if lying down but with the hind parts merely squared to enter into the wall, as was the case with the bull and the sun-stones. Most strikingly, there was again this mysterious cup-shaped pit on top of the lion's head.

Some moments later Mikkelsen came across a third lion sculpture in the same area, but this one was only a fragment showing the feline muzzle with mouth and nostrils, and the right side of the body behind. Whoever had assailed this magnificent monument of art had done a thorough job. But it was not the Moslems. For the bull was found thrown in as part of the building material for the ramp. The Moslems had destroyed the final structure, but they did not build the ramp.

One evening as Zakkaria was preparing a late dinner, Hassan was set ashore alone on the uninhabited island to catch some fish in the lagoon. He was not afraid of jinnis or feretas, but after a while we heard him shouting wildly for Zakkaria to fetch him in the rubber dinghy. Zakkaria took some time putting aside his pots and pans, and when he finally rowed to fetch Hassan the latter was beside himself with rage and fear. A jinni had come behind him and thrown sand on his head. Hassan was still brushing it out of his hair. Perhaps a flying heron, we suggested, or a big bat. But Hassan sneered at these suggestions. Herons do not throw sand. Jinnis do. Next day in broad daylight he took Zakkaria to the place to look for footprints. There were none. Only those of Hassan's big bare feet. This convinced Hassan. Only jinnis can move on a beach without leaving tracks.

Pressed by other duties both Skjölsvold and Loutfi had to leave before the rest of us, so with *Shadas* we crossed the Equatorial Channel to the airport island of Addu-Gan.

On our way south from Gaaf-Gan we made a hasty call once more at Fua Mulaku. Nilandu and Gaaf-Gan had yielded very little variety in types of potsherds compared to what we had seen here. Understandably enough, Fua Mulaku must have been a favourite call for all foreign ships passing through the Channel, because of its fertility and its unlimited water supply.

This time we had a rowing boat carried from the beach to the larger of the two lakes which made Fua Mulaku different from all other coral atolls I had seen or heard of. Lakes do not form on coral islands, but this had once been an open atoll with a passage into an inner lagoon. Local traditions still spoke of a time when ships and rafts would sail in from the sea to find shelter where today were marshy taro fields and the lakes.

The lakes were slowly filling up, and gradually turning into bogs and taro fields. On our first visit Björn Bye and I had tried to swim on the surface of the larger lake, head above water, but we came out with our swimming trunks full of brown mud. This time Johansen and I rowed out with two islanders, scaring the tall cranes and white waterbirds up into the treetops. The lake was only some 350 metres (380 yards) long but stunningly beautiful without a ripple in the water, and in all shades of green mirroring the coconut palms, banana plants and the dense wall of foliage that closed in on the water from all sides. But merely dipping the oars to row we turned up patches of fluffy reddish-brown mud. It was so soft that our island companions dived overboard and disappeared as if into chocolate mousse. They swam right down to the bottom, coming up again like chocolate covered candy men with fistfuls of a beautiful white paste of lime.

This bigger of the two lakes, *Bodhu Kulhi*, was only a stone's throw from the seashore and must have been a dream place for early seafarers, first as an open harbour, then as a bunkering place for much needed freshwater when nature closed the entrance and washed away the salt water with the annual torrents of tropical rain. For centuries, when the freshwater was clear right down to the then lifeless coral formations, this must have been the greatest and most beautiful attraction to any sailor on the long voyage across the two halves of the Indian Ocean.

No wonder then that Björn and I had picked up such an incredible variety of potsherds when we stepped ashore the first time. As soon as the children saw me picking up a sherd they ran about and picked up others. And with some sweets for reward we soon had them delivering to us so many surface sherds that we shut up shop and put together a cloth bag full of samples. This was delivered to our friend Roland Silva in Sri Lanka.

He wrote back at that time: 'It is rather interesting to note that the dates of the specimens reflect the movement of man dating to the period of the turn of the present era. I am sure this will give much support to your proposal of an early occupation of these wonderful islands on the equator.'

In our bag of Fua Mulaku sherds the Sri Lankan experts had picked out one neck fragment of which the report said: 'The ware is similar to that of Rouletted Ware, and it probably has Hellenistic connections of *c.* 200 BC–AD 200. This sherd is important.' Some other sherds were found to be akin to Sri Lankan ceramics of the third century AD; others had a possible sixth-century derivation from the Kushan Red Polished Ware of India. Still others were referred to as, 'Miscellaneous glazed wares, most probably imported Islamic and Chinese'.[47]

East and West had met on Fua Mulaku. We were sure of finding still more on this visit by sinking several test trenches near the big hawitta. But no. Near the oldest mosque? No. In the

237

field near the village? On the edge of the taro fields? No and no. Even if we dug right through the upper layer of black humus and the next of sterile gravel down to the *veli-ga* bedrock. In some places there were no potsherds at all, and then we realised we were digging where the lagoon had been. In the other test pits we usually found one basic type of simple brick-coloured ware with little variation except in the flaring of the rim and the size of the pot. Sometimes this ware was decorated with grooves. Only occasionally did we scrape up a different, plain yellow ware, or some of the Chinese type crackle-glazed green sherds. The spectacular variety showed up only in the coral sand near the landing places, or on the surface of barren places near the village with very little soil.

There could be only one interpretation. The local people had never used such a wide variety of foreign pots. These had been left over the centuries by ships' crews who spent short periods ashore in transit or during barter. The local population, then as now, had no need of other pots than the large jars at their doors and the smaller ones used in the kitchen. These, as the early Arabs wrote and local traditions confirmed, were standard merchandise brought from ports in south-west India in exchange for cowrie shells.

Even in Fua Mulaku and on Addu atoll the weather was unseasonal, with thunder-storms and violent rain; and our return trip with *Shadas* northbound across the Equatorial Channel proved to be much more difficult than rowing on Fua Mulaku's palm-encircled lake. A full storm blew up as soon as Addu atoll was out of sight, and nowhere in the oceans are the waves more inclined to jump into a wild maelstrom than where a major current opposes them, or joins them in chasing through a channel.

We were heading back for Gan and Gaddu in Gaaf atoll to continue our excavations. Since Loutfi, together with Skjölsvold, had left us in Addu atoll, an experienced sailor from Gaddu, named Fauzi, joined us for a free ride home while serving as our pilot. Fauzi confirmed what we knew, that the currents were so strong and variable in the Maldives that one should never trust a compass so long as there is a chance of getting a bearing on visible land.

Maniku Don Maniku, our quiet companion from the Atoll

Administration, became much more talkative now that he was taking on Loutfi's role as our adviser and guide. In the heavy rolling seas he tried to make radio contact with the outside world. The range of our tiny rented transmitter was not much further than a man could shout, so he was particularly proud when he made contact with the airport island we had just left out of sight. It was raining there, he reported happily, for we had no rain. But then his voice changed. Addu atoll had received a severe gale warning from Male, and a wind of hurricane force was raging just north of the archipelago, something very rare in these waters.

The west–south-west storm in the channel rose to a gale. Asim assured us that no dhoni would leave the lagoons in this weather. Black storm clouds were rolling over us. Wind and waves were with us and the *Shadas* was pitching ahead with great speed. By 8.45 in the morning, with our eyes burning from salt water, we were catching glimpses of Fua Mulaku between the showers of spray. It was a good coast to keep away from in this kind of weather, but we needed to get close enough to adjust our course for Gaaf-Gan.

The sea was growing really rough as we crossed the equatorial line where the current swept at its greatest speed. Everything loose on deck had long since been carried below and the dinghy on the cabin roof was properly secured. Cascades of water flooded over *Shadas* from bow to stern – it was like diving overboard each time the waves hit us. Johansen was a hardy sailor but he had had stomach pains since yesterday and said he was going to his bunk. Mikkelsen came up, smiling courageously before making an offering to Neptune and hurrying down below again. Zakkaria was hanging over the gunwales whenever he sampled a spoonful of his own cooking.

A man with a plastic sack over his head and down to his knees came from the bow and told me: 'Hassan no like this', and took additional shelter by crawling in under the overturned dinghy.

Struggling to keep to his feet with his transmitter set, Maniku Don Maniku was now unable to make contact with the outside world and was visibly unhappy with our own one here among the waves. As he staggered towards his bunk he made it clear that he did not trust Asim as captain of his ship. Only Fauzi, he said, a Maldivian grown up on this Channel, could bring us safe ashore. 'Only Allah can bring us safe ashore now,' answered Asim calmly and clung with all his strength to the tiller, giving orders to Fauzi who was helping him.

'The ribs are the weakest part of this ship,' shouted Asim to me, who was acting the part of a mere spectator of this impressive show. The little vessel was dancing like a woman responding with grace to every move of the sea. If she tried to resist she would break like an eggshell. Occasionally there was a loud sound of cracking wood as some steep wave got out of step with the others in the ballet, and Asim and I exchanged faint smiles. None of us was happy. I kept wishing I was on board a reed ship. If the ribs yielded or the palm-wood planking cracked *Shadas* would sink. With our reed ships we had often danced over much higher waves than this, but with a pleasant feeling of security because we rode on a buoyant bundle which could not be filled by any tumbling breaker since the water simply ran through the bottom and out again.

I swore at the early Sumerians and Phoenicians who had abandoned their secure reed ships and taught us to build sinkable vessels!

While we were in the deep troughs of the waves we saw them curl like glassy walls with hissing, foaming crests, ready to topple over and fall down upon us. But before this happened we rode up the steep slope ourselves so that only the crest hit the sides of the vessel. It was a comforting distraction to watch the flying fish. They were unable to take off on their long gliding flights. As soon as they shot out of one wave they landed in the next, and merely jumped like frogs between the crests.

But *Shadas* put on a good performance. Her lines and dimensions made her take to the wild seas like an Arctic trawler. With an overall length of 14 metres (46 feet) she was just small enough to roll freely between the waves, or over them as they lifted her up while the tens of thousands of tons of water swept on underneath. Had *Shadas* been any longer she would probably have broken her back over or between two wave crests.

In the main sweep of the equatorial current the seas around us grew more confused and rose above our heads as unpredictably as a team of stallions. Even the wind seemed to whistle and howl more angrily in the stays. But the wilder it got around us the clearer it was that Asim's ship could stand up to it, and once again I began to feel that I had lost my childhood's vision of an evil ocean. 'The friendly ocean,' I kept on saying to myself. The sight around us was, in a sense, terrifying; yet it was also a beautiful display of Mother Nature's power and of her friendly treatment of those who lived along with her rhythm and did not fight against it.

Asim and Fauzi were masters at the tiller. At times the gale was so strong that they had to change course, slow down and ride the weather, but in the early afternoon we could see palm crowns ahead each time we were lifted on a high wave. Normally from the deck we were able to see the tops of the palms at a distance of some 10 miles, and the sand from about 3 or 4 miles away. Fauzi climbed the mast and we then adjusted our course as Fauzi said it was Gaaf-Gan. Later we discovered it was Vadu.

We seemed to be among less violent waves now. The wind also stopped whistling and howling in the stays and we guessed we were getting out of the main current, perhaps under the influence of nearby reefs. As soon as we recognised the hawitta we realised it was Vadu, so we altered course completely and coasted along with the changing weather, the reef and islands of Gaaf atoll close to our port side.

Allah was good to the faithful Asim. Dripping with salt water Asim wore a smile from ear to ear in gratitude and pride as he steered us into Gaaf lagoon and we found shelter behind Gan.

When we finally headed northwards from Gan, with three lions and a bull among our cargo, the Maldive sun was ruling high in the sky again, and the ocean god was at peace with the wind, even though the latter kept on blowing in the wrong direction.

At the prescribed hours Asim checked his watch and called Hassan to take the tiller. Alone of the five Moslems on board he knelt on deck and bowed towards Mecca. Zakkaria was cleaning fish and Maniku Don Maniku fiddling with his radio while Johansen and Mikkelsen were burning their backs sorting potsherds on deck. As the islands and reefs floated by like corks on blue and green ink I sat on the cabin roof checking their names from Hassan Maniku's little booklet with the long list. The last words in his short introduction appealed to my mood at that moment:

The mystery and suspense that the Maldives hides among the many islands and the reefs . . . the thrill and the satisfaction that one derives from the exploration of these cannot be described. It has to be savoured rather than felt. For it is the joy of seeing what has hitherto been hidden from broad view.[48]

Male again. Were we any closer to the answer to the Maldive mystery?

CHAPTER XI
Whence the Buddhists?
Into the Lion's Den

IF YOU WANT to go lion hunting you do not go to Sri Lanka, or to Norway. There are, of course, no lions in those countries, yet in Sri Lanka you can see lions' paws sculpted in antiquity which dwarf those of the Egyptian Sphinx, while the national coat of arms of Norway shows a lion standing on two legs holding an axe in its paws. Why did Sri Lanka not choose an elephant, or Norway a bear?

The answer is that ancient man travelled. He was not locked up in one area like a prisoner. The national culture he created in his own homeland was not solely bred there. Some was brought from a previous abode, some was borrowed from other nations. Indeed, ancient man was as creative as we are today, but he was also able to learn, and he was open to the influence of others. The Old World lion, and its New World equivalent, the puma, were the earliest symbols of divine royalty in every part of the world where pre-European civilisation bloomed in the last three millennia BC. It is not so strange therefore that it spread to Sri Lanka with the royal seafarers who established their kingdom on that island in the last millennium before the Christian era; nor is it surprising that the travelling Norsemen borrowed a symbol so widespread in their Mediterranean hunting grounds.

The concept of the lion even reached the Maldive atolls before the Arab horse. Indeed, the lion, the bull and the sun were decorating the great hawitta on Gaaf-Gan before it was stripped of these symbols and covered with white plaster by the last worshippers to use this legendary Redin mound in pre-Moslem times. The legends about the visiting cat people *could* be local inventions, but the buried lion sculptures testified to contact with the outside world. The lion, the bull, the lotus flower, the long-eared images, the semi-precious beads, the copper spikes, the fingerprint masonry, and the classical profiles of the hawitta plinths tied the pre-Moslem Maldive artists to the culture founders on the continents. One by one, or jointly, these elements had come to the Maldive atolls with seafarers from some other lands.

But which lands?

Ever since our first confrontation with Maldive archaeology we had been looking for pieces that matched those we had brought to the Male Museum. Between each visit to the islands all of us travelled far and wide in Asia to consult museum collections, libraries, and archaeological sites in a joint effort to fill the gaps in the Maldive puzzle.

Sri Lanka had been our first suspect. It was the nearest land, and it was from here that Bell had come to argue an early Singalese epoch in the Maldives. Sri Lanka was one of the most impressive Buddhist centres; and, of course, it was, from antiquity, the home of the Lion people.

Some of us would dread to follow early man in his old-time craft in the open seas, others would hate to enter an untrodden jungle, crawl down the tunnels to his underground caves, or follow his ascent up a vertical rock wall.

Height certainly does not seem to have bothered the former Lion people. When their King Kassapa ruled Sri Lanka in the fifth century after Christ, he perched his palace on top of the Sigiryia pinnacle. The ascent to the palace went up the vertical wall of a rocky mountain that rose like a giant cylindrical hat above the jungle roof. The 200-metre-high (about 600 feet) cliff walls were not only vertical, but in many places directly overhanging so not even a mountain goat could get a foothold. Yet the king's engineers with the means available in their days had solved the problem of access.

Today Sigiryia is a central tourist site in Sri Lanka's 'Cultural Triangle'. I went there as a tourist, but with the advantage of having the scholar responsible for the excavations as my guide. Senake Bandavanayak was himself a descendant of the Lion people and what he could tell me was the story of his own kin. I was surprised to learn that even this site was abandoned and little known until the ever intrepid H. C. P. Bell, in 1894, began to clear the jungle and started the first dig.

Through the remains of a fifth-century pleasure garden with marble fountains and ponds fed by underground aqueducts, we reached the foot of the 'Lion's Rock' and began climbing broad stairs between huge picturesque boulders. An eagle's nest and not a lion's den, I thought, as we next began to climb steep and narrow stairs which clung to the wall and led us sideways up the vertical rock face.

High up, where the cliff began to curve out to form a shelter above our heads, the king's masons had built a comfortable gallery. A narrow inclining floor, flanked by an outside parapet built from bricks and covered with glassy plaster, was as smooth and solid now as when it was built a millennium and a half ago.

Here was a well-preserved portrait gallery of the Lion people from the period. And here real excitement began for one who had been chasing in the wake of seafaring Long-ears across three oceans. For here they were, true-to-life portraits of stunningly beautiful women, half natural size. Thanks to the protection from the overhanging cliff and the high rampart, the lines and colours were as clear as if painted by a modern artist. As to elegant design and use of colour, the ancient master had very little to learn from, and much that he could teach to, his modern colleagues. Some of the finest masterpieces of decorative and descriptive art in antiquity were preserved on the plaster-covered cliff wall in King Kassapa's natural skyscraper.

No men were represented there. The models were all women, and women seemingly chosen for their extraordinary beauty. Naked but for colourful loin cloths tied around the hips well below the navel, their slim waistlines and prodigious breasts would certainly qualify them as winners of any sex-bomb contest. No wonder the rampart forming the opposite wall was covered by later inscriptions praising the beauty of the bare-breasted young ladies. Senake translated some of the texts for me. Most of them had been inscribed in Singalese by sporadic visitors from the seventh to the eleventh centuries. One man had wondered how King Kassapa dared to expose his treasured women to common eyes. Only one woman visitor of the time was less appreciative: 'A deer-eyed young woman on the mountainside arouses my anger. She has a string of pearls in her hand and in her looks she assumes rivalry with us.'

Two other maidens hold large lotus flowers, Egyptian fashion, in one hand, gracefully opening or picking the petals with the other. There are also some holding large trays filled with colourful flower arrangements. Their skin is fair. Their profiles are almost Greek, but their eyes faintly oriental. Their stately bearing, the graceful pose of their slender arms and hands, their long fingers with pointed nails, all combine with their jewellery and majestic headwear to show that they were ladies of the upper class in their society. Nobility is also indicated by a custom common to them all: they were Long-ears! They all had pierced and vastly expanded ear lobes, and filled the slots with huge discs that made the flesh of their ears dangle almost to their shoulders. Repulsive to us, but a link in our mystery.

They were richly adorned with elegant necklaces and armlets, and each wore a majestic jewel-studded head-dress that recalled the most elaborate in Maya nobility fashion. Bright-coloured stones like red agate and green jade were worked into gold frames artistically designed as sun-symbols and lotus flowers.

As in the Maldives, the solar motif and the lotus flower were used as favourite symbols by people who extended their own ears. And higher up the cliff was a lion, a symbol so important to the king that it gave the name to his entire fairy-tale abode, and even to his own people.

Beyond the gallery of the fair maidens the royal steps have crumbled away from the cliff side, but a narrow modern iron bridge took us to where the original flight of stairs still led up to a broad terrace.

Whichever way I turned I was impressed. When I turned my back to the rock I gazed upon a panoramic view of rare beauty over a hilly tropical world rolling on until the jungle was lost like a green sea against a coast of wild mountains that rose like tall islands on the horizon. When I turned away from this view I found myself between the two paws of a lion so gigantic that, before the head and chest had tumbled from their positions against the rock wall, it would have been a landmark to friend and foe from many miles distant. This feline monster was so colossal that each toe, by itself, was twice the size of a real lion. It had been built out of solid brick and then sculpted and covered with stucco with such care for detail that even the hair of the fur showed up right down to the huge sharp claws. A broad flight of stairs led up between the lion's paws, and it had once run on up through the lion's chest and head. Since this part had crumbled and laid bare the rock face, a series of iron ladders and guard rails now led the braver visitors up on to the palace ruins and to a large rock pond on the summit.

In front of the lion's paws was a modern netting-screened iron cage capable of holding a pair of real lions, although not large enough for a single paw of the man-made one dominating the terrace.

'What for?' I asked surprised.

Senake pointed up.

Up on the cliff face above our heads were some colossal nests of rock wasps.

'Sometimes they attack visitors up here,' explained Senake. 'The cages are for people, not for the wasps! It is quicker to get into the netted cage than to climb down.'

Senake thanked me for not insisting on climbing to the summit. The only thing we missed, he assured me, was seeing the huge size of the limestone building blocks King Kassapa's men had brought up on top.

Before we began the climb down I took a last look at the front legs of the lion which were outstretched. Could it be that this huge man-made lion had been inspired by the Sphinx in Egypt? After all, Egyptian papyrus ships used to frequent this island long before Kassapa built his fort. But Kassapa needed no outside inspiration for his lion; he believed he was himself descended from that species.

That story I was to learn the same night from a group of Sri Lankan scholars. Sri Lanka had a wealth of written records left by Buddhist monks who were collecting legends and historic facts more than 1,000 years ago. As in the Maldives, the texts were bound into regular books, some had pages of copper sheets hinged together, some had pages of palm leaves bound between wooden covers. Recent excavations had brought to light some precious books of thin sheets of pure gold. Apart from China, no other nation in Asia can pride itself on such a detailed history recorded meticulously over more than 2,000 years.

These old chronicles show that Sri Lanka was reached in the late sixth century BC by Aryan invaders who came by sea from the Gulf of Cambay on the north-west coast of India. These seafarers called themselves Singalese, or Lion people, because their leader, King Vijaya, claimed to have lion blood in his veins. According to this tradition, his royal grandmother had wedded a sacred lion. Upon conflict with his father the king, son of the lion, Prince Vijaya had taken to the sea in two ships with 700 followers, men, women and children. Vijaya's ships called first on some other islands, but finally they ended up on the north coast of Sri Lanka and established their first settlement near Puttalam on the west coast. The subsequent Sri Lankan calendar is counted from the year of this landing. While we, at the time, had reached our year 1982 (after Christ) the Singalese had reached their year 2525 (after Vijaya's arrival). The Lion people accordingly reached Sri Lanka about 543 BC, and their language reveals that they are of Aryan stock.

But were these Lion people the first to reach Sri Lanka?

Had nobody else managed to cross from the nearby continent before the sixth century BC?

The Singalese archaeologists have admitted there was mounting evidence that at least one earlier civilisation was already present on the island when the Lion people arrived; but little has so far been done to unravel its identity. In the Buddhist period the monks who wrote Sri Lanka's chronicles did much to erase any memory of these earlier Sri Lankans. They referred to them as three classes of 'demons': the *Yakkha*, the *Naga*, and the *Rakkhasa*, who worshipped water, fire and fertility.

As in the Maldives, these people also from religious pride try to erase their own early history, I thought to myself as I parted from my Singalese company to go to bed. But today, when modern science was finding human traces of these presumed demons, they too had to be taken into account in our search for Maldive origins. Whoever they were, I thought, they must have been descendants of boat builders, for this great island had never been linked to the continent in human times. Thus, in looking to Sri Lanka for possible pre-Moslem arrivals in the Maldives we could not concentrate solely on its Buddhist period. Even the Lion people sailed the seas before they became Buddhists, and they did not convert to Buddhism until the third century BC, that is, three centuries after their arrival. In this early period the Lion people must have maintained their ancestral religion as they brought it from the former Indus Valley civilisation, modified, perhaps, through contact and intermarriage with the Yakkhas and their contemporaries who already possessed the land.

The Yakkhas, who were they?

'The Yakkhas were the true engineers behind Sri Lanka's hydraulic civilisation,' I said to myself, repeating what one local scholar had tried to hammer into my mind a few days earlier when he insisted I read his publication.

'A crackpot,' I thought when I saw the title: 'The Ancient Hydraulic Civilisation of Sri Lanka'.

Never heard of *hydraulic* civilisations. Neolithic yes. And even megalithic. But not hydraulic. Yet the scientists who had that day shown me the impressive dams and waterworks of the Lion people had also called their culture 'hydraulic'. So apparently it was a legitimate term in this region.

If the Yakkhas had been real people like the Lion people, they must have shared their fate with the Redin of the Maldives. Like the Redin they had faded away in the memory of later invaders until they survived only in legends as mythical beings.

If the Yakkhas had left archaeological traces behind them, then the 'demons' of the land referred to in Buddhist records had very likely suffered the same fate as the American Indians when they were 'discovered' by the Christians: they were not all killed by the invaders, but through intermarriage and contact they lost their identity. Their descendants and their culture were assimilated, to live on as inherent parts of the later Singalese society. This society was characteristic for the Sri Lankan nation and for them alone. The Buddhists had done in Sri Lanka what the Moslems had done in the Maldives. They had intentionally underplayed the importance of their own national past. In their eagerness to give credit to the founder of their own religious faiths, both nations had played down the cultural level and the impressive age of their own root ancestry.

I grabbed the book from my suitcase to see what the 'crackpot' had to say about the Yakkhas. On the first page I read: 'I dedicate this book to the Yakkhas, to whom we owe a greater debt than is still realised'. The author was A. D. N. Fernando. It was a newly published copy of *Journal of the Sri Lanka Branch of the Royal Asiatic Society*,[49] of which the author was Joint Honorary Secretary. Assuredly he was not a crackpot, but a serious scholar. One sentence in particular caught my eye: 'Historical records indicate that three tribes called Rakkhasa, Yakkha and Naga were living in Sri Lanka when Prince Vijaya, the founder of the Sinhala nation landed in Sri Lanka in the sixth century BC. When he disembarked from his ship, he saw the Yakkha Princess Kuweni at the spinning wheel, seated beside a tank.'

The author cited the *Mahawamsa*, the Great Chronicle, the most important early Buddhist book of Sri Lanka.

The *Mahawamsa* states that Yakkha kings were given a respectable place in society by King Pandukabhaya [of the Lion people] and they sat on the same stage together to witness the annual celebrations of the populace. It was King Pandukabhaya who brought the country together into a single entity, with the appeasement of the Yakkhas. According to the Mahawamsa, the claims of the original Yakkha chiefs to the land of their birth were equitably settled. The Yakkhas no doubt were one with Pandukabhaya and Pandukabhaya was in turn beholden to the Yakkhas for their help from his early childhood and for their assistance and total support in unifying Sri Lanka. With the aid of their Yakkha technology he planned and executed the construction of Anuradhapura.

The walled city of Anuradhapura was thus built by the Lion people and the Yakkhas joining forces. This happened in the fourth century BC, still a century before the Lion people became Buddhists. Anuradhapura, with its colossal buildings and waterworks, became the capital and cultural centre of Sri Lanka from the moment of its founding, through the lives of 113 Singalese kings and up until the thirteenth century AD; but the senior partners in the founding of this capital, the Yakkhas, gradually disappeared into oblivion, and when the Singalese a century later turned to Buddhism, the Yakkhas became slowly degraded to demons.

As I read Fernando's report I was increasingly impressed. Here, clearly, was a brave Sri Lankan scholar who had tried to

250

penetrate the religious veil which, since mediaeval times, had shrouded the greatness of the local past. Fernando wrote: 'One must not forget that the *Mahawamsa*, the great chronicle, is essentially a Buddhist chronicle and is like the Bible to the Christians. In its writing sometimes a stand is taken to suggest that everything began with the Buddhist era, just as the Christians like to think that everything began with the chosen people.'

Fernando goes on to extract from the *Mahawamsa* evidence of an advanced degree of Yakkha civilisation. To show their skill in metallurgy, reference is made to a temple with 'gold images of 4 great kings, 32 maidens, 28 Yakkha chiefs, devas, dancing devetas playing instruments, devas with mirrors in hand and a host of other devas with flowers, lotus, swords and pitchers'.

The Yakkhas were city builders even before they helped the Lion people build Anuradhapura. The chronicles mention that Lankapura was the ancient city of Sri Lanka before the Lion people arrived. *Pura* means 'city'. *Lanka* means 'resplendent' in both Sanskrit and Pali, the ancient languages of the Indian subcontinent.

According to records the city of Lanka was engaged in revelry and gaiety to mark the marriage of the Yakkha king's daughter in his palace, when Vijaya and his lion soldiers struck. After the conquest of the Yakkha metropolis, Vijaya proceeded to establish five townships. Some, if not all, were probably in existence already, as five townships could hardly have been required for his 700 men. That the Yakkha were neither cave dwellers nor satisfied with mere makeshift shelters appears from Fernando's observations:

If we visit the old Yakkha settlement and fortress of Ariththa (presently Ritigala) we find large monoliths, but well carved to perfect rectangular shapes, each single monolith 18 feet × 6 feet × 1½ feet [in metres approximately 5.5 × 1.8 × 0.45] like table tops and well placed as if it were in a conference hall, with absence of any Buddhist religious remnants. The presence of numerous Asanagaras with huge monoliths, the prevalence of Yakkha technology in hydraulic engineering in the 4th century BC all point to the advanced state of megalithic culture of the Yakkha in the pre-Buddhist era.

From an aerial survey in 1979 Fernando discovered the ancient sixth-century BC Sri Lankan metropolis of Vijithapura. It covered 250 acres of ground. But his most important discovery of Yakkha remains came two years later. Sri Lankan engineers were then involved in a major hydraulic project to build a dam that would create a lake many miles long and drown a large valley. As the bulldozers set to work they began to scrape against bricks already in the ground, and to everybody's amazement it turned out that prehistoric engineers had made the same calculations and built a dam at the very same spot. Fernando, who saw the massive prehistoric brick wall appearing, notified the authorities, and further excavations were conducted under the supervision of Sri Lanka's Department of Archaeology.

After reading Fernando's report I went to Maduru Oya to visit this discovery myself. Here was indeed the testimony to an engineering activity that antedated the records of the Buddhist monks, yet of a magnitude that would impress a Pharaoh. The grandeur of these waterworks indeed justified the term 'hydraulic civilisation'. But the gigantic size of the stones shows that it could equally well be called megalithic. If we focus our attention on their skill with water rather than with stone, or vice versa, we fail to acknowledge the full dimensions of the technology known to these people. For the lack of a scholarly superlative I felt it legitimate to speak of a megacivilisation. And within this grouping would fall a number of those prehistoric cultural colossi that had left their ancient remains on the rivers and coasts of northern Africa and of west and south Asia.

The first objects that caught my eye were the huge blocks lining a twin gallery that ran right through the 10-metre-high (about 33 feet) brick wall that once shut off the valley. The separate openings of these two parallel outlets were formed by three enormous stones set on end and covered by a single monolith of massive dressed granite that weighed over 15 tons. There was more than ample room for a man to crawl comfortably through these square tunnels lined with megalithic blocks. To reduce the pressure on the ceiling the massive brick structure of the dam wall was built with a gable arch above each gallery, an ancient technique known, as Fernando points out, from the Middle East to pre-Columbian America. Like so many other prehistoric dams left by the Lion people or their predecessors in Sri Lanka, the main achievement was to overcome the problem of regulating the flow of water from the artificial lakes which measured 10 kilometres (6 miles) or more in length. Millions of tons of water had to be controlled in times of flood and drought to serve the many miles of irrigation canals in the dry lands down below. The ability to tame such vast masses of water was a device described by Fernando as the key to the Yakkha success: 'This key was the controlling valve or sluice. This was the master invention that made it possible for the development of the hydraulic civilisation in our country. In Sri Lanka, it is called the *bisokotuwa*, a totally indigenous innovation.'

The *bisokotuwa* is a vertical shaft with a square cross-section built into the dam wall and enclosing a wooden valve which can be raised and lowered. It divides the water conduit into an inflow and an outflow channel that could be regulated. The recently discovered dam had this shaft faced smoothly with granite and encased in broad flat bricks bonded with resin. Outside again was an extra covering of watertight clay mixed with sand. Describing the complicated system of the twin inlets, Fernando remarked: 'The area of cross-section of the inlet is smaller than the area of cross-section of the outlet conforming to the well-known principle of hydraulics in the construction of sluices. In short the ancients were fully aware of the scientific and technological principles involved in such construction.'

During excavations part of the valve shaft had collapsed and exposed to view a beautifully sculpted terracotta relief plaque never meant to be seen by human eyes as it was encased in the inner chamber. The plaque measured roughly 1 metre by 1.5 metres, and was of a Yakkha cult depicting five figures who appeared to be dancing devetas. 'It was as if these dancing devetas were heralding the waters that rushed past them to the outer world to feed the rice fields below.' They were dancing between two perfectly executed cylindrical columns of classical form with square plinths. The author finds a similarity to the relief-moulded animalistic figures on walls in seventh-century BC Babylon, but these Sri Lankan terracotta relief figures 'are executed on bricks laid together with hardly any spacing between and held together with natural resin. The small human figures that are carved are of extremely fine quality. They are neither plastered nor glazed and appear to be tool cut and worked on the brick itself by a Master Craftsman'.

According to Fernando, the relief plaques appear to have been used in a ritual ceremony before being locked up, as the figures had been slightly defaced by a blunt tool but with no intention of total destruction. Outside the shaft, and on either side of it, were found two other terracotta sculptures, smaller but similarly cut with great skill as high reliefs on tiles. Each represented an image head of the Yakkha cult. The round face and rather demonic features were not unlike the pre-Buddhist demon-gods of the Maldives. The resemblance was even enhanced by these Yakkha images having extended ear lobes with huge plugs.

The absence of any written record or of any Buddhist remains at the site, together with the very nature of the dam construction and the actual evidence of Yakkha rituals both within the sluice and outside it, place the date of construction before the period of Buddhist influence. The Yakkha, then, were a highly organised and technologically advanced people.

As will be recalled, the oldest known practice of ear extension can be traced back to the mariners of Lothal, the port of Mohenjo-Daro in north-west India. The Yakkha then, like the subsequent Lion people, were part of the great family of civilisations which, in one way or another, had benefited from the influence of the Indus Valley civilisation.

A question naturally arises. How great was the ethnic and cultural difference between the Lion people and the Yakkhas, who preceded them and were apparently so easily absorbed? Could it be that both represented people of much the same Indo-Aryan stock that followed each other in successive migrations down the west coast of India?

I was beginning to suspect that the answer to this question had a bearing also on the Maldive riddle.

I was lucky enough to be taken to Anuradhapura by no less an authority than Roland Silva, the architect–archaeologist in charge of excavations and reconstructions of the whole of Sri Lanka's Cultural Triangle. We had become friends since we first met in Björn Bye's home while planning our first visit to the Maldives. With such a guide the old metropolis seemed to come back to life; walls rose and got back their roofs, and the colourful crowds of visitors filled the streets and steps of the sanctuaries, as in olden times. What we could see were enormous vaulted domes which rose like gigantic igloos above the forest, some whitewashed and shining in the sun, others conquered by the jungle growth to resemble grassy hillocks. It was a fairy-tale world that, with ample reason, drew spectators from all over the world, although Sri Lankans themselves were now in the majority. They were all impressed at the almost incredible dimensions of these structures built by man in bygone centuries when no force other than elephants and combined man-power was available to the architects and engineers. Here were well-preserved stupas, also called dagobas, built in the first centuries AD yet larger than any of the buildings of the contemporary Roman Empire. Each was built as a solid mound of brick vaulted like a soap bubble with mathematical precision, yet enshrining nothing larger than some relics of the Buddha. The bulkiest of them all, the Jetavana stupa, was completed in the third century AD with a height of almost 120 metres (nearly 400 feet), at which time there were no larger buildings in the world except the two greatest pyramids of Egypt.

Roland Silva pointed to a group of young girls all in brightly coloured robes. The people of the past must have dressed much like that, the women in saris and the men with dhotis wrapped around their waists. The *Mahawamsa* chronicle states that Anuradhapura, in addition to all its colossal shrines, had four outer suburbs, large monasteries, hospitals, hot baths, a public cemetery, and the king employed 500 street-sweepers and 200 sewage cleaners. No mean city. I had to agree with my distinguished guide that the local sense of aesthetics reached a climax in an elegant WC where the marble floor itself was an artistic masterpiece of relief sculpture surrounding two neat pedestals above a sunken conduit.

The hydraulic system functioned thanks to the Yakkha and Singalese founders of the city who had dug out a swampy area and built a dam. From the reservoir water streamed through clay pipes and open conduits into the city aqueducts and the irrigation canals of the entire surrounding district. The monks had even built a swimming pool larger than Olympic dimensions for their own ritual and pleasure bathing.

Page 1: A basketful of money. The Maldive boy shows the local variety of cowrie shell which was formerly cultivated on palm leaves in the lagoon and exported by ship loads to serve as currency and charms among widely scattered nations in Asia and Africa. Maldive 'money shells' have been found hoarded with burials from 1500 BC in the Indus Valley harbour city of Lothal, and through Arab and Finnish-Ugric middlemen a few specimens had even reached the Atlantic coast of Arctic Norway by AD 600, prior to the Viking voyages.

Page 2: A variety of sculptured stones fallen from the former facing walls lay on the ground or below the surface around the pyramidal mound of Gaaf-Gan. Most common was the sun motif which appeared in various forms and compositions *(a, b, d)*. A single stone *(c)* was carved like a giant shell. The religious decor on stones found protected underground was often partly or entirely covered by a thick coat of plaster, as for example the winged sun shown in *(b)*. The once sacred symbols had been covered up in a secondary period when voyagers with another faith had arrived to rebuild and reuse the old structures. This could have happened when the Buddhists arrived and converted pre-existing temples into stupa, for when the Moslems arrived they never used these mounds, but destroyed them.

Page 3: The traditional dhoni was built locally for traffic between the islands. The square sail *(above)* was formerly universal in the Maldives, but now yields to the modern lateen rig, as seen below where workmen load archaeological material from Nilandu for transport to the National Museum in Male.

Page 4: The peculiar fitted stone masonry of the walled mounds and sunken baths was the work of the legendary *Redin* according to Maldivian traditions. Whoever the Redin might have been, they were certainly great architects and master masons. They left behind colossal structures and evidence of a specialised masonry technique otherwise characteristic of some of the world's earliest civilisations. The walls the Redin had built around their lofty temples had been stripped in the Islamic period, but the walls of the sunken baths had usually been buried complete.

Page 5: Loutfi with the head of a Hindu water god found among ravaged ruins in the jungle of Kondai island. The limestone head represents the important Hindu god *Makara* in its oldest and least modified form, typical of highland Nepal. Characteristic features of the head are the curled snout, large molar teeth, a plumed crown, and a mean expression in the monster's slanting eyes.

Page 6: A pre-Moslem ancestor gallery excavated in the Maldives. They all antedate the twelfth century when Islamic law abolished human portraits. The curly-haired Buddha *(lower left)* was born as a Hindu prince and thus inherited the royal Hindu custom of ear extension, which the Hindu nobles and their ancestor gods had copied from the original sun-worshippers of the Indus Valley civilisation. Who were the long-eared gentlemen with moustaches and feline corner teeth who navigated the Indian Ocean before Islamic and even before Buddhistic times?

Page 7, a: Sun symbols were just as common as they were special for the islands along the Equatorial Channel, whereas the Ox sculpture *(b)* was found alone inside the rubble fill of the Gaaf-Gan temple mound. Like the lion sculptures from the same temple, the hind part of the ox was shaped as a square block to be inserted in the wall, leaving only the forepart emerging in high relief. The horns were carved as on an Indian water buffalo.

c: The spool-shaped earplugs extending the lobes of the ancient images were like those excavated archaeologically in the pre-historic Indus Valley port of Lothal.

d: When we discovered the missing fragments of a stone plaque with rows of pictograms and symbols on the equatorial island of Vadu, we found one important clue to the complex origins of the Maldivians. A strikingly similar plaque had been found on the northern tip of Sri Lanka which had originally been settled from the Gulf of Cambay in north-west India. Our discovery thus confirmed ancient written records in India and Sri Lanka sug-gesting that the old Indus Valley harbour city of Bharuch had been the home port of the 'Lion people' who landed on the northern tip of Sri Lanka, as well as one major branch of the earliest settlers in the Maldives.

Page 8: Farewell to the Maldives. The sun-god of antiquity follows its eternal path across the equatorial sky. This once sacred highway led us straight to our first discoveries, just as it would have guided the first sun-worshipping mariners who had to pass through the Equatorial Channel of the Maldives when they spread civilisation around the southern tip of the Indian subcontinent.

As with so many other prehistoric cities of the same epoch, a modern visitor could not avoid feeling the unity of mankind through time and space. The last millennium of technological progress has changed the world around us more than it has affected the sentiments which our daily environment imposes upon us. Inside and outside their city walls, the long-eared Lion people of Sri Lanka, their nobility and priesthood, their scholars and scribes, their architects and doctors, their farmers, miners and sailors, their potters, weavers and painters, their carpenters, smiths and gem makers were all there with their work and struggle, with their appetites for food and love, with dreams of health, wealth and security which some possessed, others did not, then just as now.

'We have not been able to match this type of architectural and engineering skill even in modern times,' said Roland Silva as we walked up the steps to a platform supporting a huge stupa.

'This building is about 370 feet high and built 2,200 years ago. With all our modern aids we are still struggling to get over the 200-foot level in building construction. Our tallest building in Colombo today is a bank 212 feet high.'

We were walking along the raised platform supporting the colossal white hemisphere, and everybody around us was looking up to see the giant egg-shaped dome with its stupa tower against the sky. I began instead to look down at the large slabs that formed the stone pavement we walked on. They were big, but they did not all seem to be of the same kind of stone, nor were they cut to match. Then suddenly I noticed a slab that made me halt. I called Silva back. We had stepped on an old stone with a relief clearly visible; the symbol of the sun carved as concentric rings around a central disc. But Silva could not explain how that one slab had such a design while the others had none.

I began nosing around the platform, and soon I detected some other slabs with the identical motif. In one place there was a cluster of them haphazardly placed among other slabs, none of which seemed to have been originally cut to fit together.

'These are reused slabs,' I said, and Silva agreed. Surely they had not originally been carved to serve as pavement. I told him that I recognised the motif. It was as if these slabs had actually been removed from the walls of the large hawitta on Gaaf-Gan.

258

There were no such sun-stones in the walls of the stupa, and none in any of the ruined buildings we had visited here in Sri Lanka. I had been particularly careful to search for parallels to the Maldives. And here they were.

'These slabs are reused,' I repeated to Silva who was admittedly puzzled at their presence. 'They have been taken from an earlier temple by the builders of this Buddhist stupa.'

Silva called a colleague. None of them had previously paid attention to these stones. They admitted they must have belonged to some other building originally, but nobody had searched for pre-Buddhist remains in this area. Yet they should be expected, for Anuradhapura had been founded as Sri Lanka's capital before it became a Buddhist centre. Nobody knew where the temples were which the Yakkha and the Lion people must have built when they founded the city. The printed guide to the site merely stated that, before the first stupa was built, there had been a pre-Buddhist shrine at the site called the 'House of Great Sacrifice'.

Not a stone was visible in the stupa itself as the entire dome was covered by a thick coat of shining white plaster. It had cost 100 million rupees for UNESCO to repair and strengthen this Buddhist structure. In the future there might also be means enough to search for remains of the earlier temple from the pre-Buddhist period. Perhaps it could be found in the immediate vicinity. Perhaps the remains were already locked up as fill inside the massive stupas; but that latter alternative only came to my mind later when we found that the original hawitta on Gaaf-Gan had also been covered by a coat of white plaster on top of the older sun-stones. Hidden inside lay the lion sculptures as mere fill.

However, on this visit to Sri Lanka, neither we nor anybody else yet suspected that three small lion sculptures lay buried inside the Maldive hawitta. For this reason I saw no connection when I noted a regular stock of lion sculptures on the platform of the large stupa at Anuradhapura. Together with other sculptured building stones they lay huddled together in the open, as if for temporary storage more than for exhibit. They apparently belonged nowhere, as there was no place for them on this plain unornamented stupa. These left-over or displaced sculptures included complete lion statues, lion heads, and lion reliefs. One lion had the concentric rings of the sun-symbol on its chest, others had the same symbol on their joints or on a raised paw. One relief showed the sun-symbol enclosed in a curl formed by the tail of the lion. They all seemed to have been found out of context. Were they of Buddhist origin, or from the pre-Buddhist period of the original Lion people?

'Remember that Buddha's family name was Sakyamuni,' said Silva, 'and that family name was traditionally linked with the lion and the sun, so the sun-symbols could be Buddhist.'

I knew. Silva had shown me the huge sculpture of the sleeping Buddha in nearby Polonnaruva. The long-eared stone giant rests with his head on a lion-decorated pillow and has concentric circles as sun-symbols on the soles of his feet. Both the lion and the sun were Buddha's legendary ancestors, because the lion and the sun were believed to be the progenitors of the royal Hindu lines from which Buddha descended.

This complicated our efforts to solve the Maldive mystery in the months that followed. Who is who among the priestly descendants of the lion and the sun? Buddhists or Hindu? Where did one line end and the other begin? Whenever I tried to find a way through the tangled mystery, the lion and the sun, as well as the lotus flower and the Long-ears, would reappear together. Their tracks seemed to run in an enclosed ring like a knot that had no loose end with which to tie up the pre-Moslem epoch of the Maldives.

CHAPTER XII
Following Footprints
Buddha's Road from a Hindu Cradle

IN THE SEASONS between our busy digs in the Maldives, our team of travelling detectives spread out to learn more about Buddhist, Hindu and early sun-worshippers' remains in India, Pakistan, Nepal, Thailand, Burma, Malaysia, Singapore, Indonesia and the Philippines. Gradually it became increasingly apparent that the theory that all pre-Moslem activity in the Maldives could be ascribed to Buddhist arrivals from Sri Lanka left many gaps and unexplained facts. The Maldivians themselves had never looked upon their Sri Lankan neighbours as their paternal kin; but, more conclusive, perhaps, there was not a single reference to the Maldive Islands in the chronicles of Sri Lanka. Yet these were very detailed and covered all events of even the least national importance from the time that the Buddhist monks brought their beliefs to the island. Had Sri Lankan monks known of the large Maldive hawittas or been affiliated with the local kings and priesthood this would surely have been worthy of mention in the rich Singalese literature.

In spite of this silence, the Maldive hawittas, in their final phase, had been converted to plaster-covered stupas. And Buddha images in stone and bronze had now been found in these atolls.

Failing to find a loose end in the tangle I grabbed at a conspicuous knot in the string of lion descendants – Buddha himself. In spite of his mythical or symbolic descent, Buddha was no more a fairy-tale being than were the subsequent founders of Christianity and Islam. Buddha's background must somehow have a bearing on the riddle.

Buddha was born in Nepal or northern India about 563 BC, son of a Hindu king of the Sakyamuni line. His childhood name was Siddhartha. He grew up in luxury and comfort, and among the ceremonies he had to undergo as a Hindu Prince was having his ear lobes pierced and extended according to ancestral tradition. He was married and even had a son by the time he began to be overtaken by a great sense of compassion for human suffering. He left his family and for years took up a life of self-denial and meditation until his life was changed yet again. One day he was sitting as a common vagrant under a large *bodhi* tree when he felt he became 'enlightened' and awoke to the *Darma*, the 'Ultimate Truth'. To share this truth with the rest of mankind he wandered and travelled for the rest of his life with his selected followers, all living as beggars, teaching reincarnation and preaching the Eightfold Path to Supreme Enlightenment. Their moral concerns were, above all, honesty, modesty, right means of livelihood and right meditation.

He died in 483 BC. To his followers, who announced him as the sacred Buddha, he passed into the *Nirvana*, while they continued to travel far and wide by land and sea to spread his teachings.

According to the early Sri Lankan records, written by monks in the fourth century AD, either Buddha himself or one of his associates during Buddha's lifetime, was believed to have visited Sri Lanka three times. These three visits were thus ascribed to a period centuries before the Singalese themselves were ultimately converted to Buddhism.

But how did the teachings of Buddha reach the Maldives? This question has a bearing on early international communication on and around the Indian subcontinent. The various possibilities are revealed when we consider the main cultural upwellings on the mainland.

The 'zero year' of Indian civilisation was experienced by those who lived in the Indus Valley about 3000 BC. Give or take a hundred years that was the time when the world's three great river valley civilisations suddenly emerged at a reed ship journey's distance from each other: in the Indus Valley, Mesopotamia and Egypt. They all appeared abruptly, and at the peak of their cultural evolution. If we accept the Hindu teachings from their first written records, there were still older civilisations somewhere else on this planet at an earlier epoch. But until we can prove differently from archaeological remains, civilised man suddenly appeared 5,000 years ago, when he began to build cities like Amri, Kot Diji, Mohenjo-Daro, and Harappa in the Indus Valley. He was already a seafarer too, building ports along the river banks and along the coasts of the Indian Ocean.

For more than 1,000 years the Indus Valley civilisation grew and expanded to cover a vast territory, and with its maritime trade extending down the coasts of India and into the inner reaches of the Persian Gulf. Then, equally suddenly, this great civilisation collapsed. From about 1500 BC onwards all the Indus Valley cities and ports were abandoned.

We have constantly been told that the Indus Valley civilisation disappeared without a trace, but that is not true. A civilisation that has dominated much of a continent for over a millennium can neither die nor disappear without leaving an impact on the surrounding nations. Today we know this to be the case. It is becoming ever more evident that, when the original Indus Valley civilisation broke up and disappeared, a series of regional cultures took over and developed along their own lines.

This new period marked the formative stages of the traditional Hindu society and, as part of this cultural survival, a second urban civilisation appeared where the upper reaches of the Indus river approached the upper reaches of the river Ganges. And it was to this inland civilisation, in the fertile valleys between the two sacred rivers, that the royal Sakyamuni family belonged. In accordance with their ancestral mythology they claimed descent from the lion and the sun. In the sixth century BC the heirs to that family gave birth to Prince Siddhartha, the later Buddha. It is tempting to use Buddhist terminology figuratively and describe the cultural environment of Buddha as a 'reincarnation' of the lost Indus Valley civilisation. There is, at any rate, a clear geographical and chronological link which should not be overlooked.

A large gap remains, however, between Buddha's cultural environment at the foot of the Himalayas and the puzzling presence of Buddha statues in the Maldives. But early man travelled. In the fourth century BC Alexander the Great marched from Greece to the Indus Valley and sent his army back by sea from the river Indus to Mesopotamia without leaving any permanent impression on Indian culture. But shortly afterwards a local Indian warlord, King Chandragupta (*c.* 320–296

BC), rose to power and founded the Mauryan Empire by conquering most of the Indian subcontinent. With his grandson, Ashoka, we come back to the story of Buddha and the knot of our riddle.

King Ashoka came to the throne in 270 BC and before his death ruled over an area from Afghanistan to Bangladesh and from Mysore in south India to the Himalayas. During his reign he conquered the country of Kalinga on the west coast of India, which was an important trading partner of pre-Buddhist Sri Lanka. According to Sri Lankan chronicles, in this bloody war 100,000 men were slain in battle and many times that number died. The victorious emperor was so anguished by the horrors he had caused that be became converted to Buddhism. From then on the life of King Ashoka was devoted to spreading the message of Buddha. His son Mahinda became a missionary monk, converting people to Buddhism throughout south-east India. In about 250 BC his travels eventually brought him to Sri Lanka. He landed in Mihintale, 15 kilometres (9 miles) east of Anuradhapura, where King Tissa of the Lion people was then ruling.

King Tissa, in fear of the powerful mainland monarch, wanted to become a Buddhist, but according to the chronicles the monk did not care to convert any fool to the new faith and he intended to put the king to a test:

'What is the name of this tree, O King?'

'It is a mango-tree.'

'Are there any other mango-trees beside this?'

'Yes, there are many mango-trees.'

'Are there other trees apart from this mango and the other mango-trees?'

'There are many trees, but they are not mangoes.'

'Besides those mango-trees and the trees that are not mangoes, are there any other trees?'

The king answered this final question correctly and was converted by the monk. His answer was:

'Yes, there is *this* mango-tree.'

Whether or not Buddha himself came to Sri Lanka it is believed that he left his footprints in the rock there. But so did Adam, and so did the god Shiva of the Hindus. In chronological order the early Hindus, Buddhists and Moslems (who share Adam with the Jews and the Christians) have laid claim to the same sacred footprints on Sri Lanka. The fame of these footprints even reached the Maldives. During his two sojourns in the Sultanate of the Maldives between 1343 and 1346, Ibn Battuta speaks of two Moslem fakirs who returned to those islands after 'visiting the Foot of Adam in the island of Serendíb' (i.e. Sri Lanka). Ibn Battuta later went to see the 'Foot' himself.[50]

As if the natural depressions that resembled large and small footprints did not suffice to fill the needs of early worshippers, they began to manufacture other sacred footprints that could conveniently be placed in their temples. When I tried to follow the spread of such footprints I found that they were even older and more common among the Hindu worshippers in southern India. It was as if the last foot was set ready for a jump to Sri Lanka on the tiny rock island of Sri Pada in the ocean just off the southernmost tip of India. Here the Hindu worshippers had built a temple around a slightly oval and rusty coloured depression in the rock. According to Hindu mythology this was the footmark left by the goddess Parvati as she attempted to obtain the hand of the primal god Shiva. Worshippers from far parts of the country would come to the southern tip of India to venerate the footprint on this rock. But I could not help wondering why the goddess, to obtain the hand of Shiva, should step out on to this rock island off the southern tip of the continent. Did that first lord of Hindu mythology come from the sea?

Of all these Hindu and Buddhist footprints none pointed more clearly towards the Maldive Islands than a large and beautiful pair set neatly side by side on a stone plaque found on Sri Lanka. The plaque was hanging in the entrance hall of Sri Lanka's National Museum, one of the largest and oldest museums in Asia. It had been found at Kantarodai near Jaffna on the extreme northern tip of this pear-shaped island, that is, as far away from the Maldives and as close to the Indian mainland as it is possible to come. Yet the link to the Maldives was as clear as any fingerprint. On this plaque were nearly all the strange signs we had taken for hieroglyphic writing when we found them on the broken fragments of limestone in the Male Museum. Here, in Sri Lanka's National Museum, the plaque was complete and given a place of honour in the entrance hall. In the Maldives it was broken, had pieces missing, and was hidden from sight behind the door of the closet containing Hindu and Buddhist images.

Here were the same symbols: the fish-hook, the conch, the fish, the jar, even the sun-wheel and the frame with lotus motif and row of swastikas. But the signs were scattered about on the plaque in no order. On the Maldive fragment they were grouped together in a line, like script. In both cases, however, they were obviously symbolic and not merely decorative.

On the Sri Lanka specimen they were carved as if to increase the magic strength of the elegantly carved impression of two large feet. 'A double *paduka*,' explained the helpful lady Director of the Museum. 'A pair of Buddha's footmarks.'

On the Maldive fragments it was difficult to detect any footprints until we found the missing pieces in Vadu. When all the pieces were fitted together the outlines of two large feet appeared. In the same refuse pit we also dug up a chunk of broken limestone which had a carved depression of a single footmark but with no decoration or symbols.

But were all these footprints intended to represent those of Buddha?

Very likely. But not definitely so. Hindu images were also found in the Maldives. And the Sri Lankan plaque had been found at the northern tip of the island where the Tamils predominate. The Tamils have remained Hindu right up to the present day. And Tamil kings also reigned for a time in Sri Lanka. After King Tissa was converted to Buddhism in about 250 BC, his descendants lost the throne, but the official tourist guide to the former capital of Anuradhapura scarcely acknowledges the interregnum: 'After King Tissa we pass on quickly to the reign of Elara. Just as the Singalese arrived in Sri Lanka four centuries before, now a new wave of invasion from India arrived, which put Tamil kings on the throne.'

These Tamil kings, in fact, ruled Sri Lanka until 161 BC when the throne returned to the Singalese. More than likely, since this faith survives among their descendants, these Tamils were Hindu. No fixed date can be assigned to the old plaque on the wall in the National Museum, however. It carries no information but that it predates the period of Buddhist images in Sri Lanka and must belong to a very early period.

There is, indeed, recorded evidence that some kind of sacred footprints were already found on Sri Lanka by the early Singalese. When King Gajabahu, who reigned from AD 114–136, built the 115-metre (380-feet) high stupa of Abhayagiri, he built it over an existing footprint then assumed to have been left by the Buddha. This made Fa Hien, a fifth-century visitor to the capital of Sri Lanka, assume that: 'The Buddha came to this country and by his supernatural powers placed one foot in the north of the royal city, and the other over the top of the mountain.' This mountain footprint was that which Ibn Battuta considered had been left by Adam, and which the Hindus maintained was that of Shiva.

Who had carved the plaques now discovered with the strange signs on the footprints; or, if they were not carved locally, who had carried them to such widely separated places as the northern tip of Sri Lanka and the shores of the Equatorial Channel in the Maldives? The reactions to our finds of the first religious footprints in the Maldives suggested that we should leave the answer to others, for Moslem, Singalese and Tamil opinions are involved, not to mention those of Christian scholars of the school which is touchy about the subject of ocean travelling before Columbus. At this point it will suffice to state that on these occasions pre-European, indeed pre-Islamic, seafarers had been able literally to carve their footprints in stone, footprints which are covered with signs and symbols that nobody can ascribe to coincidence or to the similarity of climate or the human mind.

Seen one by one the symbols on these stone plaques could be independently devised: the sun-wheel, the swastika, the lotus motif, the fish, the fish-hook, the conch, the jar, etc. But put them all together on a pair of footprints carved on a stone plaque, and coincidence can be excluded. On the Maldive plaque the small signs are carved in a line like writing, while only the large central sun-wheel and the lotus petals and swastika are used as combined symbols and decoration. On the Sri Lankan specimen the little signs are scattered independently over the surface as if no concept of script is present and the symbols have retained only magico-religious significance. Advanced forms of phonetic script had been developed both in Sri Lanka and in the Maldives in the epoch when these tablets

267

were carved. Why did none of them write in their own characters any sacred phrase or message that they wished to convey?

Clearly these symbols represented the survival of a proto-script or pictorial way of conveying thoughts to an already initiated viewer. Were these signs carved by Buddhists or by Hindus? I have tested them on people of both religions, and each recognises them as symbols belonging to their own faith. In that case, the Buddhists must have inherited them from the Hindus. For Buddha was a Hindu reformist who carried on much of the tradition in which he was brought up, just as the later Christians, and after them the Moslems, never totally abandoned the old Hebrew Testament.

How much the Hindus must have passed on to the Buddhists began to dawn upon me when the task came to separate the footprints of the one from those of the other.

The sun-wheel on the plaque was seen by Sri Lankan Buddhists as the sign of Buddha, for it was the symbol of his mythical solar descent. But in the provincial museum of Trivandrum in southern India I was shown a tall bronze statue of the Hindu god Vishnu. He was long-eared like Buddha, had a sun-disc on his back and held in one hand a large sun-wheel with spokes, just like the one carved on the footprint plaques of Sri Lanka and the Maldives.

'This sun-wheel we call a *chakra*,' explained the local curator. 'It is a very common symbol in our Hindu religion.'

Next to this big bronze image was an equally large wooden statue of the same god, Vishnu, covered with sun-symbols and with a large sun over his head. In his left hand he carried a conch.

'The conch is the special symbol of Vishnu. We call it *shanka*,' said the curator. 'All the gods are descended from the sun, but *shanka* is the special symbol for the god Vishnu.'

Other visitors joined us and wondered why I was so interested in Hindu signs. I pulled out a photograph of the slab fragment from the Maldives, and showed them the carvings of the sun-wheel and the conch. One of them pointed to the pot with three arrows.

'That is a *purna ghata*, it means a full pot,' he said. 'A vase of plenty,' another tried to explain.

These people were not scientists. But to them this was not science. It was their religion.

'And these two fish-hooks?' I asked.

'One is a fish-hook, but not the other. That one is the barbed rod the gods use to catch human spirits.'

'And the fish?'

'It is the symbol carried by Shivaite goddesses.'

The visitors commented on the signs one by one. They were only hesitant about the one that resembled an hour-glass or a beaker that curved inwards halfway down. But then the curator called our attention to a bronze dancer surrounded by a ring of fire. In one hand he held a symbol precisely like the one on the Maldive plaque. It was a Hindu figure, but nobody knew what the object was.

'And the swastikas all around these signs?'

'Hindu. You don't see it much here in the south, but it is common in northern India.'

'But this must be Buddhist.' I tried to provoke a reaction by pointing out the running band of lotus petals around the plaque.

'But they got it from us,' they laughed, and showed me what I had already seen in the museum: deities on thrones adorned with bands of lotus petals, and plinths with lotus motifs. Certain gods in their reincarnation were born out of lotus flowers.

There seemed to be little more to ask about. The concept of a double footprint I had already seen in a Hindu temple. The god Vishnu himself lay as a large sculpture in the middle of a pond resting on his mythical ocean raft of serpents with a *chakra* sun-wheel in his hand. On a pedestal by the pond was a plaque with his double footprints, to which devout visitors still paid homage.

I now brought out my pictures of the many-headed stone demons dug up at the site of the virgin sacrifices in Male. The museum visitors were hesitant, but all agreed they had seen something similar. Indeed, all around us in the museum there was something similar. Several of the wooden Chola statues from this part of south-west India depicted demonic deities with the tongue stretched out, long feline corner teeth, bulging eyes and round discs inserted in expanded ear lobes. We were close, but not quite there. No closer, in fact, than the wooden masks of Indonesia and the traditional pre-Buddhist dance masks that are still copied for sale to tourists in southern Sri Lanka.

But one of the group pointed to a sign carved on the Maldive stone image. It was the very ancient and well-known symbol of a thunderbolt shown as a sort of double-ended trident.

'That's a *vagra*,' he said, and the museum curator showed us a statue of the Hindu god Indra holding just such an object in his hand. Indra was the chief Vedic god of India, a warlike Aryan god who vanquished the sun, and his weapon was this thunderbolt. But Indra had also been adopted into Buddhist mythology. In fact, at Polannaruwa in Sri Lanka, I had seen a large statue of a seated Buddha where the decoration on his pedestal was an alternating band of lions and 'thunderbolts'. So, were it not for the fact that the Maldive *vagra* was carved on a non-Buddhist multiple-headed image, it could be ascribed to either of the two religions.

On a shelf in this same museum were two tiny seated bronze figurines which immediately brought to mind their Maldive counterparts. In the Maldives one of the two images clearly represented the Buddha, but not the second one. Here were obvious relatives of that second type. The bronze images were shown seated on a round pillow with one leg up and one down, with tall ceremonial headwear, and with necklace, waistband and rings around the upper arms, all just as in the Maldives.

As a final test I showed the interested group my photographs of these two Maldive specimens. There was no hesitation and full agreement: 'One is a Buddha seated with both legs crossed in the *padmasana* position. The other with the tall head-dress is a Hindu deity seated with one leg up and the other down in the *sukhasana* position.'

This confirmed what we had concluded ourselves. For the moment we did not seem to be getting much closer to the real answers, rather the problem seemed to become more involved since these symbols and the religions were so entangled. Here, on the Malabar coast of south-west India, were parallels that were missing in Sri Lanka but still far from what we were looking for. It was the continental shore closest to the Maldives, yet it did not seem to be the missing link to the outside world.

I had expected clearer evidence of contact between southern India and the Maldives, partly because we knew there had been trade relations in recent centuries and partly because there was a reference to the Maldive Islands in the local Chola history.

This related that their King, Rajaraja I, in his lifetime between AD 985 and 1014, conquered the entire mainland coast of south-west India. He even 'subdued the many ancient islands, 12,000 [*sic*] in number'. Also his 'powerful army crossed the ocean by ships and burnt up the king of Lanka'. The numerous islands must have been the Laccadives and the Maldives, since Lanka was Sri Lanka where he conquered Anuradhapura, built the new capital at Polonnaruva and erected Hindu temples there.[51] But this successful Chola naval raid on the Maldives seemed to have left no lasting trace.

I visited all the ancient temples and archaeological sites right down to the southernmost tip of the continent. Everywhere there was something to see and to learn, beautiful landscapes and friendly people, but little that revealed a relationship with the Maldives.

My only aid in touring all the temples down to the south cape was a road map and a taxi driver happy to wait anywhere, as we did not have a single word in common anyhow. We could only exchange gesticulations of disgust or content when we shared our Kerala meals. Once I asked him to stop when I heard the deep tones of a conch trumpet up in the hills. It lured me to climb some almost endless mountain steps past a couple of *lingam* stones and up to a lofty cave. There I was entertained by two monks who worshipped the monkey-god Haneman through his reincarnation as a monstrous ape which appeared on the cliffs above when they called him. Two stone guardians with long slit ears flanked the cave entrance. Carved on a monumental stone lintel between them were red painted con-centric circles which the monks identified by pointing to the sun.

One thing was evident. Both in Sri Lanka and here, on the Malabar coast, I had come across sacred sculptures of the phalloid form we had excavated in the Maldives. Here, among the local Hindus, they were still in ritual use as *Shivalingam*, the *lingam* of Shiva. I saw them, large and small, venerated in the Hindu temples, even by elegant ladies and young girls who touched them, put red paint or flowers on them without blushing, while local scholars tried to convince me that it was wrong to associate the *lingam* with sex. It was only the symbol of the god Shiva. I was shown an ancient wall painting in a palace depicting the seafaring Shiva resting on his snake raft with his right arm stretched out to touch a *lingam* painted separately at his side. It was illustrated as a dome on a square-stepped platform, like a miniature stupa. Here we were again; similar sculptures excavated in Sri Lanka were considered to be miniature stupas. The image was the same, the difference was in the interpretation.

Who then had brought this image to the Maldives? I returned to Sri Lanka and then again to the Maldives with a feeling that the question was still open.

Ask a Maldivian where he believes his own people originated, and he is likely to leave all possibilities open. Belonging to a nation of ocean navigators, he knows that a thousand miles more or less is not the decisive factor for watercraft at sea. It is the buoyancy of the boat itself, and the weather. For a trained seafarer, even food and water provisions are far from decisive factors. So: Sri Lanka? Yes perhaps. But why not the Arab world where Islam came from? Tangiers in North Africa, or Tabriz in Iran? Everything is possible.

The only two sources from which we could draw reliable information on previous opinions about Maldive origins were Bell and Maloney. The former was an experienced old-time archaeological commissioner of Sri Lanka while the latter, as a professional modern anthropologist who ignored Bell's ruins, had studied the living people.

It was tempting to suspect that, of the two, Bell would have the best cards when it came to reconstructing past events on the islands. He had gone straight to the old ruins left by the prehistoric population, while Maloney had drawn his indirect conclusions from a study of the islanders living today. In spite of the actual observations made by Bell, Maloney shared the common view that archaeology had no future in the Maldives due to the sterile sand and low water table. Although he was wrong in this assumption, the more we learnt from our own investigations, the more I became inclined to suspect that it was Maloney who was on the right tack.

Bell, working in a difficult epoch and hampered by the Moslem monopoly on Maldive history, tried to explain the original Maldive culture as a direct offspring of the Buddhist civilisation on Sri Lanka. Maloney did not share Bell's opinion, and he showed that Bell had personally been the first to admit the total absence of references to the Maldives in the historic records of Sri Lanka. In fact, Bell had even written:

> As an alternative, though less probable supposition, it may perhaps not be unduly rash to surmise for the earliest Aryan colonisation of the Group a date synchronic with that of Ceylon itself (viz., four or five centuries before the Christian era), by a distinct but kindred body of the same adventurers, instead of assuming a subsequent direct immigration from this Island.[52]

Although Maloney's object of study was *People of the Maldive Islands*, he stressed that half of his own efforts had been devoted to the problematical background of their culture history. Because, he says, 'this had not been traced, and previous observers have not seen the great complexity of the historical streams that evolved into Maldivian culture. This has also been necessary as a corrective to Bell, whose work was meticulous but sought to trace everything back to Sinhala roots'.[53]

Maloney gave Bell full credit for the old Maldive texts he had collected and for having shown that most Divehi words in the modern Maldive language were etymologically related to old Singalese. But since these words were clearly of Indo-Aryan origin, the Maldives could have received them directly from north-west India instead of secondarily by way of Sri Lanka. Although Bell did not consider this a likely working hypothesis, Maloney did. Any major influence from Sri Lanka, Maloney said, would have taken place in the earlier days of the Naga and Yakkha, before Sri Lanka had yet been settled by the Singalese.

This suggestion, independent of archaeology, was based strictly on historical, linguistic and cultural evidence. While the Sri Lanka records are silent about the Maldives in Buddhist times, there are hints referring to such oceanic islands in the brief texts referring to the earlier Yakkhas and Nagas:

> According to the Sri Lanka chronicles there were Naga kings on the coast near Colombo in pre-Buddhist times, of whom one had a Naga kingdom extending 'half a thousand yojanas into the sea'. There is also the legend that Yakkhas and other

'non-humans' were expelled from Sri Lanka to another island, by the grace of a previous Buddha, in order to allow Sinhalas to occupy the land.[54]

The early Buddhist monks who wrote these Singalese chronicles left no clue as to who this previous 'Buddha' was. He helped to facilitate the Lion people's conquest of the island by sending most of the previous population away, but this happened long before Buddhism was finally established on Sri Lanka, when King Tissa and his Lion people were converted. Literate monks, who in their day had been bright enough to put King Tissa to a test like the one about the mango-tree, would not record the story of the fate of the Nagas and the Yakkhas except as an allegoric reference to some actual event. The two earliest Singalese chronicles, the *Mahawamsa* and the *Dipawamsa*, both refer to the same incident.

In the *Mahawamsa* it is recorded that a Naga king named Maniakkhika reigned on the west coast of Sri Lanka at Kalyani, which is just north of the present capital Colombo. He had a big retinue of Nagas. His sister's son, King Mahodara, ruled 'in a *Naga*-kingdom in the ocean that covered half a thousand *yojanas*'. King Mahodara was quarrelling with his nephew Culodara about the throne at the time when 'the Enlightened One' interfered. Converted to the 'true doctrine' these kings gave up their thrones to this early Buddha, who then established eighty Naga territories 'in the ocean and on the mainland'.

The *Dipawamsa* chronicle too, also from the fourth century AD, spoke of this 'Enlightened One' who paved the way for the Lion people:

> The Teacher, who was free from passion, saw the most excellent island of Ceylon. At the time the plain of Lanka had big forests and great horrors: different kinds of *Yakkhas* . . . *Rakkhasas* . . . *Pisakas* . . . The assembled army of *Yakkhas* saw the Exalted Buddha standing; they did not consider him to be the Buddha but another *Yakkha*. The Buddha told them: 'All of you ask me for fire; I shall quickly produce great heat as prayed for by you, big fire and great heat'.

This wording would seem to indicate that, according to the

Singalese chronicler, the Yakkha may have been fire worshippers now punished by the 'Enlightened One' for their paganism.
For the 'Buddha' gave the Yakkha the fire they wanted, but in
excess. The heat became 'unbearable in the islands. The *Yakkhas*
soon sought for refuge, east, west, south, north, above, below,
and in ten directions'.

Seeing the Yakkhas grieved and frightened, the 'Enlightened
One', compassionate and merciful, thought of happiness for
these unworthy creatures, and brought them (or brought them
to) the land of Giri dipa, Giri island. This was a

> low land . . . like the plain of Lanka . . . in the midst of the
> sea . . . Beautiful, pleasing, green and cool, having lovely and
> excellent groves and forests here, trees stand bearing fruits
> and flowers, empty and solitary, there is no master. In the
> great and deep ocean, in the midst of the water of the sea,
> waves always break, surrounded by the inaccessible chain of
> mountains, it is difficult to go inside against the wish.

This reference to 'mountains' and one more reference to 'the
island of *Giri* with rivers, mountains and lakes' certainly takes
the mind of any hasty reader well away from the Maldive atolls.
But Maloney was no hasty reader. He noticed that in the
Maldives the word *giri* means 'reef', which, of course, is a
mountain under water. He even counted thirty-six reefs in the
Maldives which are named *Giri*, or have the suffix *-giri*. Thus it
all makes sense! The calm lagoons are the many lakes, the rivers
are the rapid currents that run in and out of the lagoons, and in
the crystal clear water these islands show up as what they really
are: lofty crater-shaped peaks rising to the surface from the
bottom of the sea. Although the surface of these submerged
mountains is low above the sea and flat like the plain of Lanka, it
is difficult to get inside the surrounding *giri* because of the
narrow entrances and the constant surf.

According to these descriptive Sri Lankan texts the Singalese,
after their arrival, never left the country again. They were not
the ones to be blessed with the other islands. The 'Enlightened
One' gave them to the Yakkhas and their contemporaries among
the unworthies: 'He let all *Rakkhasas* . . . live in *Giridipa* . . . not to
return again', and 'Well satisfied *Yakkhas*, well contented

275

Rakkhasas, having obtained the excellent island as desired, all being greatly delighted'.[55]

The chronicles make no clear distinction between the Nagas, the Yakkhas and the Rakkhasas – they were all more or less demons. And yet they were very human demons for the first Singalese king upon arrival married the Yakkha princess Kuweni.

In Singalese *naga* literally means 'snake'. Maloney shows that there is good reason to assume that the Nagas in the ancient Singalese chronicles actually were the early Tamils. The main abode of the Tamils has always been the Jaffna peninsula at the northern tip of Sri Lanka, which is called Naga-dipa or 'Naga-island' in Pali, Tamil and even in ancient Greek literature. From the beginning of Singalese history the Tamils were there to intermix with the Singalese and they repeatedly took their turn to reign. Maloney found what he termed a very heavy component of Tamil in the Singalese language and, despite their Indo-Aryan background, they have adopted many of the social features of the Tamil. Assuming that the legendary Naga were Tamil, Maloney writes: 'Naga legends are traceable back to the mythical city of Patala, probably the same as that known to the Greeks, in Alexander's time, at the mouth of the Indus, and might hark back to proto-historic, Dravidian-speaking seafarers whose commercial interests stemmed from the time of the Indus Civilization.'[56]

Whoever the Nagas, the Yakkhas and the Rakkhasas were, separate tribes of one common stock or altogether different people, we may draw the conclusion from the written Buddhist records that they were the ones who contributed to the organised settling of the Maldives.

All this seemed to tie one loose end of the Maldive tangle to early Sri Lanka where a similar loose end was left out at sea by Singalese records. It would seem that Providence, or the 'Enlightened One', an early Buddhist, had reserved these beautiful atolls for a branch of the industrious hydraulic civilisation sailing from the nearest coast. It would thus be tempting to consider the riddle solved.

But not quite so. There are more loose ends in the Maldive tangle than those which can be tied up in Sri Lanka.

CHAPTER XIII
Whence the Hindu?
To the Harbour of the Long-ears

LANGUAGE IS a useful clue in tracing former contacts. The Divehi language that is spoken today with slight dialectic variations throughout the Maldive archipelago is different from any other known language. Yet, as Bell showed, a root relationship clearly links the Maldives to Sri Lanka. Divehi is basically an Indo-Aryan language, and so is the Singalese spoken in Sri Lanka.

The Singalese had spoken an Indo-Aryan language because they came sailing directly from the north-west Indian coast. Inasmuch as the Maldivians are found not to descend from the Singalese, at least some of their ancestors must have come from that same north-west Indian coast. This would make the Maldive islanders cousins of the Singalese, and descendants of people from north-west India, yet blended with the pre-Singalese from Sri Lanka who possibly spoke Tamil. And Maloney actually found that the Divehi language of the Maldives contains many Tamil words. Most of the terms in the kinship system he shows to be of Tamil origin, and also most of the Maldive terms pertaining to the sea, boats and navigation. Dhoni is, for instance, a Tamil word.

Most important of all, the Maldivians themselves in their oldest official record, admit to having had Tamil predecessors. The first recorded king, Koimala, who brought their ancestors to the Maldives in pre-Moslem times, had to get permission to settle in Male from an earlier people on Giravaru island in the same atoll. This pre-Divehi people from Giravaru has survived until the present day, and believe themselves to be descended from Tamil people called *Tamila*.[57] What is noteworthy is that the Giravaru believe their Tamil ancestors to have been Buddhists.

277

A Tamil-speaking substratum confirms the recorded non-Singalese early movement out of Sri Lanka. But with an Indo-Aryan component pointing to continental north-west India, a new loose end is indicated and also a new lead to follow up. Straight to the Gulf of Cambay, in fact, the ancestral home of the Lion people.

So far the archaeologists, historians and linguists, winding in strands of evidence from all over the Indian subcontinent and Sri Lanka, have found that the ends converge on the general area of the Indus Valley civilisation. From this early centre the forefathers of Hindu royalty and their descendant, Buddha, had inherited the custom of ear extension and their belief in divine descent from the lion and the sun.

The former practice of ear extension in the Maldives was scarcely noticed until, by chance, the Buddhist and Hindu stone images were shown to us. The first sun-symbols were found when we stumbled upon the fallen facing stones from the Gaaf-Gan hawitta. And nobody knew that the lion had ever been a concept on these islands until we found the lion busts in the rubble-fill of the same hawitta and an islander found a small lion figurine by digging a well on Dhigu Ra island.

Legends about large cats with human attributes raiding the islands from the sea had made us think of the Lion people. And in Addu atoll on the Equatorial Channel Maloney collected a legend about a man-beast which caused him to compare the old beliefs in Sri Lanka with those on the north-west coast of India. The Maldive version was:

There was a king of India who was a hunter. Once, while out hunting with a net, he saw a creature like a human, but which walked on all fours, and which disturbed the people. This creature would also take hunters' nets and steal their prey, so the king couldn't get any catch. . . . One day, the king, with the help of many men, put the net over the creature, which could not get out because of the large stone weights. The king took the creature to the palace and looked after him well, and because he knew no language, the king taught him language, which took a long time. The creature started helping the king by showing him treasures in the forest, and the king came to respect him. The king had a daughter who fell in love with this creature [in an alternate version the king forced his daughter to marry the creature]. The king, being angry, put the couple on a ship and sent them off into exile. Their ship came to Laam [Haddumati] Atol, where the exiled pair saw a crow which cried. They thought the crow was not a good omen and it was therefore undesirable to land there, so they went on to Male. They settled in what is now Sultan Park and started a Kingdom.

Also in Noonu atoll, at the opposite extreme of the archipelago to the far north, Maloney heard a legend about a king who taught a man-beast to walk in some foreign land, assumed to be Sri Lanka. The man-beast married the king's daughter and caused political trouble, so he was forced to leave. 'He and the princess arrived in *Rasgetimu* and they lived there for some time. Then the people there asked them to rule.'[58]

Rasgetimu is an island in the Ra atoll, next to Noonu atoll where the legend was collected. It is an island so located that an arrival from Sri Lanka would be excluded as the voyagers would have to cross the Noonu reefs or resort to a pilot helping them through the labyrinth to reach the opposite, outer side of the Maldives. In contrast, Rasgetimu is ideally located for a landing by voyagers from north-west India.

Maloney shows that the sultans in Male abhorred this idea of their own descent from a man-beast, and they suppressed this version about the progenitor of the first king, as opposed to the Buddhists in Sri Lanka who proudly preserved the lion as their totemic symbol. The only origin legend permitted to be inscribed on their official copper-sheet books by the Moslem sultans of Male, was the so-called Koimala record reported by Bell. According to this official genealogy only a single king ruled in the Maldives before Islam was introduced:

Once upon a time, when the Maldives were still sparsely inhabited, a Prince of Royal birth named *Koimala Kalo*, who had married the Ceylon King's daughter, made a voyage with her in two vessels from *Serendib* Island. Reaching the Maldives they were becalmed, and rested awhile at *Rasgetimu* island in North Malosmadulu Atol. The Maldive Islanders learning that the two chief visitors were of Ceylon Royal descent invited them to remain; and ultimately proclaimed *Koimala* their King at *Rasgetimu*, the original 'King's Island' (M. *Rasge* 'king', *timu* 'island'). Subsequently *Koimala* and his spouse migrated thence to *Male* . . . and settled there with the consent of the aborigines of *Giravaru* island, then the most important community of Male Atol.

The Moslem record claims that this first king sent his two ships back to Sri Lanka to bring over other people of 'the Lion Race', whereupon his son 'reigned as a Buddhist for 12 years, and was then converted to Islam, ruling for 13 years more before finally departing for Mekka'. Then his daughter in turn reigned as a nominal sultana until her son 'married a lady of the country. From them the subsequent Rulers of the Maldives were descended'.[59]

Even Bell concluded that this record boiled down to a minimum what was many centuries of pre-Moslem Maldive history. The possibility of a twelfth-century prince from Sri Lanka taking over the Maldive throne cannot be excluded, but if so this event has totally escaped the Sri Lankan records. Furthermore, no Sri Lankan prince would first land in Rasgetimu up in the far north-west, precisely where local records attributed the very same story to the man-beast and the princess. The interesting detail in this sultanic version is that it admits that earlier aborigines lived both in Noonu atoll and Male atoll. And that, in their effort to claim descent from a prince of the Lion people rather than a man-beast, they end up with a feline as their royal progenitor in any case.

It is not surprising that Maloney later collected in Male an oral version in which Koimala was the son of a prince exiled by a king in India. 'The Indian King was angry with his son and sent him off with his wife in two boats; they had 700 soldiers. They came to Rasgetimu in Raa Atol, and when he became king there, people called that island Rasgetimu (King's Island). Then the king and queen came to Male, and Koimala was born there of that Indian couple.'[60]

Only at the time of my own research in the archives of the Moslem Cultural Centre was a second copper-plate book from the twelfth century translated and made public. This was the earlier cited *Loamaafaanu* manuscript which made no reference to any king named Koimala at all. On the contrary, this early text lists the names of the five last kings of the Lunar Dynasty who succeeded each other on the throne in Male from AD 1105 until Islam was embraced and the first mosque built. None was named Koimala.

This seems to confirm Maloney's suspicion that *Koi-mala* was a composite term alluding to a whole group of individuals and not to a single monarch. He showed that *Koi* was the Divehi word for 'Prince' and *Mala* could well be derived from Mala-div, the Male islands. *Koi-mala* would then be the 'Princes of Male', and thus represent all the pre-Moslem rulers lumped together until the day when Islam was introduced. He showed that *Koya* means 'Prince' in southern India, derived from the Dravidian root *Ko*, 'King'.

With the arrival of Koimala in Rasgetimu island reduced to an allegory about the beginning of an immigrant dynasty approved of by an earlier population, Maloney was justified in accepting the man-beast version as the genuine origin myth: 'All image of a lion got lost in the Maldives because of isolation, so it was replaced in the myth by the man-beast, while in Sri Lanka some image of the lion was maintained by contact with north-western India'.

Could the lion myth have come from Sri Lanka to the Maldives? In the case of a direct transmission it would have gone in the opposite direction. The Maldive version has it that the man-beast came straight from India to become their king. The Sri Lanka version has it that the one who came there, after discovering some islands on the way, was the grandson of the lion. The names of two of these islands were recorded by the early monks and may have some significance. The seafaring migrants, not only men but also women and children, sailed in two large ships. The *Dipawamsa* chronicle says: 'The ship in which the boys ascended, came to an island uncontrolled, which was then named as *Naggadipa*. The ship in which the women ascended, came to an island uncontrolled, which was then named as *Mahila* kingdom (*Mahilarattham*).'

According to the *Mahawamsa* chronicle, the men landed on an island called Naggadipa and the women in Mahiladipaka. Both chronicles concur that the men first raided their own home coast and there plundered Supparaka (or Suppara) and Bharukaccha

(Bharuch), two ports in the Gulf of Cambay in north-west India. It was from the port of Bharuch that Vijaya and his men had sailed to Sri Lanka.

It is reasonable to suspect that Naggadipa was identical with Nagadipa, the Naga island that formed the northern tip of Sri Lanka. The Mahila kingdom, or Mahiladipaka where the women landed could then hardly be anything but the Mala-dipas, the Maldives.

Did the voyaging princess remain in the Mahila island kingdom where the records said she landed, and does this explain the old Maldive custom of being governed by queens? And does this explain why the prince, landing with only men in Nagadipa, looked for a new wife? According to the *Mahawamsa* chronicle, upon settling in Sri Lanka: 'He married a *yakkhini*, queen of the island, and later a princess of the Pandiyan kingdom of southern India, and was progenitor of the Sinhalas.'[61]

Piece by piece, written records and oral traditions of these civilised founders of nations seem to tell us much of what actually happened. Maloney, following his linguistic lead up to Bharuch and the other ports in north-west India, found some reference to early seafaring from this coast in the ancient *Jataka* texts of India. These record events presumably linked to the previous lives of the Buddha, and thus antedating Buddhist times:

> *Jataka* No. 213, the Bharu Jataka, is set in Gujarat, for King Bharu must have ruled around Bharukaccha, modern Bharuch, often mentioned as a port in the early literature. This Jataka says that King Bharu caused ascetics to quarrel, and, therefore, the spirits that dwelt in the realm of Bharu were angry with the King. They hence brought up the sea, and the inhabitants of the kingdom perished thus. The ancient commentary accompanying this passage adds the following significant note: 'And those who at that time spoke the truth, blaming King Bharu for taking a bribe, found standing room upon a thousand islands which are yet to be seen today about the island of *Nalikera*.'

Nalikera means 'coconut' and Sri Lanka was renowned for its extensive groves of this palm which had been introduced from

Malaysia and the Pacific. The thousand islands so small that those who left because of quarrels with the King barely found standing room can only be the Maldives, in the sea off the coconut island. There is, indeed, a written reference to a king in the Bharuch area who is said to have sent a major group of his people in exile to oceanic islands.

Another *Jataka* (No. 360), referring to the same port, speaks about a certain Queen Sussondi who got carried off to a Naga island called Seruma. The King sent an emissary by the name of Sagga by ship to 'explore every land and sea' in search of her. Sagga embarked with merchants from Bharuch sailing for the Golden Land (south-east Asia). But a monster caused their vessel to shipwreck and the royal emissary saved his life by floating on a plank until he landed on a Naga island where the Naga king lived who had abducted the royal lady from Bharuch: 'The queen saw Sagga on shore, and said, "Do not be afraid", and "embracing him in her arms, she carried him to her abode and laid him on a couch", fed and dressed him, and "under the influence of her passion she took her pleasure with him". After a month and a half, merchants from Banaras landed there to get wood and water, and Sagga went with them.'

Very possibly this queen from Bharuch, who was overjoyed in her island exile at seeing a man of her own people, although unwilling to return home with him, might be the one who also left Bharuch according to Sri Lanka's royal chronicles, when a ship of ladies ended on a different island and the men came alone to found the Lion Dynasty.

Maloney's comment was:

The motif of Sagga being enticed by a queen there fits in with the matrilinear traditions of the Maldives, which also have long had a reputation for being sexually permissive. A subsequent ship stopped for firewood and water, and on this point again the Maldives are suggested; ships in ancient times would hesitate to get wood and water from mainland coasts controlled by local kings or pirates, but would stop over at one of the uninhabited Maldive islands for these supplies.[62]

Finally, a third *Jataka* (No. 463) speaks of a blind seafarer born

283

into a family of master-mariners, again in Bharuch. Local merchants wanted him on their ships, believing he brought good luck. Once he had piloted a ship under the guidance of a 'Great Being' and with 700 passengers on board. He came back after four months of being tossed about in stormy seas, and reported having visited the mythical seas of *Khuramala*, *Aggimala*, *Dadhimala*, *Dalamala*, and *Nilavannakusa*, as well as the *Valabhamukhu Sea* 'where the water was sucked away'. The 'Great Being' with the 700 passengers reminds one of the 700 who left Bharuch with the exiled prince according to Sri Lankan chronicles, and such an event may explain why a fragment of such a story about a blind pilot is found worthy of record in the Indian religious *Jataka*. Another hint is found in the names of the seas. Four of them have the suffix *mala*. Where else in the open ocean off Bharuch does one find such a quantity of seas but in the Mala-dipas, the Male-islands? The last of the seas described could well fit the shallow waters in the Bay of Mannar with the Palk Straits where the 700 voyagers would have to enter if, as Sri Lankan records state, they landed at Nagadipa on the north tip of their island. Here the sea is noted for the tidal currents that suck the reefs and banks bare.

Bharuch had played such a central part in these early written records, both in the chronicles of Sri Lanka and in the *Jatakas* of India, that I had now to visit there.

It was with a great feeling of expectation that I went to a tourist agency in New Delhi and asked how to get to Bharuch. But they had no information on it. However, if I definitely wanted to go I had better fly to Ahmedabad and ask there.

I did so. In an excellent local hotel the owner lent me his car and a most entertaining Indian driver. It was a day's drive on a good road through much of the state of Gujarat. There was little to see, in the flat landscape along the road, of the past grandeur of the world's first civilisation, but the colourful country life with Indians of all castes and physical types, ox-carts and elephants, made the drive enjoyable.

The first part of the road I knew. I had been to Gujarat twice before in my previous efforts to make myself familiar with the maritime aspects of the Indus Valley civilisation. After a couple of hours we passed the fairy-tale palace of the Maharaja of

Baroda. I recognised the spires behind the tropical trees in the park, for I had been a house-guest there of my friend Fatesingh-rao Gaekwad on my previous visits to Lothal, which is on the other side of the bay.

Like a fjord, the long Gulf of Cambay runs into the north-western corner of India and almost splits Gujarat into two. Lothal is on the west side and Bharuch on the east side of this navigable fjord. Although the landscape was flat the road never went close along the shore. The driver said there were terrific tidal currents and a great difference between the high and the low water levels, so the fishermen could come in at high tide and leave their vessels dry on the mud-flats when the tide went out. One had to be an expert mariner to benefit from the currents and the tide, and people on this coast were as much at home in the water as on land.

I knew. This was one of the places where maritime activity reached an early peak, and this was the harbour area of the Long-ears.

Everything I saw and heard was absorbed with interest as I checked the landscape and people for possible clues to the maritime riddle. The faces, the stone blocks abandoned on the roadside, the vegetation. The temple images. But we were living in a different epoch. There were some curly-snouted Makara-gods on the temple facades, but fairly recent and not so characteristic as the one we had found on Kondai island in the Maldives, which resembled the more ancient ones of Nepal.

Certainly, there were many individual people who could be taken for Maldivians. But then again, the Maldive islanders represented such an obvious blend of physical types that this was to be expected. Occasionally we saw a man with golden plugs in his ear lobes, and one had only empty holes left big enough to put a finger through. These were certainly no Long-ears, but perhaps their ancestors had been. For after the Baroda Palace we reached the University where last time Professor R. N. Mehta had shown me a drawer full of large ear-spools, excavated from Lothal. This time we drove past with the knowledge that at least this piece of the puzzle fitted.

We were heading for a desolate place known as Bhagatrav. It was near Bharuch and had been a port in the Harappan period, that is a port of the Indus Valley civilisation. It had been located and excavated by S. R. Rao, the Indian archaeologist who had dug Lothal.

I kept an eye out for the ponds and ditches along the road. All were filled with tall green reeds. Where there were wetlands, extensive areas were covered with these reeds. We stopped so that I could check one with a knife. It was the same kind as we had used for building the reed ship *Tigris*: *Typha angustata*, the reed used by the first ship builders both in Mesopotamia and the Indus Valley. There was indeed plenty of it. We had floated for five months on this reed, and there was still a lot of buoyancy left. Since then I had collaborated with Indian scientists at the University of Bombay. They had tried to cover bundles of such reeds with various blends of waterproofing used on the west coast of India in former times. They mixed pitch from various trees with shark oil and asphalt. The most interesting part of the experiment was the conclusion. The best result was obtained with the blend recorded on the ancient Babylonian tablet about the Flood: two measures of pitch to one each of oil and asphalt. From a nineteenth-century Indian botanical work they had also found out that *Typha elephantina*, an extra large local species of the same reed, was formerly used by fishermen for boat building in this area. Certainly, as on the tidal flats in Bahrain, flat-bottomed reed bundle vessels would be ideal for security and smooth beaching in this bay. No wonder ship building and navigation started in this area long before boat builders learnt to split planks for ships with ribs and hull.

We reached Bharuch, where there was nothing to see but a merchant city bustling with activity like all other Indian ports. It lay away from the gulf, but on the wide estuary of the navigable river Narmada. We crossed the long bridge over that holy river at the outskirts of the city. Here excitement began. We left the road and were lost in a network of dirt tracks between tiny villages and muddy fields. In passing, I noticed with excitement the symbol of the winged sun painted on the front of a couple of the village shops, but the driver was keen only to get out of this maze of backroads and my attempt to explain that this was what I had come for was to no avail. Obviously here was a modern survival of a motif I had failed to find in its ancient version outside the Maldives.

Soon I found it again. We had stopped in the temple square of a tiny village called Obha to ask for the ruins of Bhagatrav. Nobody knew, but when we went to ask the schoolmaster, we saw the same concentric rings with three horizontal bars on either side painted on the gate to his little school. Only once before had I seen this symbol outside the Maldives, and then again in modern form. It was painted on both sides of the door to a small farmhouse on Sri Lanka, next to the ruins of Anuradhapura. When the owner came out and we asked him where he had copied the motif from, he was evasive and said it was merely 'an idea of the painter'. Now, when the Gujarati teacher came out, we asked him the same question. He had no answer. Nobody in the village knew what the symbol represented or why it was there. But below the winged sun was painted the word WELCOME in Gujarati letters. It was hardly a coincidence that this particular Maldive sun-symbol should have survived in modern form in the two old homelands of the Lion people.

On the temple facade across the square there was a large lotus in relief above the door, and over the lotus was a rising sun with wings. Beside the sun was a swastika. Nobody knew why the swastika was there either. An old man believed it was the symbol of the Hindu god Ganesh, but later, when I asked a scientist in Bharuch, he said that these people no longer knew that originally this had been a local symbol for the sun.

The teacher pointed out the whereabouts of Bhagatrav, where scientists had dug up Harappan remains. It was only two minutes' walk across the dry mud-flats outside the village. At the site there was nothing left to see. Wind erosion had buried whatever the archaeologists had exposed and only some exceedingly old and worn potsherds lay scattered in the area. They were too plain and simple to tell any story, but the red and the grey ware, and also the rim shapes, concurred well with the common surface sherds in the Maldives.

With a scant harvest so far – except for the 'winged sun', lotus and swastika found surviving in a village at the spot where Bhagatrav is buried – we returned across the bridge to Bharuch and spent that night in a wayside rest-house. I awoke the next morning to the caws of at least a hundred crows. Never had I seen so many crows. Here in these Gujarat villages and towns they seemed to be protected as part of the old city sanitation system.

287

I have liked crows ever since I had a tame one as a boy. Now I looked at them with new eyes. I had just read a report on early navigation in this part of India written in the first century AD by the Greek geographer and author of *Periplus Maris Erythraei* ('Circumnavigation of the Erythrean Sea'). He states that crows served as navigation aids to the early seafarers from Bharuch. They took them along on their ships and let them loose at sea to study their flight. If the crow took off without returning they knew there was land nearby and where it was. This had made me ponder over the strange fact that the crow was a common bird in the Maldives, where other birds are extremely rare. During our meals at the hawitta in Gaaf-Gan crows were sitting in the trees waiting to clear away the remains. Crows cannot fly as far over the ocean as to reach the Maldives, and on Gaaf-Gan we saw no other feathered species but seabirds. Yet the crow was mentioned in the myth of the discovery of the Maldives. When the man-beast and the princess reached the first island they saw a crow. They took this as a bad omen and continued to the next. Perhaps they figured that the crow was a sign to the effect that other mariners had come there before them.

That morning the crows were a good omen. Thanks to a personal introduction from Indira Gandhi I had a letter to Sri B. M. Pande, Superintendent Archaeologist of the Archaeological Survey of India, with headquarters in Baroda. As one of the watchmen led me through the patio to his office, I caught sight of a small group of stone statues of very great age, as evidenced by the erosion. I could hardly believe my eyes. There was a squarish stone image, a head about 60 centimetres (2 feet) tall with a face on each of its four sides, just like the main pre-Buddhist image dug up in Male. I had barely greeted Sri Pande in his office before I invited him out on to his own patio and pointed to the image.

'That is a Shiva,' he said. 'We have just brought it from a site we are excavating near Goraj on the Deo river. In the area of the old Bharuch kingdom.'

The faces were so eroded that traces of the corner teeth and tongue could scarcely be seen in the coarse sandstone, but on one of the sides a huge disc was clearly visible in an ear lobe. The size and all the details of the sculpture were so intimately related to the Maldive counterpart that a close relationship was obvious.

'The old name for the site is Maha-Deo-Pura, the City of Shiva,' said Sri Pande, and a few hours later we were at the spot. Excavations were going on under the direction of Pande's assistant, Narayan Vyas. Right on top of the old ruins lay a whitewashed 'modern' temple built two centuries ago by a forefather of my friend in the Maharajah's Palace.

The first thing that hit my eyes were two lion heads which flanked a lotus over the entrance. I knew I was in lion country. A less prominent place had been given to three free-standing statues of bulls that had been dug up at the site, painted white, and placed outside the walls. Whatever they may have represented to the prehistoric sculptors, today these hump-backed oxen were undoubtedly accepted as Shiva's bull Nandi in this Hindu temple. Inside was only a huge phallus stone, a *Shivalingam*, standing in the centre of the floor, and a small niche with a statuette of a four-armed Shivaite deity holding two fishes by the tail.

Outside was the deep trench with men down at the bottom digging and brushing clean the remains of walls buried metres deep in soil and refuse. The lowest walls were of bricks with mouldings estimated to date from the pre-Chalukyan period, at least from the second or third century AD. The rounded shapes of the mouldings recalled those in the Maldive Islands, but everywhere at this site and for about a mile around there were also beautifully shaped and polished building blocks of hard stone, some reused in the nearby village houses and some merely scattered about.

I noted straightaway that the whitewashed *Shivalingam* temple which stood on top of it all had a foundation built from such reused blocks, exactly as the Moslems had taken facing blocks from the earlier hawittas in the Maldives. These fine stones were shouldered and shaped in masterly fashion as in the 'fingerprint' masonry and, what was more, they had once been held firmly together with 'butterfly' clamps such as in the sunken wall we had discovered on our first Redin island. Here, however, most of the stones had been brought together secondarily, so that the butterfly 'wings' rarely matched. Nonetheless here they were, each 'wing' cut deep into the edge of the stone as a truncated triangle. Here, then, too, near Bharuch, was the first and only example of this metal-clamp fitting I had so far seen in the vast gap between the Phoenician port of Byblos and the Maldive Islands. The routes of transference could be many and indirect, but there was an obvious connection.

Good-sized stone statues and images from the prehistoric cult site had been dragged about everywhere – some lay in the field, a few were set up in the nearby village and many emerged from the eroded embankment of the sacred Deo river. As with the three bulls, a big stone elephant had been found by the present population to be worthy of respect. It had been brought to the village, painted white, and set up beside the main temple. A remarkable discovery was that it possessed a cup-shaped depression, big enough to put my fist into, centrally placed on the back. This was the peculiar detail which Maldive and Hittite lion sculptures had in common. But neither the villagers nor the scientists had any explanation for its motive or function, although there could only be a common magico-religious tradition behind it.

There were about half a dozen man-made hillocks inside this vast archaeological site. At the foot of one of them Vyas showed me how the ploughed soil was full of prehistoric potsherds. In its slopes were scattered traces of former brick-built terrace walls, showing that this had been a solid temple mound measuring about 20 metres (about 65 feet) square, or larger if we assume that part of it is buried in the ground. In a depression on top lay a big overturned stone phallus, and a stone with a square post-hole of the type so commonly found in the ruined hawittas of the Maldives.

Indeed, to judge from its appearance, this temple mound would just have been another hawitta if found in the Maldives. Further inland in Gujarat, in a dense forest area peopled by hostile tribes, Vyas had seen a number of similar but better preserved terraced structures. They were built out of large bricks into the form of a step pyramid or ziggurat about the size of these mounds but covered by a thick coat of hard white plaster.

What a sight this must have been in the days when the kings of Bharuch reigned in this part of Gujarat and fostered the maritime branch of the Lion people that sailed away to settle distant islands. Today, here as in the Maldives, there was evidence of destruction everywhere, by conquerors who abused the religious heritage of their predecessors and devastated their temples.

But in the Maldives a totally new religion had been introduced with Islam. Not so in the harbour area of the Indus Valley civilisation. Here each new religion was based on the previous one. While the landscape was littered with demolished 'hawittas' and abandoned images of all sorts, at least some symbols – like the lion, the bull, the lotus, the sun, and the swastika – had been assimilated into the rites of the victors. In the Maldives they had all been abolished and buried. Perhaps the four-faced Shiva image from this same site would have been acceptable too in the new Shiva temple on top of the ruins, had it not been carried away as a museum trophy by modern Indian scholars!

I had no language in common with the workmen down in the deep trench, but before I left I wanted to demonstrate my appreciation of their work. Instinctively the same word came out of my mouth as I had been using constantly during the last few weeks to our workmen digging in the Maldives. It was just about the only Maldive word I knew:

'*Barábaro,*' I said smiling, and pointed at the fine mouldings they were scraping clean.

'*Barábaro!*' they all shouted back joyfully, and I do not know who was more surprised, they or I. I had forgotten that *barábaro* was the word for 'good' or 'fine' in the Urdu and Gujarat languages of this very part of India also, the same as in the Maldives. It was also one of the many terms that had led linguists to look to this northern part of India for the roots of the Divehi tongue.

I returned from Maha-deo-pura, the 'City of Shiva', with a feeling that language and myth had done archaeology a good service in pointing to this area as a common source for the Sri Lanka and Maldive royal ancestry.

That night I went to bed thinking about the hawitta, the stupa, and the ziggurat. Certainly, the ziggurat of Mesopotamia was the oldest known form of these solid ceremonial mounds. In its earliest Sumerian period it was a solid stepped and truncated pyramid with a temple on top, as in ancient Mexico.

Formerly nobody used to think in terms of any of the people in antiquity moving outside their national boundaries; but now we know there was extensive long-range contact and trade. A mini-ziggurat had been discovered on the island of Bahrain, and another near the prehistoric copper mines of Oman. There is ample reason to suspect that even the central height of Mohenjo-Daro had been a terraced temple mound before Buddhists in later times rebuilt the summit. The prehistoric mounds I had seen and heard about that day in Gujarat were shrines built in that same way: as solid terraced elevations.

In Trivandrum the architect–historian D. A. Nair cited words attributed to Buddha himself. When on his death-bed his disciples asked him how he wanted to be buried, he replied: 'In a stupa, for I am a Hindu Prince.'

The *Encyclopædia Britannica* describes the stupa: 'The hemispherical form of the *stupa* appears to have been derived from pre-Buddhist burial mounds in India.'

Indeed, I had seen the variety of the most ancient Hindu shrines in Nepal. The oldest were best defined as ziggurats: a sun-oriented, terraced and truncated pyramid with a long flight of ceremonial stairs up to a small temple on top. The main part of the structure was thus solid. In later forms the temple itself grew in size and importance, while the solid base was reduced to two or three superimposed terraces.

The great hawitta on Gaaf-Gan was remembered as having formerly possessed a small stone room on top. Accordingly it had been of the ziggurat or Hindu temple type. The one Bell had seen in better condition than we on Laamu-Gan was said to have had a spire shaped like seven superimposed kettles, and clearly it was a Buddhist dagoba or stupa. But, as we have seen, perhaps the Buddhists had modified the upper part of a previous structure, such as Bell had found on the same island. The well-preserved lower section of that hawitta had nothing to do with any dagoba or stupa, according to Bell himself.

There was still more to the Maldive story than any of us had realised.

The next day I drove through endless fields of cotton plantations to visit the famous sun-temple at Modhera which is a major tourist attraction in this part of India. As we travelled, we met long rows of patient oxen in pairs dragging bulky loads of cotton down to Bharuch and other ports on the coast, and the driver proudly pointed out that cotton was one of the most important exports from Gujarat, by land and by sea. The large-wheeled wooden carts, with an ox on either side of a common shaft, were precisely as the famous little pottery models made by the Mohenjo-Daro artists 4,000 or 5,000 years ago. Even loads of cotton were drawn by the Mohenjo-Daro double ox-span. It was in these very fields that man had first started cotton cultivation.

Cotton was also one of the main plants of the ancient Maldivians. From the earliest records it appears that *kafa*, cotton, was cultivated, spun and woven on horizontal looms into exceedingly fine texture. The earliest Portuguese wrote that finer cotton fabrics were not found anywhere else. Maldive cotton cloth was exported to India for its high quality. On special islands all the people worked to make cotton textiles. Every Maldive person who died had to be buried in cotton grown in his own garden, and every family had two or three cotton trees.

I knew that cotton had long been a major fingerprint in the tracing of early cultural migrations, indeed no other plant has to the same extent brought botanists into frontal collision with anthropological dogma. In 1947, I had barely returned from landing in Polynesia from Peru on the *Kon-Tiki*, when I was confronted with the 'cotton problem'.

The world's leading experts on cotton genetics, J. B. Hutchinson, R. A. Silow, and S. G. Stephens, had that same year completed the first chromosome analysis of all wild and cultivated cotton species, and they had made a revolutionary discovery. All Old World cotton types had 16 large chromosomes. The New World cotton types, however, could be separated into two groups. The wild and unspinnable American cotton had 13 small chromosomes, but the cultivated American cotton had 26 chromosomes, 13 small plus 13 large. This species with long, spinnable lint had been produced by the pre-Columbian civilisations in Mexico and Peru, and did not grow wild. The predecessors of the Mayas, the Aztecs and the Incas had managed to cross-breed the useless local wild cotton with one from the Old World, and thus obtained an excellent spinnable hybrid.

How had the early American Indians in Mexico and Peru obtained seeds of the large-chromosome Old World species to

293

cross-breed with a useless local plant? The polemics began. The botanists suggested a human crossing of the Atlantic before Columbus. Impossible! Of course no boat could have sailed across before European mediaeval times. The cotton seeds must have drifted across all alone. Or blown with the prevailing trade winds.

The botanists had, however, demonstrated beyond any shadow of doubt that the 26-chromosome cotton brought into existence in America by man, had been carried from America by prehistoric voyagers to the Galapagos Islands and to the Marquesas Group in Polynesia. The feud was therefore restricted to the seeds that had crossed the Atlantic. They could have been wild and not necessarily of the cultivated species.[63]

The weakness in the archaeological protest was to infer that a seed would float more easily over the Atlantic alone than in a sailing vessel which would benefit from wind and current alike. In addition, it was hard to visualise American Indians waiting on the beach to pick up a cotton seed. They would have had to know that it would yield spinnable lint if crossed with a wild local bush which so far had served no useful purpose.

The weakness in suggesting a human means of transfer was that cotton was not cultivated by the Phoenicians, the Norsemen or other European or African people who sailed the seas. Not even the Egyptians or the Mesopotamians cultivated cotton in early antiquity. Cotton as a domestic and mercantile product was restricted to the Indus Valley civilisation until, suddenly, it started in Mexico and Peru among every civilised tribe and nation in pre-Columbian times.

Seeing the Gujarat oxen now drawing their loads towards the local ports just as they did millennia ago, I began to see implications behind the early growth of cotton even in the Maldives. Ibn Battuta had also spoken of the cotton on those islands and praised the Maldive cotton fabrics as the finest in the world even before the Europeans' arrival. Had the seeds of spinnable cotton floated alone to these oceanic islands in pre-Columbian time? Hardly. As raft voyagers in tropical currents we have seen how the surface is full of scavengers; not only the large plankton eaters, but the tiny fish and minute pelagic crabs that scurry about everywhere and nibble at the least little crumb floating on the surface. We shall never know who, but man brought the cultivated Indus Valley cotton by sea to the Maldives.

The botanist R. A. Silow, basing his conclusions on indisputable genetic evidence, had boldly suggested that, at some time since cotton cultivation began, it must have found its way from the Indus Valley to America. But how? Neither he nor I nor anybody else had considered the Maldive Islands. With this oceanic kingdom having had contact with the Gulf of Cambay at least a millennium prior to the voyage of Columbus, and probably long before, the geographical barrier crumbles. Vessels already able to bring cotton to the Maldives were at a favourable starting point for clearing the southern tip of Africa and being carried on by the natural elements to the Gulf of Mexico.

The sun-temple at Modhera proved to be worth the visit although it was several hours drive into the inland of Gujarat and quite different from what I expected. Built as late as the eleventh century AD, it represented a completely different culture period from what I had seen near the coast in Bharuch. The superstructure of the building, known to have consisted of a roof shaped like a stepped pyramid, had gone, and one was left with an impression of a multitude of colossal, richly ornamented columns supporting what remained of the massive pyramid's base. But the impressive structure still standing was sufficient to demonstrate the superb craftsmanship of the early Gujarati engineers, and it was considered amongst the best of Indian art and architecture.

A local guide pointed out that the temple faces due east and is so designed that the rising sun at the equinoxes shines into the shrine through the doors of the *mandapas* and makes the entire structure 'radiate in the glory of the presiding Sun-god'. That main solar image was missing, but there were twelve other huge statues of the sun-god, as well as twelve smaller ones, carved, as our guide explained, after the idols of Mithra, the sun-god found in Iran and Middle Asian countries.

By this time I had made an observation of my own which took me away from the little group of Indians following the guide. Here were some mortice marks of former 'butterfly' joints again, but displaced and out of order. This ancient sun-temple was built at the site of an earlier, demolished structure. Some of the large blocks forming the floor were still in the original position so the adjoining 'wings' of the 'butterfly' mortice matched from stone to stone. A few others had been set in the wall at random with no regard for the right combination of the old marks. This meant that, in antiquity, this type of specialised stone fastening must have had a wide distribution in this part of India. It also showed that this fancy eleventh-century sun-temple was not the original form in this area.

The concept of a stepped pyramid as a religious structure was known to the builders of this temple, as was shown not only by the roof but also by the dominant motif outside. At the east entrance I caught up with the guide again who had finished explaining the myriad large and miniature figures in combat and love that filled the walls and columns. In front of the temple, on its east side, he showed us an enormous ceremonial bath. Its dimensions matched the temple itself. Known as the *Surya Kunda*, or 'The Sun's Tank', it was a water-filled rectangular basin with walls rising in steps and terraces up to the surface of the ground, touching the base of the sun-temple. Not only was this bath of the sun built like the mirror image of a ziggurat, upside down, but, as if to make the recurring motif clear, a multitude of tiny step pyramids were built as decoration, one next to the other, along every terrace.

In the central position on the west wall was a sculpture of Vishnu resting at sea on board his eternal serpent raft. It was a rather unlikely vessel. I could not avoid thinking of Con-Tici, the pre-Incaic sun-god of Peru, and Quetzalcoatl, the Aztec sun-god of Mexico. They also travelled on this peculiar type of watercraft. In the legends of both areas they were bearded white foreigners who had come to bring to their forefathers sun-worship and the arts of civilisation. Even cotton cultivation. In Aztec tradition Quetzalcoatl travelled the ocean on a raft of snakes. In the iconographic art of the pre-Incas on the coast of North Peru Con-Tiki is also shown travelling with his entourage on a serpent raft. A coincidence? Those of us who crossed the Atlantic on the bundles of the reed ship *Ra* had felt as if we were travelling on a bunch of undulating serpents.

Did these people share their legend because they had a common watercraft, or did they have a common watercraft because they shared their legend?

On the road back to the Gulf area the driver stopped to show me some of the *oao* (*vav*) – enormous underground waterworks – for which Gujarat is renowned. Basically they are wells built as temples, artistically decorated and accessible by ceremonial stairways. Sometimes the well is huge and the water so far down that the stairways go from one level to the next like the access to a modern underground station. These amazing engineering feats are extremely ancient, and some go back to prehistoric times. Gujarat was clearly within the expansion area of the interrelated hydraulic civilisations that flourished throughout western Asia from the third millennium BC. Sumerian texts are full of references to the great navigation channels and complex irrigation systems which their kings built and continuously dredged with enormous effort. On the island of Bahrain, Danish archaeologists had already discovered amazing underground aqueducts of a most ingenious sort otherwise famous from Persian archaeology. And on the other side of the Hormuz Strait I had been stupefied by the prehistoric *falaj* of Oman. Built as stone-lined tunnels they ran for many kilometres under barren deserts at the depth of 10 metres (over 30 feet), with shafts for maintenance running at intervals up to the surface. To get the required pressure one *falaj* started way up a canyon and came down on one side higher than the river, then dipped in a tunnel under the river bed and came up to continue as high up as before but on the opposite side. These early people knew how to manipulate water. No wonder the voyagers to Sri Lanka arrived as hydraulic experts and those who ended on the Maldive Islands at least excelled in building elegant baths, regulating freshwater at their will through bottom vents. Most modern castaways would perish at the beach of the salt lagoon before they could figure out how to draw fresh water from the solid limestone bedrock of a coral atoll.

Filled with admiration for all this evidence of early human intelligence, taste and dexterity which I had seen in Gujarat, I stood the following day in the baking sun and stared down into the stagnant water in a huge prehistoric tank built from baked bricks. According to a local poster it was 218 metres long, 37 wide and 4.15 deep (in feet, 715 × 121 × 13½), with vertical walls on all sides. There was no stairway into this unusual basin, but one short wall was interrupted with an open gate with traces of the locks of a former spillway. This was no ceremonial bath. There were no benches along the sides. This was the prehistoric port of Lothal, the vertical walls of which had been built from oven-fired bricks to resist salt action. Rao, who made this discovery in 1954 and led the excavations, wrote:

> The largest structure of baked bricks ever constructed by the Harappans is the one laid bare at Lothal on the eastern margin of the township to serve as a dock for berthing ships and handling cargo. . . . In no other port of the Bronze Age, early or late, has an artificial dock with water-locking arrangements been found. In fact, in India itself, hydraulic engineering made no further progress in post-Harappan times.[64]

When I last came to see this port I was struck by the narrow entrance which could admit no vessel larger than could easily be drawn up on the beach. Puzzled, I told Professor Mehta who had brought me to the site that there must have been another way in, another canal entrance.

'That is what Rao concluded also,' said Mehta laughing, 'but we have dug test pits outside the other walls and found the same hard, sterile ground everywhere. There cannot have been another way in. That's why some of us now wonder if it was only built to collect rain water.'

'Impossible,' I exclaimed. 'You have just shown me the large anchor-stones Rao found inside, and the old well a few steps away. Nobody would dig a well next to a water basin. And if they cared to collect rain or flood water it was simpler and more efficient to dig a catchment with sloping sides, like a pond where man and beast could get at the water as the level sank. They would not build high vertical walls where the water had to be hoisted up in buckets!'

Everybody around agreed. And yet no ship could have got through such a narrow entrance into this splendid harbour. Still, there was the large mud-brick wharf at the dockside with all the warehouses beside it. It seemed so obvious from all that Rao had found and demonstrated that this was a dock, that I asked for permission to dig an additional test pit. Two men came with shovels and dug a hole in the ground outside the wall where the narrow entrance was and a few feet to the side of the present channel. Up came old potsherds and disturbed earth. Secondary fill. The entrance canal had once been much wider. This observation prompted us to make a close check on the well-preserved masonry inside the entrance wall. Like modern bricklayers the early Lothal masons had placed their bricks precisely to make the midpoint of each lie across the join of the two below. But a few steps to each side of the present opening in the wall was evidence of joins that did not match so well, as if sections had been added as an afterthought. The purpose could only have been to reduce the width of an entrance that had originally been much larger.

The outside test pit and the brick alignments inside the adjoining basin wall gave dimensions to the original entrance which permitted the passage of full-size reed ships into the Lothal port in its early phase. In a second phase, however, the gate into the large harbour had been reduced to a modest spillway narrow enough to allow closure by wooden lock gates. Why?

Lothal today lies some distance from the Gulf of Cambay across large dry mud-flats. Even the local river is too far away to send flood water into the basin. We know that the sea level in this area has gone down since Harappan and Sumerian times, as witness the Sumerian port of Ur now lying buried in desert sand far from the river and the gulf. We also know that the extreme difference between high and low tide in the Gulf of Cambay is 10.5 metres (34½ feet). Even today the local vessels are built with shallow keels and bulky bottoms so that they do not roll over when they are beached as the tide goes out. Ancient Lothal was ideal for twin-bundle reed ships which could float right into the docks at high tide, when their decks would be high above the wharf. As the water disappeared during low tide the ship would rest firmly on the dry bottom with the deck now level with the wharf. The thickness of the bundles of our little reed ship *Tigris* was 3 metres (just under 10 feet).

This third visit to Lothal came after we had been digging in the Maldives and found a variety of imported prehistoric beads. One was the incredibly tiny type of bead for which Lothal is renowned among scholars. Here, a few short steps from the wharf and the ruins of the warehouses, lay the remains of the prehistoric bead factory where Rao had encountered hoards of

299

such beads, 1 to 1.3 millimetres in diameter. Inside the small local field museum there was more Lothal jewellery to which I had paid little attention on my previous visits. This time I stared in amazement. There was one glass case containing a necklace made of globular brownish agate beads interspaced with whitish stone or shell beads shaped like oblong barrels perforated lengthwise. Precisely the two types of bead we had found in the Maldives. And the special shape and size given to each of the two materials was also consistently the same as in the Maldives. The description said: 'Indus beads of semi-precious stones, which were in great demand in Sumer, Bahrain, Elam and Egypt, were processed at Lothal and exported to distant lands. The raw material, namely agate, chert, jasper, etc., was obtained from the *Ratanpura* mines in South Gujarat through the Harappan ports of *Mehgam* and *Bhagatrav*.' Embedded in the courtyard of the bead factory Rao had found jars containing 800 cornelian and agate beads in various stages of manufacture.

Directly, or through later middlemen, these were the kinds of beads that had reached the Maldives. According to local archaeologists, the dock area of Lothal city fell into disuse when an abnormal flood sealed up the basin possibly as early as 1900 BC, thus bringing an end also to Lothal's prosperity. Before that time, however, Lothal had managed to obtain the hoard of Maldive cowrie shells which I noticed on exhibition in another case next to the beads.

Import and export. That is what the ships permitted and how civilisation began.

CHAPTER XIV
The Verdict

WE WERE sitting in an upstairs room in the Kon-Tiki Museum in Oslo – Skjölsvold, Johansen, Mikkelsen and I. Downstairs were the balsa raft *Kon-Tiki* and the papyrus ship *Ra II*, both in a sense responsible for bringing all of us together with a common interest: island archaeology.

With us also was Knut Haugland, Curator of the museum and my closest collaborator ever since we waded ashore together in Polynesia after the voyage on the balsa raft. He was an indispensable member of the team. He had worked the museum up from being a makeshift shed for the raft to a scientific centre with revenue from a stream of visitors that subsidised scholarly research. Abbas Ibrahim, the Maldive Minister for Presidential Affairs, had just been visiting us. The museum was going to exhibit samples of the stone carvings we had excavated, some of the many which were duplicated.

Now our team was meeting to discuss how to proceed, for Skjölsvold, Johansen and Mikkelsen were to write up the scientific details about their excavations, and the Kon-Tiki Museum would publish their drawings and reports.

'So, who discovered the Maldives? Have you found the answers?' asked Knut jokingly.

'We have one answer,' said Skjölsvold. 'And it may surprise many people. These islands were not just found by primitive drift voyagers. They were settled by civilised people who were already sailing the open sea in antiquity.'

'They were already great artists and architects before they sailed to the Maldives. And that was earlier than the Viking Age in Europe,' added Mikkelsen.

'Maybe even as early as the Late Stone Age in Europe.'

Johansen nodded with a smile at an unopened bag of potsherds he had placed on the table between us.

'Perhaps. But at least we now have the first proof that the Maldivians were building with classic designs 1,000 years before the time of Columbus. I have just got our first carbon datings from the laboratory,' continued Skjölsvold. 'Somewhere around AD 550 a temple complex was built on Nilandu. Maybe even rebuilt, since it contained worked stones from another construction.'

We recalled the buried walls of the Nilandu hawitta with mouldings worthy of a European cathedral. We also recalled the fine large shell found right at the bottom of the sand-filled interior. That, and another large shell, as well as a good charcoal sample found by trenching the buried wall around the temple area, had now been carbon analysed. The results of all three came out roughly within the same centuries. However, together with the buried shell Skjölsvold had also found the fine reddish limestone blocks tossed in with the fill. They came from an earlier building.

'How old that building was we have no means of telling. But it certainly shows that something was going on in Nilandu long before the Moslem period,' concluded Skjölsvold.

We had found no datable material inside the Gaaf-Gan hawitta, which we did not trench. Only the sculptures. Some bones which we dug up outside that hawitta were from Moslem times, about AD 1500, that is from the days of Columbus, 1,000 years later than the rebuilding of the Nilandu hawitta.

'AD 550. That is six centuries before the official settling of the Maldives according to their own historical records.' The archaeologists had good reason to be satisfied with their first test digs, but Haugland was puzzled.

'Where could people have sailed from with experience in architecture 1,000 years before European caravels even ventured beyond sight of land?'

Asia, Africa, America. It was my turn to report on what I had seen in the maritime centre of north-west India. In Lothal and around Bharuch. In the original home of the Lion people who built seaworthy ships and sailed away from their home ports in the sixth century BC. The memories of their marine adventures had long since turned into legend when put on written record about AD 500, at the time of Nilandu building activity. The people of Bharuch were master architects long before the royal expeditionary force with men and women was sent into exile in search of other land. That happened 2,000 years before Columbus. They were already used to making mouldings like those of Nilandu. They were experts in carving solid rock into beautifully shaped blocks fitted to perfection. Joined with 'butterfly' clamps. Used to organising mass labour for building large sacred mounds. They kept up their ancestral tradition of sculpting lions and bulls, and used the sun, the lotus and the swastika as religious decoration. Quarried chert and agate and made beads like those we had found, for export. They even shared a strange word like *barábaro* with the people on the Maldives. I had found just about all we were looking for, even the four-faced Shiva. But not the footprint tablet with the pictographs. That pointed to Naga-dipa, the Tamil territory on the northern tip of Sri Lanka where the Singalese Lion people had first landed.

'Do you still believe the pictographs you found on the broken footprint tablet derived from the Indus Valley script?' asked Knut.

Not directly. But indirectly, yes. All those signs had a symbolic meaning. They were pictographs. And they were all borrowed from symbols that had spread from the first civilisations in north-west India. From the ports of Lothal, Bhagatrav, Bharuch and the many subsequent Hindu kingdoms in the same area. This maritime centre in north-west India was known to be the cradle of all the cultures and kingdoms that gradually grew down to the southern tip of India and eastwards to Java and other distant lands. The Maldive Islands, clearly, were basically another branch of that great and early cultural expansion.

'Do you know,' inserted Mikkelsen, 'that phalloid stones date back to the Indus Valley civilisation?'

'We saw a perfect phallus stone from Mohenjo-Daro in the National Museum in Karachi,' added Johansen enthusiastically.

Whether our phalloid Maldive stone images derived from mini-stupas or from *Shivalingams*, they had an early progenitor in the Indus Valley cult. Even *Encyclopædia Britannica* has an entry on Siva (Shiva) suggesting that an Indus Valley seal representing an ithy-phallic (erect phallus) figure seated in a yogic posture may be a prototype of this important Hindu deity, 'or at least represent an early association between the ascetic and the phallic that has persisted in the mythology of Siva up to the present day'.

'We had them in Norway once,' laughed Johansen. 'The Holy White Stones from pre-Viking times were *just* like the Asiatic ones. They are dated to around AD 500.' This was his speciality and he showed us pictures of Nordic phallus stones resembling what we had found in the Maldives, probably from the same period. We all, agreed, of course, that this was a good example of independent origins.

But then came the riddle of the cowrie shells. People in Scandinavia could, of course, have hit upon the idea of carving sacred phallus stones, even with the stupa-like form. But how could they get hold of cowrie shells?

I had hardly notified my friends about the cowries found as funeral gifts in Lothal, when I received a letter from a reader in Finland. She wrote that she had seen Maldive cowrie shells in the National Museum of Helsinki, excavated by archaeologists from prehistoric tombs in Finnish Karelia! Asked to provide more information, she contacted the responsible authorities at the Helsinki Museum and came back with a surprising reply: cowrie shells were commonly found archaeologically all over the Finnish-Ugric area. They had been used in ancient Finland mainly as ornaments on the harnesses of horses. They were known as 'serpent-heads' by the Mari-people of the Upper Volga river, and historical records show they were obtained as payment for furs they brought to the mercantile state of Bolgaria which occupied the coast of the Caspian Sea around the Lower Volga about AD 600–1250. These merchants obtained the cowries from Arab traders. Their routes from the Indian Ocean via the Persian Gulf continued overland to the markets of Tabriz and to the Caspian Sea. It was merely an extension of the early Maldive trade in entire shiploads of cowries to which the early Arab sources referred centuries before the Maldive kingdom became Moslem. Among the Arab writers was Ibn Fadlán who visited Bolgaria in AD 922.

The Estonian historian L. Meri wrote about this amazing trade route: 'A violent wave of cowrie-shell fashion washed over the Finnish-Ugric nations, which could not have any notion of these "serpent-heads" coming from the Maldives, from the distant Indian Ocean, from the place of origin of these shells.'[65]

Reading this information to my friends I thought we had reached the outer limits of the cowrie shell trade in time and space. But no.

'We can add to this that Norwegian archaeologists have excavated cowrie shells on the Atlantic coast north of the Arctic Circle. Eleven of them were found at Lödingen in northern Norway in a tomb dating from the sixth century AD!'

It was Mikkelsen who made this incredible report. Then Johansen added: 'And in 1975 a number of cowrie shells were also found in a woman's tomb from about AD 600 at Luröy, an island off the coast of northern Norway, exactly on the Arctic Circle!'

Mikkelsen waited for me to digest this surprising information from our own home country. Then he quietly produced a publication by a Swedish archaeologist, B. Nerman, who had excavated pre-Viking tombs on the island of Gotland off the east coast of Sweden. He had found cowrie shells from the Indian Ocean in three different women's tombs dating from AD 550–800. One was perforated for suspension and seemed to have been worn on a belt. It had caused much surprise in Sweden that the island of Gotland could have had contact, even though indirect, with people in the Indian Ocean at that early time. But then another Swedish tomb from that same period was found to contain a beautiful bronze Buddha sitting on a lotus flower.

We all agreed that people travelled long before everybody's journey was put on written record. But Knut asked: 'Couldn't the cowrie shells have come from the Atlantic?'

'No!' I could answer. 'The money-cowrie, *Cypraea moneta*,[66] is a strictly Indo-Pacific mollusc. You don't find it anywhere else.'

'Maybe they came from East Africa?'

'Ibn Battuta showed that East Africa imported cowries from the Maldives, and he himself exported shiploads to Asia. Only in the Maldives were they cultivated for mass export. The Arabs called the Maldives the Money-islands even before they introduced Islam there. Three centuries before Ibn Battuta, Al-Biruni wrote that cowrie shells were the monopoly of the Maldives.'

From the northernmost corner of Europe our review of

Maldive trade quickly turned to the Far East at the opposite end of the Old World.

'Ancient Chinese ware,' said Johansen and sorted out a pile of familiar green potsherds. 'This is what we dug up in Nilandu, Gaaf-Gan and Fua Mulaku. I showed it to oriental archaeologists on my tour of south-east Asia. They all identified it as Chinese from about the eighth century, when the ancient trade with China increased and ceramic was the principal export.'

Johansen had also learnt that J. Carswell of Chicago's Oriental Institute had visited Male where he had picked up hundreds of surface sherds from the Chinese Sung and Ming dynasties (AD 960–1279 and 1368–1644). Carswell had been surprised to find all this evidence of traffic from the Far East in the Arab period, since he had hardly found any Islamic pottery. Also a certain J. V. Allen had found some surface pottery on an island just south of Male, which the oriental experts believed might be Sassanidian, that is from the innermost part of the Persian Gulf. The rest of Allen's sherds had been identified as south-east Asiatic and Chinese.

We heard of nobody else who had picked up Maldive potsherds except Ivar, the 6-year-old son of our Male friends Eva Jonsson and Mohamed Hameed, who might have found the prize specimen. Playing with his parents he had dug in the sand of another Vadu island, Kaaf-Vadu, just south-west of Male, when he pulled up an ancient sherd of fine hand-pressed and painted grey ware, with a very special leaf ornamentation. This ware and its decoration recalled the particular pottery of the ancient Indus Valley civilisation. The tiny islet of Vadu seemed to hide many secrets of the past in its deep sand. I had briefly visited the local tourist resort to see a little bronze Buddha somebody had found when digging sanitary installations.

We were still admiring little Ivar's sherd when Johansen pulled out a small box to show us his trump card. He had now also visited Vadu island, and he told us his story while unwrapping the pieces in his box.

As part of our joint programme, Johansen had just been back alone to the Maldives, hoping to visit the island of Maalhos in Alifu atoll, west of Male. The reason was that a Swedish tourist had gone to that island the same year because he had heard rumours of a stone head said to have been found there seventeen years ago. The Swedish visitor told us that when he arrived the islanders first denied the existence of any sculpture. But in the end they showed him a stone mask which lay upside down on top of a refuse mound. It had been dug up from an ancient well. He insisted that the head be sent to Male. And there we were shown the limestone mask, about 30 centimetres (1 foot) tall, just as we were leaving. Beautiful. The realistic face had the symbol of the 'third eye' on the forehead, and above its ornate headband rose a tall ridged cap.

The sole purpose of Johansen's return to the Maldives had been to dig test pits in the area where the stone mask had been found. But for some reason our friends on the Council did not allow him to go to Maalhos, and he ended up on the islet of Vadu instead, where the boy had found the precious sherd we now had in front of us. Everywhere in the sand of Vadu Johansen had been able to pick up ancient potsherds. The island must once have been important. He knew the tradition that it had once been much larger, so he waded into the lagoon. Just with his hands he had been able to scoop up potsherds from the sand at the bottom. These were some of them.

He showed us some ancient sherds of fine hand-pressed, unpainted pots of grey ware with a very specific surface decoration of so-called cord-stamp impressions.

'I showed these to the archaeologists in the National Museums of Singapore, Kuala Lumpur and Manila. I did not say where I had found them. But this is what I found in the Vadu lagoon. Independent of each other they all said it was neolithic pottery, of a type that ceased to exist about 2000 BC.'

In silence we all looked at our wide variety of sherds one by one as they were passed around. Some such Maldive sherds may one day perhaps tell the story of how prehistoric Madagascar had been peopled from Indonesia.

Then came my turn to tell what I had learnt from our Moslem friends on the National Council. They had finally confided to me the full story behind the large Buddha stone head that had brought me to the Maldives in the first place. It was correct that it had been part of a complete statue smashed up by religious fanatics. And it had been found on Toddu island just west of Male, off the northern tip of Alifu atoll. But there was more to the story than that.

The head had been discovered inside a small stupa. That stupa had also been in good shape, hidden for eight centuries inside a mound covered by palms and dense vegetation. The people knew the mound as *Bodu gafusi*, 'the big stone pile'. But in 1958 a noted Male official, Mohamed Ismail Didi, sailed for Toddu with the full approval of the authorities and the Moslem Council. Under his direction, untrained villagers cleared and excavated the mound. The dome of the small stupa, a couple of metres (6 feet) high, was still preserved, and so was the fine stone enclosure carved in imitation of a log fence. Didi had personally written a report on his discovery, in Divehi language and with Divehi letters, which Shadas had helped me to translate. The well-preserved Buddha was found hidden in a chamber under a large stone slab. They also found a relic casket, like a stone pot, and inside was a silver bowl surrounded by black powder, possibly ash. There were also two inscribed silver sheets, about 30 × 5 centimetres (12 × 2 inches) and a small gold cylinder, like a charm container, some gold fragments and pieces of gold wire, besides three rings, two coins, and a substance like native medicine. They had cleaned and polished the coins to see what they represented. 'There was a figure of a deer or a horse, we could not be certain . . . on the other side of the coin was the head of somebody. The other coin was not clear enough. We took photographs of these coins.'

Nobody knew what had happened to the contents of the relic casket. The coins had disappeared with the rest. Vandals had systematically effaced the little stupa. But the photographs of the coins had been saved by our friend Hassan Maniku, and one showed the laureate head of Apollo on one side and Minerva driving her chariot with four galloping horses on the other. This coin had been perforated, probably to be worn as an amulet. In 1980, A. D. W. Forbes of Aberdeen University had done research in the Maldives and obtained prints which he sent to Dr N. M. Lowick of the British Museum Department of Coins and Medals. In the archives of Loutfi's office I had just been shown the typescript of Forbes' detailed report: 'Dr Lowick promptly identified the coin as a Roman Republican *denarius* of Caius Vibius Pansa, minted at Rome in 90 BC . . . The coin could have circulated in the Roman Empire at any time up to AD 100.'[67]

'A coin from 90 BC. Of course it could have been worn as an

amulet for some time,' commented Skjölsvold. 'Yet we know there was direct contact between the Maldives and ancient Rome.'

He was referring to the reign of the Roman Emperor Flavius Claudius Julianus who died in AD 363. His comrade-in-arms, Ammianus Marcellinus, listed the most distant envoys that came to pay homage, as he saw them seated at either side of the court: 'On one side the people from across the Tigris and the Armenians invoked peace, on the other the nations from India and even the Divi and the Serendivi sent their nobles with gifts in competition to come first.'[68]

Serendivi was Sri Lanka, Divi the islands in front.

'The Romans learned how to sail to these islands from the Egyptians,' I added, repeating my favourite quote from Pliny the Elder. We had a copy of Pliny's *Historia Naturalis* on the bookshelf which I reached for to read a well-marked page. Pliny wrote this work before he died at the eruption of Vesuvius in AD 79, and Roman ships were already visiting Sri Lanka and the opposite coast of India then, that is, at the time when Roman coins like the Maldive one from 90 BC were still in circulation. To get to Sri Lanka Roman ships had to pass through the Maldives.

But what I was looking for was Pliny's mention of sailings to the Prasii, a trading people of the river Ganges on the far side of India. After a description of Sri Lanka with all its towns and products, Pliny goes on: 'This island was formerly believed to be a distance of twenty days' sail from the nation of the Prasii, inasmuch as the voyage to it used to be made with vessels constructed of reeds and with the rigging used on the Nile, but at later times its distance was fixed with reference to the speeds made by our ships as seven days' sail.'

Those who insist that Egyptian reed ships never left the Nile must have overlooked this record; and without it I would have been much less keen on testing reed ships in the oceans. Apart from the estimated distances in sailing time, the Egyptians had taught the Romans the secrets of crossing the Indian Ocean in accordance with the seasonal variations of the monsoon. Pliny was campaigning for the Romans to take over the Indian Ocean trade, instead of giving the profits to middlemen in Egypt: 'And it will not be amiss to set out the whole of the voyage from Egypt, now that reliable knowledge of it is for the first time accessible. It is an important subject, in view of the fact that in no one year does India absorb less than fifty million sesterces of our empire's wealth, sending back merchandise to be sold with us at a hundred times its prime cost.'

He instructs the Roman merchants to sail about twelve days up the Nile to Keft, where camel caravans are organised for another twelve days' journey to Berenise on the Red Sea. There were organised watering posts at intervals and apparently a vivid traffic with caravan stations capable of accommodating 2,000 travellers.

Travelling by sea begins at midsummer before the dogstar rises or immediately after its rising, and it takes about thirty days to reach the Arabian port of Cella . . . from that port it is a forty days' voyage, if the Hippalus is blowing, to the first trading-station in India . . . Travellers set sail from India on the return voyage at the beginning of the Egyptian month Tybis, which is our December, or at all events before the sixth day of the Egyptian Mechir, which works out at before January 13 in our calendar, so making it possible to return home in the same year.[69]

'We are told that Vasco da Gama learned about monsoon sailing from the Arabs,' I added. 'It is true. But we must not forget that the Romans had learned monsoon sailing in the Indian Ocean from the Egyptians 1,500 years earlier.'

'What a sight for the Maldivians,' said Johansen, 'to see the proud Egyptian papyrus ships with colourful square sails stand through the Equatorial Channel along the highway of their sun.'

No doubt they did not simply pass through. We all agreed that no mariner would cross the full span of the Indian Ocean without stopping for fresh provisions and water. Perhaps the Maldive women copied the beautiful collar pieces of their dresses and the men the elegant bows of their dhonis from Egyptians in transit.

'Who said the Maldivians lived isolated in the ocean?' asked Mikkelsen. 'They had settled at a crossroad of all the main maritime nations.'

If reed ships from the Red Sea came here, those from the Persian Gulf had still easier access. And those from the Gulf of

Cambay would seem like next-door neighbours.

Were it not for the practical sailing directions of Pliny recorded in the interests of Rome, written sources would have ignored Egyptian sailings to Sri Lanka and beyond. Had not Queen Hatshepsut's fleet sailed down the Red Sea to the legendary 'Punt', or the Pharaoh Necho despatched an exploring expedition around the continent of Africa, neither the Egyptians nor their neighbours would have considered a merchant sailor worthy of inscriptions or record. The short texts of the Indus Valley civilisation have not been deciphered and are only known from seals, but the one seal showing a large reed ship and the many seals with Indus Valley script excavated all over Mesopotamia tell a story by their mere presence. The Mesopotamian clay tablets, in contrast, abound in references to large ships and to distant lands months away in sailing time. But the geographical names given are not those we use today, and only those constantly mentioned like Dilmun (Bahrain), Makan (Oman) and Meluhha (the Indus Valley) have been tentatively identified. Some others were much further away and we can only guess at their identity. Certainly, by the sixth century, ships were not noticeably improved from Sumerian or Babylonian times, and yet by then the Arabs had taken over the trade in Maldive cowries up the Tigris river and to the caravan routes beyond.

Maloney, a man with wide horizons, observed that the Maldivians had the strange traditional habit of counting with twelve as the base number. A provocative system of problematic origins, he says, and, asking where this duodecimal system could have come from, he discounts Sri Lanka and India and proposes: 'We probably have to look ultimately to Mesopotamia, from which the use of the numbers 6 and 12 spread in several directions.'[70]

He suggests that perhaps this feature of Sumerian and Babylonian civilisation was transmitted through prehistoric Gujarat by way of Persia and Sindh, and thence by sea to the Maldive Islands.

I told the others that, after my visit to Bharuch and Lothal in Gujarat, I was convinced that at least the Hindu element in the Maldives had come from that north-western corner of India. And probably, the Hindus were not even the first to have made

311

that journey straight south from the Gulf of Cambay to the Maldives. Perhaps earlier sailors in the days of Mesopotamian and Indus Valley seafaring had been led by the sun to the Equatorial Channel, and survived in legend as the Redin. Maybe they were the ones who had broken the pots in the Maldives prior to 2000 BC and brought cowrie shells to the port of Lothal in that same period?

Skjölsvold stressed, and we all agreed, that Buddhism must have had a firm footing in the Maldives before Islam was introduced. These Buddhists could have come directly from Burma, like the bamboo raft we had seen. There is indeed ample evidence to show that the Maldives had contact with Buddhist nations as far east as south-east Asia and China in early pre-Islamic times.

Yet Sri Lanka seems the more likely source. There they have written records of a major migration to coral atolls in the ocean. And it was caused by a powerful visiting Buddhist about 500 BC. Even though the Maldives had never been under Sri Lankan dominance in the Singalese period, neither politically nor religiously, these two independent nations must have known about each other and even have had some unofficial commercial contact. As Mikkelsen pointed out, this was shown by some of the potsherds he and Johansen had excavated at the Nilandu temple complex. They were identified as of Sri Lankan origin, and datable to the period from AD 700 onwards.

Buddhists from Sri Lanka and Hindus from north-west India thus seemed to have had an equal share in the peopling of the Maldive archipelago, and even roughly in the same century, some two and a half millennia ago. Whoever might have been on the islands before them was expelled or absorbed.

The Maldive Islands, which most of us around the table had hardly heard of before, now began to appear like a barrier reef from which octopus tentacles spread to remote corners of the Old World. Into the Red Sea and the Mediterranean as far as Rome. Into the Persian Gulf and beyond as far as Finland and the Arctic coast of Norway. Into the Gulf of Cambay, and around India in the opposite direction past the straits of Indonesia to distant China. Directly and indirectly the prehistoric Maldives had been involved in global trade.

But where did the very first Maldivians come from?

'Let us leave all possibilities open,' concluded Skjölsvold. 'We know that Sri Lanka and the ports in the Gulf of Cambay have played important parts in the prehistory and even the history of the Maldives. But too many others have come here or sailed through before European history began, so . . .'

'So, the best conclusion therefore,' said I, 'is that the ocean is and always was an open road since man began to build ships.'

'So you can't give us the name and address of the first man to reach the Maldives,' said Knut.

'Who was the first sailor to cross the English Channel!' asked Johansen.

Knut smiled: 'But the first one to reach a tiny atoll in the Maldives really deserves a place in maritime history.'

Notes

1   Bell (1940).
2   Maloney (1980) pp. x, 48.
3   Maniku (1983).
4   Bell (1940) p. 119.
5   Ibid, p. 122.
6   Ibid, p. 104.
7   Ibid, pp. 126–7.
8   Ibid, pp. 105, 106.
9   Heyerdahl (1958).
10 Bibby (1969).
11 Heyerdahl (1980) chap. 5.
12 Heyerdahl (1980).
13 Maloney (1980) p. 172.
14 Maniku (1983) p. 33.
15 Bell (1940) p. 116.
16 Ibid, p. 125.
17 Ibid, p. 111.
18 Ibid, p. 131.
19 Ibid, p. 151.
20 Ibid, p. 105.
21 Ibid, p. 112.
22 Ibid, p. 95.
23 Maloney (1980) p. 417.
24 Bell (1940) pp. 17, 76.
25 Gray (1888) p. 444.
26 Maloney (1980) pp. 420–1.
27 Gray (1888) p. 478.
28 Ibid, pp. 484–5.
29 Ibid, pp. 236–7.
30 Bell (1925) pp. 132–42.
31 Maloney (1980) p. 155.
32 Gray (1888) pp. 434–6.
33 Battuta (1354) vol. II, p. 344.
34 Forbes (1983) p. 71 footnote.
35 Bell (1940) pp. 18–19.
36 Ibid, p. 203 and Hassan Maniku in an unpublished manuscript on 'Islam in Maldives' (Male, Dec. 1982, ref. no. MOE/82/CISSEA/12, p. 3) quotes the old Maldivian chronicler Hassan Thaajuddeen (d. 1727) who also uses the wrong name, Shamshuddeen al Thabreezi, but adds the interesting information that he left Thabreezi in the eleventh year of Khaleefa Mugthafee Li-Amrillah's reign, which would be AD 1147. If this was

correct, the traveller from Tabriz must have made various calls on his journey from Tabriz to arrive in the Maldives as late as 1153.

37 Gray (1888) pp. 446–8.
38 *Loamaafaanu* manuscript, English translation by National Council for Linguistic and Historical Research, with foreword by His Excellency Maumoon Abdul Gayoom, President of the Republic of Maldives, Male 1982.
39 Gray (1888) pp. 439–50.
40 Ibid, pp. 468–71.
41 Ibid, pp. 472–3.
42 Bell (1940) pp. 26–7.
43 Maniku (1977) p. 3.
44 *Rasge-timu* means 'King's Island'. The Maldive legend referring to this island as the first settlement of Maldive rulers is discussed in Chapter XI.
45 Maloney (1980) pp. 165–6.
46 Ibid, pp. 146–7.
47 Letter from Sri Lanka Ministry of Cultural Affairs, 29 August 1983. Signed Roland Silva and S. U. Deraniyagala.
48 Maniku (1983) p. 3.
49 Fernando (1982).
50 Gray (1888) pp. 454–7.
51 Sastri (1955) p. 183.
52 Bell (1940) p. 16.
53 Maloney (1980) pp. ix, 48.
54 Ibid, p. 57.
55 Ibid, pp. 41–9.
56 Ibid, p. 57.
57 Ibid, pp. 54–67.
58 Ibid, pp. 31–2.
59 Bell (1940) p. 16.
60 Maloney (1980) p. 30.
61 Ibid, pp. 33–6.
62 Ibid, pp. 38–41.
63 Hutchinson *et al.* (1947, 1949); Silow (1949); Heyerdahl (1952) pp. 446–53.
64 Rao (1965) pp. 30–7.
65 Letter of 31.10.84 from Esa Anttonen based on information from Ildiko Lehtinen; L. Meri (1984) p. 174.
66 Burgess (1970) p. 343.
67 'A Roman Republican Denarius of *c.* 90 BC from the Maldive Islands, Indian Ocean.' Manuscript by Andrew D. W. Forbes. National Centre for Linguistic and Historical Research, Male.
68 Ammianus Marcellinus, Book XXII, 7.10.
69 Plinius, Book VI, pp. 398–401, 416–19.
70 Maloney (1980) p. 53.

Bibliography

Battuta, Ibn (c.1354) *The Travels of Ibn Battuta*. Trans. with revisions and notes from the Arabic text, edited by C. Defrémery and B. R. Sangvinetti, by H. A. R. Gibb, Vol. II (Cambridge: Hakluyt Society, 1962).

Bell, H. C. P. (1925) 'A Description of the Maldive Islands: *c*.1683', *Journal of the Royal Asiatic Society, Ceylon Branch* (Colombo) no. 78.

Bell, H. C. P. (1940) *The Maldive Islands. Monograph on the History, Archæology, and Epigraphy*. Published posthumously (Colombo: Ceylon Government Press).

Bibby, G. (1969) *Looking for Dilmun* (New York).

Burgess, C. M. (1970) *The Living Cowries* (New York, London).

Fernando, A. D. N. (1982) 'The Ancient Hydraulic Civilization of Sri Lanka in Relation to its Natural Resources', *Journal of the Sri Lanka Branch of the Royal Asiatic Society* (Colombo) N.S., vol. XXVII, special no.

Forbes, A. D. W. (1983) 'The Mosque in the Maldive Islands. A preliminary historical survey', in *Etudes Interdiciplinaires sur le monde insulindien* (Paris) Archipel 26, Archéologie Musulmane.

Gray, A. (1888) *The Voyage of François Pyrard of Laval to the East Indies, the Maldives, the Moluccas, and Brazil*. Trans. and annotated by Albert Gray assisted by H. C. P. Bell (London: Hakluyt Society) 2 vols.

Heyerdahl, T. (1952) *American Indians in the Pacific. The Theory Behind the Kon-Tiki Expedition* (London, Chicago).

Heyerdahl, T. (1958) *Aku-Aku. The Secret of Easter Island* (London: Allen & Unwin).

Heyerdahl, T. (1980) *The Tigris Expedition* (London: Allen & Unwin).

Hutchinson, J. B., Silow, R. A. & Stephens, S. G. (1947) *The Evolution of Gossypium and the Differentiation of the Cultivated Cottons* (London, New York and Toronto).

Hutchinson, J. B., Silow, R. A. & Stephens, S. G. (1949) 'The Problems of Trans-Pacific Migration Involved in the Origin of the Cultivated Cottons of the New World.' Abstract from the Seventh Pacific Science Congress, New Zealand, Feb. 1949.

Maloney, C. (1980) *People of the Maldive Islands* (Madras).

Maniku, H. A. (1977) *The Maldive Islands, a Profile* (Male).

Maniku, H. A. (1983) *The Islands of Maldives* (Male).

Meri, L. (1984) *Hõbevalgem* (Tallin).

Plinius Secundus, Gaius (1944–62) *Historia Naturalis*. The Loeb Classical Library (London: Heinemann).

Pliny the Elder – see Plinius Secundus, Gaius.

Rao, S. R. (1965) 'Shipping and Maritime Trade of the Indus People', *Expedition* (Philadelphia: University of Pennsylvania) vol. 7, no. 3.

Sastri, K. A. N. (1955) *The Colas* (Madras: University of Madras).

Silow, R. A. (1949) 'The Evolution and Domestication of a Crop Plant' (Melbourne) Austral. Inst. Agricult. Sci. vol. XV, no. 2.

Index

318

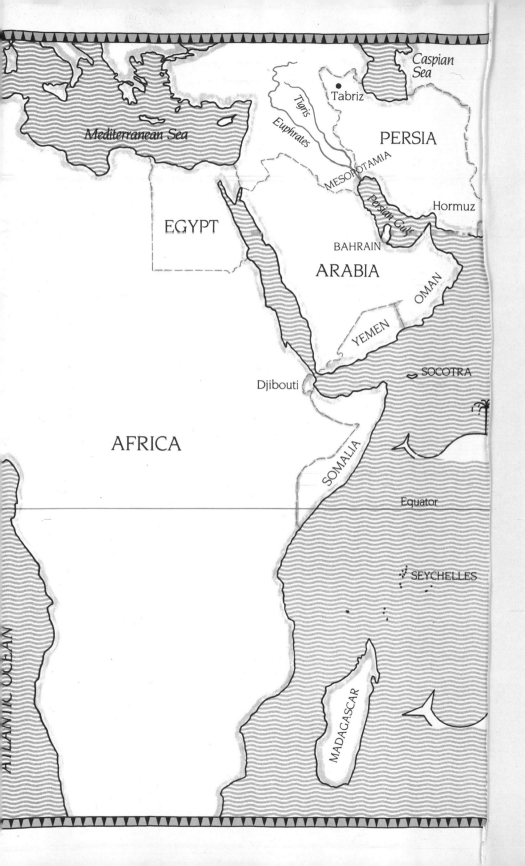